STRATIFICATION AND DIFFERENTIATION

SKILLS-BASED SOCIOLOGY

Series Editors: Tim Heaton and Tony Lawson

The *Skills-Based Sociology* series is designed to cover the Core Skills for Sociology A level (and equivalent courses) and to bring students up to date with recent sociological thought in all the key areas. Students are given the opportunity to develop their skills through exercises which they can carry out by themselves or in groups, as well as given practice in answering exam questions. The series also emphasises contemporary developments in sociological knowledge, with a focus on recent social theories such as postmodernism and the New Right.

Published

EDUCATION AND TRAINING
Tim Heaton and Tony Lawson

MASS MEDIA
Marsha Jones and Emma Jones

STRATIFICATION AND DIFFERENTIATION
Mark Kirby

HEALTH AND ILLNESS
Michael Senior with Bruce Viveash

Forthcoming

POLITICS
Shaun Best

THEORY AND METHOD
Mel Churton

RELIGION
Joan Garrod

CRIME AND DEVIANCE
Tim Heaton and Tony Lawson

WEALTH, POVERTY AND WELFARE
Sharon Kane

FAMILY
Liz Steele

Skills-Based Sociology
Series Standing Order ISBN 0-333-69350-7
(outside North America only)

You can receive future titles in this series as they are published. To place a standing order please contact your bookseller or, in the case of difficulty, write to us at the address below with your name and address, the title of the series and the ISBN quoted above.

Customer Services Department, Macmillan Distribution Ltd
Houndmills, Basingstoke, Hampshire, RG21 6XS, England

STRATIFICATION AND DIFFERENTIATION

Mark Kirby

MACMILLAN

I would like to dedicate this book with thanks to my parents, **Cyril** and **Iris Kirby**, who have supported me longer than anyone else, and also to my nephew, **Jamie Waters**

Contents

Acknowledgements

Writing a book like this requires the help of lots of others, which I would like to acknowledge. First, thanks to Tim Heaton and Tony Lawson for inviting me to contribute to their series and for the vast amount of editorial work and advice which they gave me.

Secondly, thanks to the library staff at Amersham & Wycombe College for dealing with a whole series of requests and continuing to give excellent service to staff and students alike.

Thirdly, thanks to my colleague, Nick Madry, and my other colleagues at Amersham & Wycombe College for putting up with me.

While writing this book, I was also involved in the publication of a textbook, *Sociology in Perspective*, and discussions with the authors of that book helped clarify the contents of this one, so I would like to thank them all.

Catherine Gray and Keith Povey have both worked hard to turn my scribblings into something which can be published and I would like to thank them both for their expertise and advice.

Finally, thanks to Tanya Hope, Eddie Sanderson, Dan Pritchard and Alison Kirton for letting me try out some of the ideas in this book on their students, and thanks to Julian Dean, Rachel Hek, Dr Lesley Hoggart and Dr Costas Lapavitsas for being good friends.

I hope you enjoy the book and your sociology course.

MARK KIRBY

The author and publishers wish to thank the following for granting permission to reproduce copyright material in the form of extracts, figures and tables:

Addison Wesley Longman Ltd; Aldgate Publishing Ltd; Blackwell Publishers; Harriet Bradley; the Child Poverty Action Group; Guardian News Service Ltd, part of the Guardian Media Group plc; HarperCollins Publishers Ltd; Heinemann Educational Publishers, a division of Reed Educational and Professional Publishing Ltd; Independent Newspapers (UK) Ltd; Nik Jorgensen and the Association for the Teaching of the Social Sciences; Charlie Kimber and Socialist Worker; Tony Lawson; Macmillan Press Ltd; Thomas Nelson Publishers; the Observer; Office for National Statistics and GRO(S); Open University Press; Philip Allan Publishers Ltd; Andy Pilkington; the Policy Studies Institute; Polity Press; Random House UK Ltd; Routledge; University College London (UCL) Press.

We are also grateful to the Associated Examining Board (AEB) for allowing us to use questions from past A level Sociology examination papers, and the University of Cambridge Local Examinations Syndicate (UCLES) for past A level Sociology examinations papers set by the InterBoard Syllabus (IBS). All answers and examination hints are the sole responsibility of the authors and have not been provided or approved by the AEB.

Every effort has been made to trace all copyright-holders, but if any have been inadvertently overlooked the publishers will be pleased to make the necessary arrangement at the first opportunity.

1 Introduction

The philosophy behind the book

This book considers social stratification, which is a central component of any sociology course. The aim of the book is to update your knowledge in this area and, by encouraging you to become an active participant in your education, help you develop the skills needed to succeed in your A level or AS level exams.

Skills

The subject core for sociology A level developed by the Schools Curriculum and Assessment Authority (SCAA now QCA) identifies the central skills of identification, interpretation, analysis and evaluation, which candidates must demonstrate in all A/AS level sociology exams. The Dearing Review of 16–19 qualifications laid down a new sociology core and two assessment objectives for sociology (AO1 and AO2) which will apply from the year 2001. The details of these skills are as follows: AO1 – knowledge and understanding; AO2 – identification, analysis, interpretation and evaluation.

The skills of identification and interpretation are concerned with looking at material in one format, such as tables, graphs or text, and communicating your understanding of this material. Application is concerned with relevance, that is, given the vast amount of both sociological and non-sociological material in existence, whether you are able to select the references and material relevant to the subject you are pursuing and use that material in a focused way to consider specific questions.

Analysis requires you to consider all the various elements of and arguments relating to a sociological problem in order to isolate and examine the effect of each. It therefore requires a detailed understanding of the links between diverse arguments in sociology.

Evaluation requires you to consider the strengths and weaknesses of concepts, theories, arguments and evidence in sociological debates and consider which argument has the strongest case.

It is important to be aware that all these skills require familiarity with and an understanding of sociological knowledge. However simply to know something is not sufficient. The skills approach requires you to show that you not only know and understand sociological facts, conclusions and debates but that you can interpret, apply and evaluate them as well.

The best way to develop these skills is to practise them yourself. (You cannot learn to swim without getting wet!) This book therefore contains a series of exercises that are related to the three skills identified above. If you carry them out and therefore approach this book as an active resource bank rather than simply passively taking it in (or not!) you will find that your performance in these skills will improve. You will be able to identify the skills that each exercise is designed to develop by looking out for the following symbols: $\boxed{i}$ for identification and interpretation, $\boxed{a}$ for application and analysis, and $\boxed{e}$ for evaluation. In order to help you understand the interconnections between the various subjects in this book there are also two link exercises for you to complete. These will help develop your understanding of social stratification and other areas of sociology where such information plays a part in contemporary debates.

Updates on knowledge

Knowledge and understanding are in many ways the foundation upon which to build the other skills identified above. This book therefore tries to present, in an accessible way, information about contemporary debates and issues within the broad area of social stratification. The aim is to focus as much as possible on contemporary debates without ignoring their classical basis. However it is clear that in some ways sociology (and society) have moved on from the older frameworks established in the 1950s, 1960s and 1970s, and therefore a question mark must be placed over continued reliance on old sources for an understanding of contemporary society. The book therefore focuses on developments in sociology during the 1980s and 1990s.

The book does not claim to provide a comprehensive and exhaustive summary of all there is to know about sociology in this period. It would be educationally bad to argue that students should rely on just one text for all their sociological knowledge in a particular area. You should therefore use the book in conjunction with the many others that provide an insight into social stratification. It is also the case that in order to develop your sociological skills you need to involve yourself in finding out what has happened in sociology and society during this period. I hope that this overview will prove helpful and encourage you to widen your net and look elsewhere to update the material found in this book, for example by reading newspapers, journals or other books.

The exam

Clearly a book such as this should aim to help you pass the examination that lies between you and your A-level certificate. In order to do this, the book includes examples of past exam questions, sometimes with answers and sometimes without, but in all cases with activities for you to do to help improve your sociological skills and therefore ultimately your performance in the examination. You may find that you can conduct these activities in a classroom context with the support of your teacher, but you should also attempt them on your own, either throughout your course or as a revision aid.

The important thing to remember is that it is you who will be sitting the exam. You must therefore ensure that you play an active part in your education and develop the skills that are essential to passing the exam. If you just read the text and miss out the exercises you will only be doing half of what is necessary to pass the exam.

What is social stratification?

Essentially, the topic of stratification concerns inequality. It is easy to demonstrate that inequalities exist in our society and that inequality appears to have had an enduring impact on much of human history. In fact the 1980s and 1990s have seen a massive increase in inequality. It is of course important to be aware of the extent of inequality and to recognise that it is dynamic and changing. This book therefore seeks to provide up-to-date empirical evidence of the extent of inequality in contemporary Britain and some notion of how this has changed in recent years.

More fundamentally, sociologists and other social thinkers have tried to consider why inequality exists, and also whether it is a good or a bad thing. In sociological terms, inequality has been approached by considering the way in which the various resources in society appear to be unequally distributed along certain social divisions, notably those of class, gender and ethnicity. This obviously leads to the questions of why this might be so, whether such inequalities are justified and how such inequalities might be modified or eradicated. This book is structured around these three central dimensions of social division, but also integrates material relating to two other potential axes of division, namely age and disability. Geographical region and locality may also have an effect on which resources are available to individuals and groups and will therefore be considered where relevant.

We shall consider empirical evidence of the unequal distribution of resources, and also the explanations offered by various sociologists for the existence of such inequalities; explanations that often, implicitly if not explicitly, comment on the desirability of such divisions.

The book marshals the theories of inequality around a threefold structure. Although this means pigeonholing some people, it is a way of linking theories of inequality with more substantive theoretical developments in sociology. Early theories tended to rest on rather static notions of social reproduction (the way in which the social structure and social inequalities were maintained and reproduced over generations through social action and social interaction), and focused on the processes of socialisation and the construction of norms and values. This approach was challenged with the rise of structurally oriented sociological theories, notably Marxism, Weberian theory, feminism and theories of racism. More recently we have seen the emergence of theories that try to go beyond the division between social action and social structure. These themes have affected theories of inequality and most notably have led to a focus on how groups based on class, gender, and ethnic identity are actually formed.

Exercise 1.1

i *a* The chart below provides a basic summary of the various aspects of social stratification in Britain. Copy the chart and complete it by filling in the gaps with appropriate words. To start you off, some of the answers have been filled in.

Aspect of stratification	Age	Gender	Ethnicity	Class	Disability	Region/locality
Groups that are more powerful		men				
Groups that are less powerful	children youth elderly				disabled	North

Subject content

Chapter 2 considers the ways in which sociologists and others have tried to measure social class in society. We shall look in particular at the limitations of the main objective measures, as well as considering the subjective alternatives.

Chapter 3 investigates the way in which the British class structure has changed in recent years and the implications of this for how we look both at Britain and at theories of class stratification.

Chapter 4 looks at the development of theories of class inequality, much of which provides the basis for classical sociological debate, particularly the contrasting theories of Max Weber and Karl Marx. It then considers the impact of recent developments in theory, such as the notion of class formation.

Chapter 5 considers the rise of the argument in the 1980s that social class was no longer a very useful way of looking at society, both because the divisions between the classes were narrowing, and because other divisions were now more important in the overall construction of social inequality and personal identity. It also considers the evidence from studies of social mobility, which look at the extent to which people's backgrounds constrain their lives.

Chapter 6 is concerned with gender inequality. It provides evidence of the scope and nature of gender inequality in contemporary society, as well as some of the responses to it, such as the rise of feminism and the women's movement.

Chapter 7 considers theories that try to explain why women so often find themselves in an unequal position compared with men. It also discusses more recent theories that consider the social construction of sex as well as of gender.

Chapter 8 provides a detailed picture of the scope and nature of ethnic inequality in contemporary society as well as responses to it, such as the rise of black nationalism and reactions to racism.

Chapter 9 looks at theories that explain the existence of inequalities based on ethnicity, dealing with issues such as the meaning of race and racism and the contested nature of these terms. This leads on to more recent theories on the concept of race formation.

Chapter 10 outlines the evidence on inequalities relating to age, disability and locality, and considers how sociological theories of inequality have tried to incorporate these factors into their work.

2 Measuring social class

By the end of this chapter you should:

- be aware of the main ways that social class is measured in official government publications, and the problems associated with these;
- be aware of sociologists' schemes to measure social class;
- have gained a critical understanding of the problems involved in measuring and classifying social class;
- be able to distinguish between objective and subjective notions of social class;
- have considered and evaluated the main schemas for yourself.

Introduction

While social class has always been a central concept in sociology, its meaning is very much open to debate. This can be seen in the very different definitions of class adopted by classical sociologists such as Karl Marx and Max Weber, which have influenced the contemporary work of sociologists such as John Goldthorpe and Erik Olin Wright (see Chapter 4).

Leaving aside this theoretical debate for the time being we are still left with the problem of deciding exactly how we assign individuals to a particular class. The key measure of someone's social class has often been their occupation, explaining why people are often asked to state their occupation on various survey forms. While this view is common to most government surveys and indeed those produced by other bodies such as the Institute of Advertising Practitioners, the exact way in which they construct social class structures varies, reflecting various points of view about how to measure social class.

While this can seem an arcane debate about how to pigeonhole people, it reflects an issue of real importance. To say that there has been a change in the relative balance of working-class and middle-class people in the country is to enter a debate of profound sociological significance, and in order to fully consider this debate we need to know the exact way in which class has been measured to see if we agree with the statement being made. This chapter therefore considers in detail the main objective measures of social class that have been developed over the course of this century and which provide the source material for much sociological comment. In particular, the social class schema developed by the Registrar-General and used for most Census in this century is considered, as well as the more recent model developed by the Economic and Social Research Council (ESRC), and also the alternative model based on socioeconomic groups. It is important for you to know the relative merits of each to enable you to judge material that emanates from these sources.

One key problem with these approaches is that they are all based on assigning people to social classes based on asking people what job they do. So, for instance, as explained in the text, postmen are classified as being in Class 4 and conventionally therefore seen as part of the working class. However, one problem with this is that it is perfectly possible for our postman who someone has assigned as part of the working class to feel themselves to be part of the middle class. In other words, there is the possibility for their subjective class awareness to conflict with their objective placement in the social class structure according to the job they do. The extent to which such contradictions occur, and the implications of these contradictions, is explored towards the end of the chapter.

Measuring social class: objective approaches

1. The registrar-general's definition of social class

The measurement and classification of social class provided by the registrar-general is probably the most familiar model to sociology students. It was introduced in the 1911 census and until the 1991 census it was the predominant way in which social class was measured in official statistics and much sociological research.

The registrar-general's classification divides the population into six classes based on the occupation of the head of household. The occupational categories used in the 1991 census were as follows:

- Class I: Professional, etc.
- Class II: Managerial and technical
- Class IIINM: skilled non-manual
- Class IIIM: skilled manual
- Class IV: partly skilled
- Class V: unskilled

The key division in this schema is between manual and non-manual occupations. Classes I, II and IIINM comprise non-manual workers, who are conventionally grouped together as the middle class, while the remaining categories (IIIM, IV and V) consist of manual workers, who are conventionally grouped together as the working class. Whenever you come across reference to the working class or the middle class the chances are that the author is using the manual/non-manual divide as the basis of the classification.

Exercise 2.1

[a] Place each of the following jobs into its designated social class according to the registrar-general's schema outlined above:

- Electrician
- finance manager
- teacher
- nurse
- doctor
- caretaker
- secretary
- general labourer

The main strength of this classification is that it has been in use (albeit with modifications) for the best part of the twentieth century, and therefore provides a continuity of data on the changing class structure in Britain. However it should be noted that since some occupations have been redesignated over time such comparisons may be misleading. For example in 1961 postmen were reclassified from class III to class IV. It is also the case that prior to 1961 people aged between 16 and 20 were excluded from categorisation. As a result the usefulness of such data for longitudinal (across time) surveys of changes in the class structure is reduced (see Reid, 1989).

✘ However, despite these defects it is clear that surveys based on these class categories have revealed important social inequalities – such as the inequalities in health identified in the famous Black Report, which used the registrar-general's social class categories – and as such they do provide a useful, if not perfect, indicator of social inequality in Britain. In 1997 the National Heart Forum produced figures on heart disease that revealed a large rise in inequality between 1970 and 1993: 'The social class gradient in mortality from coronary heart disease in males, in the early 1990s reached threefold between unskilled and professional classes from a barely 50 per cent excess in the early 1970s' (National Heart Forum report, quoted in Mihill, 1997). Basically this means that unskilled workers were 1.5 times more likely than professional workers to die of heart disease in the 1970s, but by 1993 they were 3.0 times more likely to do so. Hence the extent of inequality in health had increased. The social class classification used by the National Heart Forum comprised six categories and was a variation of the model used in the Black Report.

The present government has set up a task force (under Sir Donald Acheson) to look at health inequalities and their report is due in 1998. Sociologists will then be able to compare health inequalities in the 1990s with the earlier data from the Black Report, assuming that the Acheson team uses similar social class categories, which seems probable.

Social class distribution by RG category, economically active population (%)

Class	Occupation	1971	1981	1991
I	Professional	4	4	5
II	Managerial and technical	18	22	28
IIINM	Skilled non-manual	21	22	23
IIIM	Skilled manual	28	26	21
IV	Semi-skilled manual	21	19	15
V	Unskilled manual	8	7	6

(Source: Census 1971, 1981, 1991, using class names operative in 1971. Office for National Statistics © Crown Copyright.)

ITEM A *Exercise 2.2*

Study Item A.

1. Identify the classes that are increasing as a proportion of the population and those which are decreasing.

2. Which of the following illustrations best represents the class structure in each of the three periods quoted above (1971, 1981, 1991)?

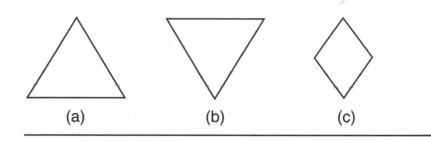

(a)   (b)   (c)

It is essentially on the basis of statistics derived from the registrar-general's classification that sociologists have talked about the decline of the working class and the rise of the middle class. As long as you accept that the manual/non-manual divide does accurately represent the dividing line between these two classes, this point is statistically true. However this view is not accepted by all sociologists. As Crompton (1989) points out, the category of manager has been highly problematic in the past. Most managers are now categorised as class II but there are some anomalies. For instance managers who are scrap dealers or rag and bone merchants are allocated to class IIINM. Secondly, the registrar-general recognised in 1960 that apart from class I and class V all other classes contained both manual and non-manual workers. As a result the boundary between the middle and the working class, usually defined as lying between classes IIINM and IIIM, may not entirely represent reality. This has led to protracted boundary debates (debates about where the boundaries between the various classes lie, mostly relating to the boundary between the middle and the working class), most notably about the position of clerical workers. The main reason for this is that clerical workers are classified as middle class because their work is non-manual, but Marxists (for example Braverman, 1974) would argue that in fact their situation is more akin to that of the manual working class. This is because both are wage labourers rather than owners of the means of production and because in some cases skilled manual workers earn more than clerical workers. Due to the importance of class IIINM in the population today (23 per cent of the economically active) the class structure would be radically different if these clerical workers were classified as part of the working class rather than the middle class.

The registrar-general's classification has also been criticised by sociologists due to its origin in the debate about genetic inequality, and therefore that the hierarchy in the classification is not arbitrary but reflects the belief that those placed at the top of the classification hierarchy (class I, professional) are somehow better (in a broadly genetic way) than the others. Statistically the picture would be exactly the same if unskilled manual workers were class I and professional workers class V, but the imagery would be very different. In other words, the schema assumes that manual workers are inferior and reflects this by putting them at the bottom of the class structure (see Szreter, 1984; Delamothe, 1989; McDonnell, 1990).

A third problem is that in some ways classification by occupation does not reflect the relative earning power of those occupations and therefore the classification does not mirror the distribution of income. Priests for example, with an average stipend of about £18 000 are in Class 1 while MPs on £35 000 find themselves in Class 2.

In reality the place within the hierarchy of a particular occupation derives from its general standing in the community and as such it might be argued that the construction of the registrar-general's index owes more to status than to social class. Also, since measures of societal prestige are inevitably subjective this might undermine the 'objective' nature of data derived from this source.

Exercise 2.3

i a One possible defence of the use of societal prestige as a measure of social class might be that the level of remuneration attached to various occupations reflects society's consensual view of the relative value of these occupations. Therefore there might be a clear link between high prestige (a subjective category) and high income (objective). Which sociological perspective is likely to pursue this argument?

It is also the case that since this particular measure of class is based on occupation, those without paid employment do not feature in it, or at least not on the basis of their own occupation, and therefore not directly. This was the subject of a debate at the Office for

Population Censuses and Surveys (OPCS), leading to a consultation exercise in 1989 about whether the measure should be abandoned on the ground that it claimed to measure social class but in fact only measured occupation. It was decided to keep the measure, largely because it was felt that 'although the classification is indeed based on occupation, it is related to other factors, and is applied to all members of a household or family, including those without occupations' (Census, 1991, definitions volume, p. 40). However the title of the measure was changed from 'social class' to 'social class by occupation', and in some of the classes the word 'occupation' became much more prominent. The problem of using occupations as a proxy for social class will be examined in more detail below.

Exercise 2.4

[a] Suggest examples of people who might be omitted on the basis of classification by occupation.

Exercise 2.5

The registrar-general's (RG) classification was devised 'so as to secure that, as far as possible, each category is homogeneous in relation to the general standing within the community of the occupations concerned. This criterion is naturally correlated with . . .   other factors such as education and economic environment, but it has no direct relationship to the average level of remuneration of particular occupations' (HMSO, 1966, quoted in Crompton, 1993, p. 53).

[a] 1. Explain the meaning of 'homogeneous'.

[e] 2. To what extent do you agree that 'general standing within the community' is a good measure of social class?

[i] 3. Using only the information in the above quotation, identify one argument in favour of using the RG categories to investigate social class inequalities and one argument against.

[i][a][e] 4. Using the above quotation and information from elsewhere, assess the usefulness of the RG scale for analysing social class inequalities.

Because of continuing criticism of the RG schema, the Economic and Social Research Council has recommended the adoption of a new class schema from the 2001 census onwards. The article in Item B outlines the basis of this new schema.

'Underclass Now Knows Its Place in Revised Social Classification'

A new pyramid of social class is proposed today to replace the one devised 86 years ago.

The Economic and Social Research Council, which is recommending the change to the Government, 'overwhelmingly' rejected the idea that social classification was obsolete as we prepared for the 21st century, but did recognise the emergence of an 'underclass'.

The change is recommended in a report from the research council to the Office of National Statistics. The chief novelty is in moving nurses up one class as 'associate professionals', apparently because nursing is due to become all-graduate. Traffic wardens are put firmly in their place.

The report lists examples of occupations at each tier of the pyramid, with broader definitions:

1. Doctors, lawyers, scientists, and employers, administrators and managers in 'large' organisations, ie, those with 25 or more staff.
2. Nurses, legal executives, laboratory technicians, other 'associate professionals', employers, administrators and managers in smaller organisations, supervisors of intermediate staff.
3. Secretaries, sales reps, nursery nurses, computer operators and other intermediate occupations in administrative, clerical, sales and service work.
4. Driving instructors, builders, carpenters and other self-employed non-professionals.
5. Telephone fitters, plumbers and other supervisors and craft and related workers.
6. Lorry drivers, assembly line workers, traffic wardens and workers in routine occupations in manufacturing and services.
7. 'All types of labourers, waiters and waitresses and cleaners' and other workers in elementary occupations in manufacturing and services.
8. The underclass of those who have never worked and the long-term unemployed or sick – as the council puts it: 'Their position is obviously the worst of all.'

The higher up individuals are, the liklier they are to enjoy favourable terms for job security, pay, and pension, as well as more control over their work andbetter career and promotion prospects.

If accepted, the scheme will replace the official pyramid dating from the mid-19th century, adopted in 1911 and almost unchanged since 1921:

1. professional;
2. managerial and technical;
3. skilled (since 1971 sub-divided into non-manual and manual);
4. partly-skilled;
5. unskilled.

The report's author, Professor David Rose of Essex University, said yesterday: 'We believe it will offer government departments a better tool for research, while serving as an important aid to social scientists and medical researchers.

'Above all, it should lead to an improved understanding of how people's jobs – or lack of a job – affect their life chances and those of their children and dependents.'

(Source: Guardian, 15 December 1997.)

ITEM B   *Exercise 2.6*

1. Make a list of the advantages of the proposed schema over the existing RG scale.

2. Note any disadvantages you feel there might be.

3. Write an evaluative conclusion about the change and its implications for measurement of the class structure.

2. The registrar-general's socioeconomic groups

Because it was recognised that the measure of social class used in the registrar-general's scale did not necessarily group together people with the same economic circumstances, a socioeconomic scale was devised and has been in operation since 1951. This classifies people into socio-economic groups, and arguably provides a closer link between classi-fication and command of economic resources than the standard RG classification. This particular classification has been used in govern-ment surveys, notably the General Household Survey.

The classification divides the population into 17 broad groups:

Percentage of the population in each socioeconomic group

SEG classification	% All	% Male	% Female
1 Employers and managers – govt and large establishments	4.9	6.2	3.2
2 Employers and managers – small establishments	10.5	12.9	7.5
3 Professional workers: self-employed	1.0	1.5	0.3
4 Professional workers: employees	3.9	5.7	1.6
5 Intermediate non-manual workers	13.6	10.0	18.2
6 Junior non-manual workers	21.1	9.2	36.4
7 Personal service workers	4.5	1.5	8.4
8 Foreman and supervisors: manual	2.0	3.0	0.7
9 Skilled manual workers	12.7	20.7	2.6
10 Semi-skilled manual workers	10.5	11.5	9.3
11 Unskilled manual workers	5.3	3.9	7.3
12 Own account workers (other than professional)	6.4	9.3	2.8
13 Farmers: employers and managers	0.4	0.6	0.1
14 Farmers: own account	0.5	0.7	0.1
15 Agricultural workers	0.8	1.0	0.5
16 Members of armed forces	0.9	1.3	0.1
17 Inadequately described and not stated occupations	1.0	1.0	0.9
Total	100.0	100.0	100.0

(Source: Census 1991,10 per cent analysis, Economic Activity in Great Britain, volume 2, Tables 19 and C. Office for National Statistics © Crown Copyright.)

The 1991 census provided information on both social class by oc-cupation and socioeconomic group (SEG), allowing us to ascertain the degree to which they diverge. Of the 17 socioeconomic groups, only 10 grouped together people classified in one class according to the RG social class scale (mainly professional workers and all the manual workers). In the case of 'employers and managers', people in these categories (groups 1 and 2) were spread across all six of the RG social class scales. This again highlights the difficulty of classify-ing managers and employers. While they would generally be classified as middle class using the RG scale, in the 1991 census 6.4 per cent of them fell into classes that are generally thought of as working class (IIINM, IV, V).

This problem with the classification of managers (most but not all of whom fall into class II), when combined with the arguments about the classification of clerical workers discussed earlier, points to the fact that of the six classes involved in the RG social class scale it appears to be classes II and IIINM that present the greatest problem, in terms of homogeneous groups of people who could be said to constitute a social class. Given that according to the 1991 census classes II and IIINM accounted for 51 per cent of the economically active and 91 per cent of those conventionally described as middle class, it would seem that the middle class (as conventionally understood, that is, classes I, II and IIINM) present the greatest problem in terms of classification. Because these groups are rising in importance in the population as the employment structure changes with the increase in non-manual occupations, it might be argued that such changes mean that the RG social class scale is becoming less and less useful as time goes on.

The assumption that there are three classes (upper, middle, working) has led to a conflict between proponents of the tripartite model and those of the binary (two-class) model of classical sociology, particularly Marxists. This has in turn led to attempts either to identify the middle class as an independent class, which undermines some classical Marxist arguments, or to reject the notion of a middle class and to argue that the middle class is effectively an adjunct of either the dominant or the subordinate class. This issue is discussed in more detail in Chapter 3.

3. The standard occupational classification

This measure was devised because governments were concerned that social class was not well indicated by the single measure of occupation. It was felt that, in the sociological literature, social class tended to be based on many indicators, rather than simply occupation. Hence the standard occupational classification was intended to 'declass' occupational schemas and measure jobs only. It classifies occupations according to the degree of skill and qualifications required. It contains nine major divisions, as shown in the following table.

Although this classification may be used to consider the changing occupational structure, the lack of distinction between the employed and those in self-employment, for example, make it a blunt instrument with which to try to carry out research. It matters (particularly for Marxist class analysis but also more generally) whether someone is a self-employed plumber or a plumber working for someone else. Insofar as sociologists wish to view classes as involving relations between people in the same occupation but with otherwise widely different characteristics, such as being self-employed, matters for a range of social attitudes and behaviours. The classification also fails in comparison with the

Percentage of the population over 16 in each standard occupational classification

Standard occupational classification	% of population (16 and over)
1 Managers and administrators	15.9
2 Professional occupations	8.7
3 Associate professional and technical occupations	8.7
4 Clerical and secretarial occupations	16.1
5 Craft and related occupations	14.5
6 Personal and protective service occupations	9.1
7 Sales occupations	7.2
8 Plant and machine operatives	10.3
9 Other occupations	8.6
Occupation not stated or inadequately described	0.9
Total	100.0

(Source: Census 1991. Office for National Statistics © Crown Copyright.)

RG scale in terms of frequency of use, and therefore for the existence of comparative data. It encompasses 18 major occupational groups, 73 minor ones and 3800 occupations (Hadfield and Skipworth, 1994).

4. The advertising industry standard

The advertising industry has developed an alternative classification for the purpose of market research because the RG scale does not have a clear link to income and it is people's disposable income that is of interest to the advertising industry. The best known classification, devised by the Institute of Practitioners in Advertising, classifies people on the basis of occupation into six classes: A, B, C1, C2, D, and E. This provides similar information to the RG classification in many respects, and the border classes (C1 and C2) are particularly confused in their makeup. For example C2 includes skilled manual workers, foremen and the self-employed.

In recent years, the idea that what we consume and how we spend our money have become important issues in sociology. This has led to a greater focus on matters pertaining to consumption. The rationale here is that two people who both earn £15 000 a year may spend that money in very different ways and therefore have very different lifestyles. This approach tends to focus on how relatively affluent people spend their money and tends to ignore the constraints on people who have insufficient money to make such choices. In the media and the advertising industry, however, many such scales exist and these have been taken up by sociologists, reflecting the postmodern idea that social class based on occupation is no longer of central relevance and that we need to classify people on the basis of consumption patterns or lifestyles (see Hadfield and Skipworth, 1994).

Furthermore, some postmodernist authors have suggested that we now live in an age when all boundaries are dissolving, and therefore traditional classifications that impose boundaries between the various groups are no longer relevant. The traditional classifications are also seen as unable to provide information on the variety of lifestyles that exist today, which may be a more important way of categorising people than their occupation or income. Malcolm Waters (1997) argues that

> 'occupation' is now critical not in terms of its capacity to put one in a relationship of exploitation but because it is a badge of status, an indicator of one's importance and of one's capacity to consume. Alongside these we can place ascribed-status membership dimensions that have now become value-infused, symbolized and reflexive (ethnicity, religion, education, race, gender and sexual preference) plus consumption statuses (yuppie, trekkie, hacker, clothes-horse, punk, gothic, jogger, opera buff etc.) and value-commitment statuses (feminist, environmentalist, Zionist, redneck, right-to lifer etc.) Identity is thus not linked either to property or to organizational position. Under conditions of advanced affluence, styles of consumption and commitment become socially salient as markers and delimitators (Waters, 1997, pp. 35–6).

Exercise 2.7

a Construct your own postmodernist lifestyle/consumption index. Devise a classification that will allow you to divide the British population into a maximum of 12 identifiable groups on the basis of what they consume and their lifestyle activities. For instance you could divide them into those who watch a lot of TV and those who do not, or those who read a broadsheet newspaper and those who read a tabloid. Whether or not they engage in sport or outdoor recreational activities could be another classification, giving you Active Sporties, Couch Potatoes, Broadsheet Boneheads and Tabloid Trivia Hunters.

Postmodernism as an approach, however, remains controversial and in some circles is becoming increasingly unpopular. Certainly there is now a backlash against it. The main reason for this is that structured social inequalities seem to be excluded from the analysis and everything is put down to lifestyle choices. The fact that these choices require higher than average earnings confirms the view that postmodernism is merely concerned with those in mainly professional jobs who can afford to spend much of their time worrying about lifestyle choices. Postmodern analysis can tell us little about poverty or the continuing inequalities of wealth, because it consistently downplays the importance of decisions about production in the lives of people. Of course it is true that the relationship between economic classes and social classes is not straightforward (that is, it cannot be assumed that knowledge of the income, occupational or property status of someone will tell you how he or she will behave in every instance), but this is not a new point and just because something is complex does not mean it does not exist.

Therefore, in relation to structured social inequality, postmodernism remains controversial and seems in danger of treating temporary advertising fads as if they were fundamental social cleavages. This inadequate response to worldwide growth in structured social inequality is partly why Habermas (1989) has likened postmodernism to young conservatism, in complete contrast to its oft-claimed radical image. His reason is that the postmodern argument that things are now too complex to initiate any collective change, and that if we do we are in danger of creating an authoritarian state, implies that we should do nothing, and therefore be conservative.

Exercise 2.8

 Copy out the table below and use it to summarise information on the various classifications used for social class analysis in Britain.

Measure of class	No. of classes	Groupings	Example of jobs	Advantages	Disadvantages
RG social class					
RG SEG					
Standard occupational classification					
Advertising industry standard					

There are two other major classifications of social class: the Hope–Goldthorpe scale and the Surrey occupational class scheme.

The Hope–Goldthorpe scale

The Hope–Goldthorpe scale resulted from John Goldthorpe's studies of social mobility (Goldthorpe, 1980, 1987). This comprises seven classes.

These seven classes were condensed into three overall groups, which Goldthorpe labelled the 'service class' (classes 1 and 2), the 'intermediate class' (classes 3, 4 and 5) and the 'working class' (classes 5 and 6). These classifications have enjoyed recent usage (notably by Marshall *et al.*, 1988, and Marshall and Swift, 1993), particularly in relation to studies of social mobility.

Classification		Percentage of sample (1987)
1	Higher-grade professionals	13.6
2	Lower-grade professionals	11.5
3	Routine non-manual	9.2
4	Small proprieters and self-employed	9.4
5	Technicians and supervisors	11.6
6	Skilled manual workers	21.2
7	Semi and unskilled manual workers	23.5

(Source: Goldthorpe, 1987.)

This model is different from the government scales of social class since it derives from Goldthorpe's theoretical ideas on the nature of social class and the class structure. As such, it represents the height of an essentially Weberian analysis and classification system. The fact that the schema derives from theoretical reflections on sociological theories of social class is a key strength, as is the fact that it is now widely used due to the dominance of Weberian sociologists (at least in Britain) in terms of the collection of data on social class from large-scale social surveys.

However there are two criticisms of this scale. First, since it is based on a Weberian view of social class, meaning that it groups together people who share a similar market position (income and economic life chances) and work situation (position within the authority relations in workplaces), it is clearly different from Marxist inspired theories of social class, which concentrate much more on what Marxists see as fundamental divisions in society. Thus the leading Marxist social stratification theorist, Erik Olin Wright (1976, 1985), has argued that because the schema is based on occupational classes rather than social classes, the fundamental conflict and division in a capitalist society, namely between the bourgeoisie and the proletariat, is obscured.

The second criticism of the Hope–Goldthorpe scale is that Goldthorpe based his analysis on the male head of household, meaning that married women are deemed to be in the same social class as their husbands, regardless of the women's occupations. Goldthorpe argues that this reflects the reality of a society where in most cases the male determines the market situation and lifestyle of a couple, but feminist sociologists have not been impressed with this argument and this has led to an ongoing debate about the classification of women in social class schemas.

6. The Surrey occupational class scheme

This classification of social class was developed at the University of Surrey (hence the name) by Arber, Dale and Gilbert (1986). The aim was to create a social class schema that would highlight the differential positions of men and women in the class structure. In contrast to Goldthorpe, therefore, women are classified on the basis of their own occupations, whether married or not. This tends to highlight the fact that occupational groups are often overwhelmingly male or female. The Surrey scheme therefore represents an attempt to present a class structure model that accommodates the feminist criticisms of Goldthorpe and others who argue that the male head of household classification system should be retained.

The categories used in the Surrey occupational class scheme are as follows:

- Class 1: higher professionals and large proprietors.
- Class 2: employers and managers.
- Class 3: lower professional.
- Class 4: secretarial and clerical.
- Class 5: foremen and self-employed manual.
- Class 6a: sales and personal services.
- Class 6b: skilled manual.
- Class 7: semi-skilled manual.
- Class 8: unskilled manual.

The division of class 6 highlights an area where there is a clear gender difference, since sales and personal service workers are overwhelmingly women, while skilled manual workers are overwhelmingly male. The scale therefore incorporates the gendered nature of occupations.

However the problem with the attempt to include women on their own terms is distinguishing between women who are in what are viewed as permanent positions, which will have a crucial influence on their lifestlyes, and those who are in transitory positions, notably those engaged in unwaged occupations. It is also difficult to classify women in part-time employment on this basis, since this may be a transitory element in some women's lives while for others it may be a more permanent state of affairs. This illustrates women's rather more complex relationship with paid employment compared with men, and also highlights the problems involved in trying to develop classification systems that can deal with this complexity.

Evaluation of occupationally based classifications of social class

Strengths

- Relatively easy to understand.
- The classifications are familiar to sociologists and regularly used in research.
- Since they have been around for most of the present century they allow comparisons between time periods.

- For many people the job they do provides all (or nearly all) of their income and occupation is therefore an important basis of social inequality.

Weaknesses

- Occupations have been reclassified over time, making comparisons misleading.
- They only measure one variable, occupation. It is debatable whether this is entirely equivalent to what people understand by the term social class
- Such scales are merely descriptive and explain nothing about class relations, that is, the nature of social relationships between the classes. Neither do they inform us about the causes of the shape of the class structure (the positions filled by people).
- It is difficult to classify people who do not have an occupation. The unemployed are classified on the basis of their last job but this suggests, for example, that an unemployed teacher has the same command over resources as an employed teacher. This is unlikely to be the case.
- Married women are classified on the basis of their husbands' occupations and not their own. This means that married women's occupations do not determine their social class.
- The classes to which occupations are assigned are not based entirely on income. Thus a person who earns less than someone else might be placed in a higher class.
- The class to which people are allotted is derived solely from what they are doing at the present time and does not take into account their origins or whether they see their present position as temporary or permanent.

Exercise 2.9

Write your own evaluation of the usefulness of objective measures of social class.

Measuring social class: subjective measures

A key problem with occupationally based objective measures of the class structure is that they take no account of what people feel themselves to be. Individuals are assigned to a class merely on the basis of what job they do. There is nothing to prevent teachers, for example, from describing themselves as working class even though on the basis of their occupation they would inevitably be described as middle class.

It is also possible to imagine dockers who feel themselves to be middle class. Reid (1989) provides some examples of the contrast between objective and subjective dimensions of class, derived from the work of Roberts *et al.* (1977) (Item C).

ITEM C

Subjective social class	Objective social class (%)					
	I	II	IIINM	IIIM	IV	V
Middle class	74	71	48	37	21	29
Working class	11	23	42	56	66	62

(Source: Roberts et al. (1977).)

ITEM C **Exercise 2.10**

[i] 1. With reference to Item C, what percentage of people in social class II (objective basis) feel themselves to be part of the working class (subjective basis)?

[i] 2. What percentage of people in social class V (objective basis) feel themselves to be part of the middle class (subjective basis)?

[i] 3. Identify the social class (on an objective basis) with the highest number of people subjectively in a different class from that to which they would objectively be assigned.

This raises the important question of which measure more accurately describes class structure, given that the findings from objective and subjective measures conflict.

It should not be assumed that this problem was confined to the 1970s. For example using the manual/non-manual dividing line as the basis for classification, the 1991 census revealed that the British population (or at least the economically active part of it) was composed of 56 per cent middle class and 42 per cent working class. However the MORI poll found in 1989 that 30 per cent of people described themselves as middle class and 67 per cent described themselves as working class (Hadfield and Skipworth, 1994). Research in 1993 by ICM found that 40 per cent of those in occupational groups A and B described themselves as working class and 14 per cent of those in classes D and E described themselves as middle class (reported in *The Scotsman*, September 1993). Clearly these findings present radically contrasting pictures of the class structure.

The issue of objective versus subjective measures has been central to many recent debates on feminist methodology. Ann Oakley (1981) justified her use of qualitative techniques to study the position of housewives and mothers by arguing that it allowed them to speak for themselves and therefore women's true experiences would be integrated into the findings. This led to the construction of a feminist approach to methodology that was based more on qualitative than on quantitative measures, continuing the tradition pioneered by Oakley but also contending that knowledge in sociology had been gendered not only by the well-known invisibility of women in many studies but by the choice of research method. It was argued by MacKinnon (1982) that men's thought is constituted in objective terms and this includes the attempt to objectify women and make them the object rather than the subject of research and knowledge. She argued that women need to retain their subjectivity both as a valuable reality and to resist this attempted objectification.

Such accounts point to the way in which knowledge is not neutral but arises from the exercise of power. Sociological accounts of inequality therefore potentially have inequality embedded within them and the debate on methodology also becomes a debate on power and inequality. Stanley and Wise (1983) argued that men decide what counts as knowledge and this represents a form of patriarchy (a system of male control) within sociology. In response, Harding (1986) stressed that the only real knowledge that women can rely on is that gained from their own personal experiences, a view that clearly arises from the feminist slogan 'the personal is political'. This implies an emphasis on qualitative rather than quantitative methods.

Feminist methodology has therefore offered a well-thought-out argument for greater emphasis on subjective analysis of inequality against the well-established quantitative tradition of examining inequality. The latter approach has been booming in recent years, largely due to the rise of the computer and the ability it offers to analyse large data sets using sophisticated statistical techniques. The near dominance of quantitative approaches in relation to the study of inequality has begun to wane. Greater emphasis is being placed on culture and identity (meaning the way people see themselves and the way this is affected by the culture or way of life around them) and this necessarily involves considering the way people think and feel.

This trend is made clear by the fact that research on class inequality is moving away from emphasis on the analysis of static measures of the class structure (essentially assigning people to a class schema and then investigating the links between class positions and various factors such as education and health), to a greater concern with the processes of class formation (see Chapter 4 of this book) and the question of whether and how people come to recognise themselves as a class. It would therefore seem that while quantitative research continues to flourish and produce evidence that inequality is still a central aspect of life, more interest is being shown in the subjective experience of such inequality and resistance to it. This is fed both by the neo-Marxist emphasis on culture and ideology (that is, a system of ideas, often with the suggestion they are false ideas) and by the feminist emphasis on the link between knowledge and power and the consequent emphasis on subjective qualitative research.

Exercise 2.11

i a e

1. In small groups, assume the role of sociologists interested in undertaking research on the way people see themselves and what words and concepts they use to describe their identity. For instance a man may describe himself as a Yorkshireman or black British or middle class or a northerner. Or a women may describe herself as working class, a woman, an Asian or British. Several combinations of these identities are possible in each case.

2. In response to your request for research funding you have been asked to justify your use of these subjective categories (rather than objective indicators) as the key concepts in your study. Write a 500-word justification of your decision and present it to the rest of the class for discussion.

The economic basis of social class

Whatever position is taken in relation to the various ways of measuring and categorising social class, and whether it should be done with the use of objective measures or based on people's subjective evaluation of their position, it is clear that the notion of social class centres on economic processes. This has led to a debate on the usefulness of social class as a concept. Firstly, there are some forms of inequality that are not economic in nature, the most notable being violence against women and racist attacks on ethnic minorities. How can one account for these forms of oppression using concepts centred on the economy? Although it is possible to argue that the economic position in which people find themselves contributes to their vulnerability to such attacks, some sociologists argue that while class might be able to explain exploitation, it cannot explain all forms of oppression.

A second problem arises with the definition of 'economic'. If this pertains only to work that is paid, then the tasks of women who have no paid employment but do housework are excluded. This issue has been central to feminist critiques of social class classifications since measures that centre on paid occupations serve to make invisible the large amount of effort put in by (mainly female) houseworkers. This work is absolutely essential to the continued existence of society, but since it is not paid it is not recognised as an economic activity (see also Chapter 6).

The debate on the measurement of class and its relation to other forms of inequality is therefore not only about how we operationalise the concept in the various forms of measurement, but is also theoretical in terms of how we consider inequality and the links between its various forms.

3 The changing class structure

By the end of this chapter you should:

- be aware of the extent of the growth in inequality in contemporary Britain;
- be aware of recent trends in the distribution of income and wealth;
- appreciate the arguments surrounding the decline of manufacturing industry and the sociological significance of this and other occupational transitions;
- have an understanding of the sociological debates on the place of the rich in the class structure;
- be familiar with the debates on the position of and the borders between the middle class, the working class and the underclass
- have practised structured exam questions.

Introduction

One of the most dramatic changes in the structure of inequality in Britain has occurred in recent years. After the Second World War there was a gradual decrease in the degree of inequality, particularly in wealth. However in the 1980s and 1990s there has been a return to greater inequality as a result of the free market policies of the new right.

While this is not surprising, what is startling from a sociological point of view is that it is occurring at precisely the same time as some leading sociologists are talking about the end of class. Bradley (1996) points out that 'class as a topic has recently become "non grata"', that is, not to be mentioned, which indeed seems to be the case. However, since it is clear that inequality has increased in recent years, other sociologists, despite the fashion of the times, have continued to talk about the importance of class divisions in society. Stephen Edgell, for example, argues that 'what needs to be explained is not the presumed demise of class, but the tenacity of class based patterns of inequality' (Edgell, 1993, p. 122).

The distribution of income

By income we mean an inward flow of money, usually at regular intervals. This can be divided into income earned from work done, and here employment or self-employment are the key sources; or unearned income, such as interest on money in bank or building society accounts and dividends on share holdings.

The main source of information on inequality in income is the New Earnings Survey, conducted by the government.

ITEM A   *Exercise 3.1*

Item A is taken from the 1995 New Earnings Survey. Your task is to look at this information and then answer the following questions:

ITEM A

Average gross weekly pay for full-time workers on adult rates whose pay was not affected by absence. Manual and non-manual refer to the type of occupation held (£s)

Region	Male manual	Male non-manual	Female manual	Female non-manual
South East	310.70	506.30	208.50	326.10
East Anglia	283.30	402.70	175.30	264.00
South West	276.50	410.00	178.00	267.30
West Midlands	285.20	410.20	186.40	264.20
East Midlands	282.40	395.80	177.20	262.80
Yorks & H'side	285.50	390.60	176.20	259.30
North West	290.40	414.40	182.00	270.60
North	286.40	385.40	180.30	258.70
Wales	284.40	386.80	185.40	264.90
Scotland	284.50	413.20	186.00	272.70

(Source: New Earnings Survey, 1995.)

---

1. Identify the group with the highest and lowest levels of pay in 1995.

2. For each of the four categories of employee in Item A, identify the region with the highest and lowest levels of pay.

3. Suggest two other social divisions that might lead to inequality in pay.

4. In no more than 100 words, write a summary of what the information tells you about inequality in the distribution of income.

5. Why might these figures not accurately reflect the distribution of income in Britain?

The 1980s and 1990s have witnessed the growth of income inequality in Britain on a larger scale than in any industrialised country, with the sole exception of New Zealand (Hills, 1995). A report for the Institute of Fiscal Studies (Johnson *et al.*, 1997) revealed an unprecedented rise in inequality, in the last twenty years, reversing the trend of falling inequality since the 1950s. Paul Johnson, one of the authors of the report, was quoted as saying that 'The increase in inequality is probably the biggest social change we have experienced in the last 20 years' (quoted in Balls, 1997). The report pointed out that the richest 10 per cent of the British population now have as much income as all the households in the bottom 50 per cent of the population. The report also pointed to the rise in unemployment and the rise in the number of households that rely on state benefits for their income: in 1993 more than 70 per cent of income in the bottom 10 per cent of households came from means-tested benefits. This report and the earlier Rowntree report on income and wealth (Hills, 1995) identify two key reasons for this development.

Firstly, the income of those with less than average earnings has risen more slowly than for those with average or above average earnings, and for the very poorest it has actually fallen. While average income rose by 36 per cent between 1979 and 1992, the income of the poorest tenth fell by 17 per cent. The 1994 Family Expenditure Survey found a similar 17 per cent fall in the income of the poorest 10 per cent between 1979 and 1994, while the income of the top 10 per cent of earners rose by 62 per cent.

Secondly, changes to the tax system have benefited the better off considerably more than the lower paid. In 1994 the Treasury calculated that the proportion of income paid in taxes by the poorest 20 per cent of households rose from 31 per cent to 39 per cent between 1979 and 1992, while for the richest 20 per cent of households the equivalent figures were 37 per cent and 34 per cent respectively, (Bevins, 1994). The Institute of Fiscal Studies (IFS) reported that the effect of tax changes since 1985 had been to boost the incomes of the richest 10 per cent by 6 per cent and cut the income of the poorest 10 per cent by 3 per cent (Elliott *et al.*, 1994).

Link Exercise 3.1

 1. Use the material in this section to draw up a summary of the changes in the distribution of income in the 1980s and early 1990s.

 2. Look at the theories in Chapter 4 and divide into groups of about 4–5 students with half the groups in your class representing positions that believe inequality has a positive role and half representing positions that believe inequality is largely negative. Use the information you have gathered from chapters 2–3 and elsewhere to conduct a debate on the following proposition: 'As sociologists, we believe that the level of inequality experienced in Britain in the 1980s and 1990s has been socially and economically harmful.'

Statistics on average income can be obtained from the New Earnings Survey, which provides information on both the mean average and the median average. The mean average is arrived at by adding all incomes together and dividing the total by the number of figures that have been added together. The median average is arrived at by placing all income figures in rank order and taking the figure that lies at the mid-point of the resulting series of numbers. This allows us to consider the distribution of income. If the median is below the mean, then the distribution of income is skewed towards the top wage earners, which was the case for all categories of workers in Britain in 1995.

In Item B, decile means tenth of the population and quartile means quarter of the population.

ITEM B

Gross hourly earnings (pence), full-time workers on adult rates

	Lowest decile	Lowest quartile	Median	Upper quartile	Upper decile	Mean
Male manual						
1994	399	482	595	746	910	631
1995	397	486	609	766	943	644
Male non-manual						
1994	503	690	967	1330	1820	1090
1995	511	706	993	1383	1907	1133
Female manual						
1994	305	351	420	523	639	453
1995	302	356	432	537	661	464
Female non-manual						
1994	406	505	652	904	1225	744
1995	413	522	683	961	1309	776

(Source: New Earnings Survey, 1995, table A16.)

ITEM C ### Exercise 3.2

Study Item B and answer the following questions:

[a] 1. Explain in your own words the meaning of the terms median, mean, decile and quartile.

[i] 2. Summarise the trends shown in Item B.

[i] 3. Identify the highest and lowest paid workers in 1995.

[i] 4. Which groups experienced a fall in pay between 1994 and 1995?

The distribution of wealth

Wealth is a stock of money, share holdings, goods with a monetary value and so on that are at the disposal of the owner and can, with differing degrees of ease, be turned into ready cash.

Westergaard (1995) has argued that the 1980s and 1990s have seen a reversal of earlier trends in the distribution of wealth. Quoting figures from *Social Trends* he argues that if we exclude the value of personal dwellings, the share of marketable wealth of the richest 1 per cent of the population rose from 26 per cent to 29 per cent and of the richest 5 per cent from 45 per cent to 53 per cent between 1981 and 1991. This can be seen in *Social Trends* 1995, which includes the following table on the distribution of wealth (Item D).

ITEM C

Distribution of Wealth in Britain, 1976–92

Marketable Wealth	Percentage of total wealth				
	1976	1981	1986	1991	1992
Most wealthy 1%	21	18	18	17	18
Most wealthy 5%	38	36	36	34	37
Most wealthy 10%	50	50	50	46	49
Most wealthy 25%	71	73	73	70	72
Most wealthy 50%	92	92	90	92	92
Marketable wealth less value of dwellings		.			
Most wealthy 1%	29	26	25	29	29
Most wealthy 5%	47	45	46	51	53
Most wealthy 10%	57	56	58	64	65
Most wealthy 25%	73	74	75	80	82
Most wealthy 50%	88	87	89	93	94

(Source: Social Trends 1995.)

ITEM D

Exercise 3.3

Study Item C and attempt the following questions:

[i] 1. What evidence is there of greater equality in the distribution of wealth?

[i] 2. Summarise the trends in the distribution of wealth during this period.

[i] 3. What proportion of marketable wealth less the value of dwellings was held by the least wealthy 50 per cent of the population in 1992?

ITEM D

In 1992 *The Sunday Times* survey of the top 300 richest people in Britain revealed that their combined wealth was £50.09 billion or 10.03 per cent of GDP.

Fifty-nine of the people on the list went to Eton and eight to Harrow; 28 went to Oxford University and 26 to Cambridge University. The list included 21 women.

In terms of regional breakdown, 136 resided in the South-East, while only four resided in the North-East and two in Wales.

In 1996 *The Sunday Times* survey covered the 500 richest people in Britain. Their total wealth was £70.58 billion, a rise of 28 per cent on the previous year. The top 20 alone were worth £22.78 billion and the top 300 had a total of £62.20 billion.

Only 75 people on this list (15 per cent of the total) were members of the aristocracy (meaning that their wealth was derived from land passed down through their families, often dating back to the feudal system of linking titles with land); 177 people had inherited their wealth; 100 had made their fortunes from industry and 148 from commerce and retailing.

Fifty-three of the people on the list went to Eton and seven to Harrow; 35 went to Oxford University and 28 to Cambridge University.

The list contained 38 women, compared with 37 in 1994 and 40 in 1995. In terms of regional breakdown, 244 came from the South-East.

ITEMS D AND E

Exercise 3.4

[i][e] 1. To what extent does the information in Item D contradict the trends shown in Item C?

[i] 2. Use the information in Item D to summarise the changing composition of the rich between 1992 and 1996.

[e] 3. Which of the factors mentioned in *The Sunday Times* survey (Item D) do you think is the most important in gaining access to the ranks of the rich? Justify your answer.

The place of the wealthy in the class structure

The most comprehensive survey of the contemporary upper class in Britain is provided by John Scott (1991). He argues that the dominant form of the British upper class, based on family links and personal ownership of land and industry, has reduced over the years. The growth of limited liability companies has led to more and more industries being owned not by individuals but by financial conglomerates and pension funds: almost half the top 250 British companies in 1988 compared with about 10 per cent by individuals.

However Scott contends that the upper class network has managed to retain control of substantial wealth and income from industry via their control of financial capital. The money from the old rich (the aristocracy) has been invested in industry by merchant bankers such as the Rothschilds and the Barings, who are themselves linked to the old landowning aristocracy. As a result the upper class has managed to survive the transition from the agricultural to the industrial economy (and, some would argue, towards a post-industrial economy).

Peter Saunders (1990), writing from a broadly new right perspective, rejects the idea that a distinct upper class still exists. He argues that the spread of share ownership and the growth in pension funds and insurance funds (via endowment mortgages) mean that a substantial proportion of the population now have at least an indirect share in the ownership of the means of production.

Scott (1991) would contend that this is an overdrawn picture, but even if it is true, ownership of company shares via a pension fund gives the individual absolutely no right of control over those shares. This right is in fact held by the nominees of pension funds, insurance companies and merchant banks who sit on the boards of the various companies in which these institutions have shares. These people are invariably directors of these institutions and therefore control rests with a small minority through their control of finance capital.

From a manufacturing to a service economy

Abercrombie *et al.* (1988) point out that there has been a dramatic shift in the industrial structure of Britain, with a decline in manufacturing jobs and a rise in the importance of the service sector: 'In 1966, 8.6 million people were employed in manufacturing industry; by 1985 there were only 5.4 million.'

The term manufacturing industry refers to firms and jobs where people actually make things, such as the car industry, while the service sector refers to jobs that do not lead to the production of tangible goods. The service sector provides services for which there is a need, such as transport, retailing, banking and insurance.

Exercise 3.5

1. Create a list of services not included in the list above.

2. Compile a list of firms in your local area that are in the manufacturing sector.

It is this shift in the industrial structure of the economy that has resurrected the debate on whether the working class is in decline and whether we are now all middle class (a view once put forward by Margaret Thatcher). This arises since the working class is usually defined as comprising manual workers. This is problematic on a number of counts. Firstly, it is only true if one accepts the functionalist or Weberian analysis of class and it has nothing to do with the way that Marxists define class. Secondly, the terms non-manual, white-collar and service worker are often treated as though they are synonymous, which they are not. A bus conductor is a service worker (he/she does not make anything) but this is also a manual occupation.

While it is important to bear these points in mind, it is nonetheless clear that there has been a massive shift and this has led some sociologists to argue that we now live in a post-industrial society. In class terms, this has led to more importance being attached to the middle class than the working class.

The post-industrial economy thesis

This argument was first mooted in the 1960s by the original exponent of the post-industrial thesis, Daniel Bell (1973). On the basis of statistics showing a decline in the number of manufacturing jobs, he argued that we were moving into a post-industrial economy. He welcomed this fact since he thought that the new jobs that would be created in the service sector would be better jobs and this would lead to an increase in the overall quality of life. This 'post-industrial' society was to be a society dominated by knowledge work (mainly work with computers and communications technology requiring technical and other expertise). He also believed that this stage would involve a move away from companies being primarily concerned with profits towards being concerned with satisfying their workforces and providing lifetime jobs. Overall, therefore, the standard of life would improve.

While it is true that the number of jobs in the service sector has grown, the new jobs have often failed to live up to the hopes of Daniel Bell and in many cases are poorly paid and require little skill. 'Employment in the service industries proper hardly matches the profile of the "knowledge society" elite portrayed by Bell. Average gross weekly earnings in US manufacturing were $396 in 1986, in services $275' (Callinicos, 1989). Callinicos argues that in California (the paradigmatic post-industrial society) service sector wages are some 40–50 per cent lower than those in manufacturing industry. Nigel Harris (1983) points out that by 1982 twice as many people sold McDonalds hamburgers in the United States as made steel.

The post-industrial thesis is open to a number of other criticisms. Firstly, it tends to portray the past British economy as dominated by manufacturing industry. However, as Callinicos (1989) points out, such jobs have never accounted for the majority of the workforce, reaching a peak of 48 per cent in 1955.

Secondly, *Employment Gazette* statistics show that in the early 1990s, during the second economic recession in 10 years, the number of employees in the service sector fell, as well as the number in manufacturing.

Thirdly, there is the question of who is doing the manufacturing now. If we look at the world-wide figures there are now more people working in manufacturing than ever before, and the number is rising continually. One of the possible reasons for the decline in manufacturing employment in the West is the move of much of manufacturing industry to newly industrialised countries (NICs): South Korea, Taiwan, Hong Kong, Singapore, Mexico and Brazil.

Such developments have led to debates about whether we in Britain live in a post-industrial, post-Fordist society. These terms are linked but distinct. An industrial society is based primarily on manufacturing industry. The concept of a post-industrial society has developed from the idea that manufacturing is declining in importance and that the service sector is now the most important part of the economy. The suggestion that jobs in the service sector have different characteristics is the key element of the original post-industrial thesis.

The terms Fordism and post-Fordism derive from an article written by the Italian Marxist Antonio Gramsci (1971). Looking at the effect of Fordism on society, he linked changes in production methods to wider changes in society and the growth of Americanism. His point was that the success of Fordist mass production (exemplified by Henry Ford's method of producing the Model T Ford – hence the name) depended not only on new production techniques but on the creation of new social relations. The output of the new industries relied on mass sales to guarantee their profitability and also on the way that industrialists such as Ford enforced clear standards of behaviour on their workers' personal lives. The link between production and other aspects of life remained in Marxist analyses influenced by Gramsci, such as the French Regulation school. Their emphasis was on the way social life was controlled and the need for capitalism to regulate not just production but the whole of society.

The term post-Fordism is used by some commentators to suggest that this system (Fordism) fell into crisis some time in the 1970s and that capitalism has had to devise new modes of regulating society to ensure continued profitability. These new ways include the promotion of more flexible work patterns and the promotion of specialised, small-scale production units to replace the mass production facilities that had fallen into crisis. It can therefore be seen that while there is a clear link between the notions of post-industrial society and post-Fordism, the latter is a wider concept that goes beyond the make-up of the production sector to consider the way this affects social relations in a society.

While it is clear that some versions of the post-industrial argument are clearly wide of the mark, particularly the notion that the level of job satisfaction is higher in service sector jobs than in manufacturing, it is true that in Britain in the 1990s more than three times as many people are employed in the service sector than in manufacturing.

One of the reasons put forward for this transformation is the process of globalisation: the growth of much closer commercial and other links between nations and therefore a greater interrelatedness around the world. The new international division of labour thesis (Frobel et al., 1980) suggests that the new division consists of manufacturing industry moving to underdeveloped Third World countries, leaving the First World to specialise in and base itself upon the service economy. If this is true, it presents problems for those parts of the First World that have historically been dependent upon manufacturing. In Britain, for example, this would clearly have an impact on areas such as Tyneside and Clydeside (with a history of shipbuilding) and the East and West Midlands (historically based on manufacturing, notably textiles and cars). Furthermore, since the welfare state is based on high levels of tax revenue, this development is seen as threatening the welfare state since if companies relocated to other countries no tax revenue will be gathered from them.

However it is important to remember that, while a fashionable notion, the concept of globalisation is highly contested. Hirst and Thompson (1995), for instance, point out that multinational companies still rely on the state for protection through law enforcement, or even military protection of their interests, for example the Gulf War can be viewed as a move to protect the interests of Western oil companies. Furthermore, according to Gill and Law (1988) the vast majority (over two thirds) of multinational investment goes to just a few advanced industrial nations, primarily Canada, the United States, Germany and Britain. Hence the bulk of investment goes nowhere near the Third World, and therefore the spectre of competition from Third World countries with much cheaper labour supplies is something of a myth if the exact flow of money is looked at. Equally on this point, one of the effects of industrialisation for newly industrialised countries (NICs) such as South Korea and Singapore has been a rise in the cost of their labour, to the point where the South Korean labour minister has bemoaned the fact that South Korean businesses are complaining that it is difficult to do business in South Korea and are contemplating transferring to Britain to improve their business (quoted in the *Guardian*, 16 January 1997).

Whether all the blame for the decline in manufacturing and the rise of what some have called the post-industrial economy can be laid at the door of globalisation is doubtful. A much more likely reason was the implementation of monetarist policies by the Thatcher government, which led to rises in interest rates and a consequent rise in costs for industry, causing a large number of British manufacturers to go bust.

The point here is that we can do something to change the situation; that is, if the decline of manufacturing industry is the result of certain domestic political policies, things can be improved through the adoption of different policies. While Britain alone cannot deal with any changes ushered in by globalisation. Therefore if you believe that globalisation is the key factor, this leads to the conclusion that such changes cannot be reversed on a purely national level. The debate is therefore important in terms of whether these changes can be reversed, and whether the nation-state is still able to influence the direction of its domestic economy. Ultimately, therefore, it is about whether your vote – which helps dictate the make-up of domestic policies – is still worth anything, or whether we are powerless in the face of global forces, or more precisely, global capitalism. Whatever your views about this, it is clear that one of the changes that has occurred is the rise of service sector workers as a percentage of the British workforce over the last twenty years.

As stated earlier, there is disagreement about how service sector workers should be categorised in social class schemes. If we view them as middle class, then it is clear that Margaret Thatcher may have had a point when she argued that we are all becoming middle class. It is also clear that the view that these workers should be considered as middle class has gained some support among sociologists. On the other hand, if we take the points made by Alex Callinicos (1989) and other Marxists, namely that a large proportion of service sector jobs are not very well paid and that many workers in this sector are worse off than manual workers, then it is possible to conclude that they are part of the working class.

2. Debating the place of the 'middle class'

John Urry (1993) traces the origin of the term 'middle class' to 1785, when it was used by a clergyman to describe a propertied and entrepreneurial class between landlords and peasants. Defining the middle class has perhaps been the most perennial topic of debate in social stratification. Its significance continues to grow as the size of the non-manual workforce grows, since this is one common starting point for defining the middle class, albeit a highly unsatisfactory one. It is unsatisfactory because it is not based on any firm theoretical position but reflects divisions that were seen as important in the past but are not necessarily so now.

In 1911 80 per cent of workers were in manual occupations, but their number fell to 52 per cent in 1981 and 46 per cent in 1991 (Abercrombie and Warde, 1994; Census 1991). In the last ten years, therefore, non-manual workers have become the majority of the workforce.

The 1991 Census shows that non-manual workers fall into one of the following social groupings:

- Class I: 6.84 per cent of the workforce.
- Class II: 31.34 per cent of the workforce.
- Class IIINM: 13.87 per cent of the workforce.

The question arises as to how to classify these non-manual workers. There are essentially six arguments that have been developed in relation to placing the middle class into the class structure:

- The middle classes argument.
- The service class argument.
- The new class argument.
- The proletarianisation argument.
- The new petty bourgeoisie argument.
- The contradictory class locations argument.

Of these the first two lie broadly within the Weberian framework, the third within a radical framework and the latter three within the Marxist one.

The middle classes argument

If we define the middle class as consisting of all non-manual workers, then it includes groups as diverse as shop assistants, lawyers, secretaries, university lecturers and civil servants, the latter ranging from clerical officers to permanent secretaries (the top grade in the Civil Service). Thus the term middle class covers a large range of occupations and incomes and therefore lifestyles and political attitudes.

One quite logical response to this is to suggest that it is inappropriate to treat all these people as identical by attaching the term middle class to them all. We therefore need to look at these groups as the middle classes rather than the middle class. This idea was put forward by Roberts *et al.* (1977), who talked of a fragmented middle class. They identified four distinct groups in their sample of male white-collar workers and concluded that the middle class is now fragmented into distinct groups on the basis of lifestyle and class images. The subjective nature of class images has led some to criticise this idea and to analyse the middle class in terms of more objective factors such as income and work situation. Nonetheless Roberts *et al.*, study has led the way for others to consider how the term middle class may be inadequate to describe such a large but disparate group of workers.

However there are some thinkers who still argue that we should consider the middle class as a united class based on common possession of educational qualifications leading to higher incomes, with their lack of property holdings differentiating them from the upper class. Giddens (1980) argues that it is appropriate to talk of a single middle class and to see the rise of this class as a major move away from the nineteenth-century class structure, which comprised just two classes: the upper and working classes. Giddens' reasoning is that they have the same market capacity (that is, they possess skills that allow them to obtain a certain level of remuneration in the jobs market) and that it is mistake to argue that a class should be conscious of itself as a class (meaning a situation where people who have the same market capacity feel themselves to be linked together in a way that stresses their common interests) in order to be defined as such. Class consciousness is therefore not the determining factor for Giddens, whereas it is central to the work of Roberts *et al.*

The service class argument

Although the term service class was originally coined by the Austro-Marxist, Karl Renner, its current use is by and large a Weberian phenomenon, the two key exponents of the term being Ralf Dahrendorf (1959) and John Goldthorpe (1982). The service class, according to Dahrendorf, is a bridge between the rulers and the ruled. Perhaps the most important exponent of the notion of the service class is John Goldthorpe. He sees it as a conservative force in society, though importantly he also argues that since 63 per cent of the service class are recruited from outside the ranks of the service class as a result of upward social mobility they do not have a great deal of cohesion and are therefore less likely to engage in collective action than the working class. Marshall *et al.* (1988) provide some evidence to support this argument. In their study of social class (with a total sample size of 1770) 53 per cent of service class respondents with a service class background vote Conservative and only 13 per cent vote Labour (from a subsample of 79 of their overall sample). Among service class respondents with a working-class background, Conservative voting was lower at 39 per cent and that for Labour was higher at 31 per cent (from a subsample of 83 of their overall sample). The greater stability afforded by a service class background seems to have led to greater class consciousness, expressed in the higher likelihood of voting Conservative.

However Goldthorpe's argument about the lack of overall cohesiveness among the service class has been criticised, most notably by Savage *et al.* (1992). They argue that when looking at the process of service class formation it is necessary to look at divisions within the service class. They contend that the fraction made up of professional workers such as doctors has a greater degree of internal recruitment (meaning that their class origins are the same as their own class position) than managerial workers and the self-employed. As a result this particular section of the service class may have much greater cohesion and class identity.

According to Savage *et al.* the key reason for this is that the professionals' position is based on the ownership of assets that differ in important ways from the assets held by the two other fractions of the service class. The professional workers' position is based on the possession of cultural assets, largely educational qualifications, which are carried with them as individuals from job to job and in a way can be passed on to their children. This notion is based on Bourdieu's idea (Bourdieu and Passeron, 1977) that those with economic capital can purchase cultural capital: in simple terms, well-paid professional workers are in a position to secure a good education for their children. In contrast managers' assets are based on occupying a particular place within a certain organisation and are not transferrable between organisations; nor can managers pass this position on to their children. Therefore professional workers are more successful in obtaining professional positions for their children and hence there is a larger degree of internal recruitment in the professional service class and greater cohesion. However Savage *et al.* (1992) do point out that managers are not passive in the face of this but try to realise their assets by, for example, moving into self-employment or pushing their children towards educational success and into a professional career.

The new class argument

The origins of this argument lie in the growth of a radical left view of society that was influenced by but different from orthodox Marxist conceptions of society. An important contribution here was the notion developed by the Frankfurt School of writers, who argued that the promotion of mass consumerism had led to the integration of the working class into capitalism. As a result, such writers rejected the traditional Marxist contention that the working class would be at the vanguard of radical revolutionary change in society and instead argued that radical change would come from the new middle-class professionals and intellectuals.

Alvin Gouldner (1979) referred to the growth of a new class that would be able to promote radical views since it would live in new ways and dissent using new forms of protest. Key to this was the idea of a group of new intellectuals whose lives would be based on the possesion of cultural rather than economic capital and would therefore stand somewhat outside the old, traditional class conflicts. Their radicalism would be based on their ability to engage in critical commentaries about the way people live and their relatively stable positions within academia (universities) would provide them with security from material want, allowing them to live their lives in new ways.

Clearly this idea was related to the growth in the 1960s of a counterculture that drew inspiration from new forms of struggle not directly related to the sphere of production, for example the black civil rights, women's liberation, anti-Vietnam war and hippy movements.

In more recent times, such views have developed into the notion that new social movements are the most important force for social and political change and that we now live in times when post-materialist values are the most important. This suggests that the old class conflicts, which centred primarily on issues such as wages and hours of work, have been replaced by attention to quality of life issues, for example by environmental movements.

The proletarianisation argument

It is thought that Marx's prediction of the decline and demise of the middle class was based on his expectation that small business people would be squeezed out by the rise of big business and would become part of the proletariat. The rise of non-manual workers has therefore left contemporary Marxists in a somewhat difficult position. The most important Marxist response to this has been to argue that white-collar clerical workers are not middle-class but have been subject to a process of proletarianisation. This means that their lives have become similar to those of the proletariat and their former privileges have been removed as they have been deskilled (control over their work has been taken away). Today routine white-collar workers find themselves in a position that is much closer to that of the manual working class than professional workers. This argument was most famously advanced by Braverman (1974), based on volume I of Marx's *Capital*.

Braverman focused mainly on the effect that the growth of scientific management, as advocated by Frederick Taylor (1947), was having on skilled industrial craft workers. His argument was that employers could not purchase labour *per se* (since that would involve purchasing persons, which would be slavery) but only labour power, and were therefore left with the problem of ensuring that they extracted the maximum amount of labour power from their workers in a given period. (The conditions under which this occurs is called the labour process.) Braverman argued that the maximisation of labour power output was being pursued through increased control over the work of individual workers and by separating the conception and execution of a task. As a result, workers were no longer involved in the planning and conception of the work they were required to do, and it is this loss that is at the heart of the notion of deskilling.

The division of labour was therefore not simply something that was undertaken in the interest of economic efficiency, but was also a way of effecting greater control over the workforce. Tasks were broken up to allow certain tasks to be completed for a lower wage rate. Scientific management was centrally concerned with the minute observation and measurement of work tasks in order to facilitate such savings, and with the need for management to take control of the work process.

In relation to the debate about the middle class, Braverman was pointing to the way that the process of deskilling was moving beyond the realm of industrial workers and encompassing others. Part 4 of his book is entitled 'The Growing Working-Class Occupations' and it includes chapters on clerical work and retail workers. The growth of the mechanised office undermined the position of clerks in comparison with manual workers. As a result, occupations that had been seen as middle class were in all essential respects now indistinguishable from those of manual workers. As the latter were considered part of the working class, clerical workers ought to be considered part of the working class too.

The new petty bourgeoisie argument

The rise in the number of workers employed in the service sector has provoked the suggestion that they constitute a new 'petty bourgeoisie', the term coined by Marx to describe small employers and the self-employed. The growth of the new petty bourgeoisie, however, is seen as the growth of unproductive workers.

Poulantzas (1975) argues that classes are defined by the class struggle (conflict between the classes), by which he means that classes arise from objective positions held in the division of labour (that is, different jobs can be identifed as belonging to a particular class on the basis of criteria laid down in Marx's work, and because this generates conflicting interests it results in class conflict). Classes are therefore determined by the positions themselves, not by the individuals who fill these positions. It is the job you do that determines your class position rather than anything about you subjectively as an individual. This is in line with Poulantzas's structural approach to Marxism (structuralists point to the underlying structures of society that determine the fate of individuals, who in extreme versions are seen as having almost no power over their own lives). However he adds the distinctive argument that classes are defined at the political and ideological levels as well as the economic level, this in an attempt to avoid the charge of economic determinism so often levelled at Marxism. Therefore in order to define the working class it is necessary to consider the structural positions that differentiate it from the new petty bourgeoisie. Poulantzas's analysis therefore also provides a definition of the 'new petty bourgeoisie'.

The new petty bourgeoisie comprise, according to Poulantzas, all unproductive workers – that is, wage earners rather than producers – and can no longer be considered part of the working class. Productive workers are those who produce things and have surplus value extracted from them by capitalists. The concept of surplus value derives from Marx's argument that the only source of value is labour, and therefore only people who produce things of value are workers. Yet they are not paid the full value of the work they do since some of it is siphoned off as income for the capitalists. It is this that Marx labels surplus value since it is surplus to the amount paid to workers, and this is the essence of the Marxist notion that workers are exploited by capitalists. Unproductive workers, in contrast, cannot have surplus value taken from them because they do not produce surplus value, and as a result they lie outside the basic capitalist class relations.

Poulantzas excludes others from the working class in line with his political and ideological criteria. Managers and supervisors are excluded because the functions they perform represent the domination of capital over labour. The third group he excludes from the working class on ideological grounds are various experts and professional and technical workers. They ideologically dominate the working class by facilitating a division between mental and manual work, and therefore allow the process of deskilling identified by Braverman to occur. Poulantzas also includes low-level white-collar workers such as clerks and secretaries in this grouping, so they too form part of the new petty bourgeoisie.

The net result of all this is a class structure where the working class are a clear minority and the new petty bourgeoisie are the largest unified class. Wright (1979, 1985, 1989) argues that if these criteria were applied to the United States, the proletariat (the Marxist term for the working class) would account for less than 20 per cent of the economically active population, while the new petty bourgeoisie would account for 70 per cent.

The theory of contradictory class locations

One of the key Marxist critics of Poulantzas is Erik Olin Wright (1979, 1985). In his critique of Poulantzas he developed an alternative conception of the middle class by arguing that certain groups, notably small employers, managers, supervisors and semi-autonomous employees (basically, professional workers) find themselves in contradictory class locations. What he means by this is that, on the one hand, they exhibit common interests with the bourgeoisie since they often act on their behalf, ensure that profits are made and part of their wages often accrues from the extraction of surplus from the proletariat. On the other hand they are employees and therefore share some characteristics with the proletariat. Because of those contradictory elements within their own positions they are not, according to Wright and in contrast with the view of Poulantzas, inevitably part of a new petty bourgeoisie and do not in fact form a class as such, but are in positions between the capitalists and the workers. While all class relations are contradictory due to the antagonistic nature of the class structure (in the Marxist view, the class structure is based on the exploitation of one group by another and this leads to antagonism in the form of a class struggle), people in these positions are in a doubly contradictory position.

Such positions emerge due to the process of proletarianisation and deskilling, which requires the employment of people to regulate and enforce the control of capital over the workforce. Wright estimates that something like 41–53 per cent of the US workforce could be categorised as filling these contradictory class positions. Of these, 25–35 per cent (41–54 per cent of the the total population) are on the borders of the working class. Potentially therefore, Wright argues, the human basis for a socialist movement (based on the idea of a radical revolutionary change in the way society is run) is up to 70 per cent of the economically active in the United States. He therefore assumes that some of those he has identified as being in contradictory class locations may be won over to radical political positions, and consequently sees these middling groups as ideologically divided (contrary to Poulantzas and also contrary to supporters of the service class thesis).

The most notable criticism of Wright's work has come from Wright himself. In a later book (Wright, 1989) he fundamentally revised his approach. The reason for this was his adoption of the arguments of a group of thinkers who developed what became known as analytical Marxism.

Analytical Marxism was developed by John Roemer (1982) and Jon Elster (1985) to try to deal with the new right idea of the superiority of free market economics by taking their assumptions (primarily about the need to start with individuals) and showing that Marxist theory still offered a better explanation of society. In particular this involved the assumption that each individual seeks to maximise his or her own individual income, and as a result analysis should be based on the actions of individuals. Since Marxist analysis is based on social collectivities (that is, social class, gender and ethnicity are structures and divisions that affect individuals' lives but are more than simply the sum of the individuals within them) this may seem a strange direction for Marxists to take. However there are other examples of this type of Marxist approach, for example Austro-Marxism.

Michael Mann (1993) argues that sociological writing and thinking about the middle class has resulted in five distinct answers to the question of where to place the middle class in the overall class structure:

1. In the working class.
2. As part of the bourgeoisie.
3. In contradictory class locations.
4. Scattered, with various elements falling into different classes.
5. A separate middle class.

Exercise 3.6

[i][a] Using information in this book and elsewhere (that is, look up the sections dealing with the authors listed below in the relevant sections of this book and in the stratification sections of other textbooks), consider which of Mann's categories on how to classify the middle class above you would place each of the following sociological thinkers:

- Anthony Giddens
- Erik Olin Wright
- Alvin Gouldner
- John Goldthorpe
- Nicos Poulantzas
- Barbara and John Ehrenrich
- Ralf Dahrendorf
- Scott Lash and John Urry
- Rosemary Crompton
- Mike Savage

[e] In each case write a short justification of your decision:

3. Debating the place of the working class

The question of who exactly the middle class are involves the question of who the working class are, since this involves the position of the boundary between the middle class and the working class. In their study of affluent workers in Luton, Goldthorpe *et al.* (1968) found no evidence of embourgeoisement because the workers they studied had not developed middle-class lifestyles and outlooks. For example, 77 per cent of their sample voted Labour, which meant that affluent workers were more likely to vote Labour than the working class as a whole.

However the findings did suggest that while these workers had not undergone a process of embourgeoisement, they were nonetheless distinct from traditional proletarians. These affluent workers were more home-centred than traditional working-class groups, and were less enveloped in the notion of the working-class community. In addition their relationship with the trade unions was not an allegiance based on principle and tradition, as was the case with traditional working-class groups, but an allegiance based on their calculation that the trade unions could help them obtain a higher level of remuneration. Therefore Goldthorpe *et al.* were critical of the Marxist argument for a unified working class.

It is precisely because of the centrality of the working class to Marxist theory that the question of the real nature of working-class life has been important. In a critical comment on the Goldthorpe *et al.*, study, Stephen Hill (1976) argued on the basis of his study of dockers (a group that was seen as traditional working class in the affluent worker schema) that the kind of instrumental attitudes found in workers in Luton were also characteristic of dockers. This put into question the image of the traditional working class presented by Goldthorpe *et al.*

The argument that the working class were in some way divided resurfaced in the 1980s. Again, the context of this was political. Just as the Conservatives had won three election victories in a row in the 1950s, they did so again in the 1980s and in 1992 went one better by winning the fourth in a row. In this climate the notion of a working class united in support of the ideals of socialism was brought into question again. While some tried to resurrect the old embourgeoisement argument (for example, Saunders, 1990), others argued that it was other factors not necessarily related to occupational divisions that were causing divisions within the working class.

The post-Fordist argument suggests that particular jobs can be divided between a secure core of workers and an insecure periphery, and that the interests of the two groups do not run together but diverge since the key aim of the core workers is to retain their privileged position over the peripheral workers. These groups are therefore unlikely to join together.

The commonsense definition of the working class as manual workers is not one supported by Marxists, who by and large tend to equate the working class with a much larger segment of society, and are therefore not threatened with extinction as industry closes down. However, in this respect, they are generally opposed by Weberians and ex-Marxists who have taken up the post-Fordist scenario. What these people have in common is a concern with divisions among manual workers, and they therefore not only reject the idea of a enlarged working class but also the idea that the working class is or is likely to become unified.

Because of the political weight placed on the working class in Marxist thought, the debate about who is working class and who is middle class is more than just a classification problem. The implication of the argument that the middle class is growing is that the weight and likely political importance of the working class is declining. This can also be seen in the growth of the debate about the underclass.

4. The underclass debate

There are two versions of the underclass thesis, but they both divorce the underclass from the working class and as a result reduce the overall size of the working class.

The first version of the underclass thesis is the cultural strand and the second is the structural strand. Proponents of the cultural view suggest that the main reason why members of the underclass suffer from poverty and multiple deprivation are the cultural norms of the family, group and environment in which they are brought up. The implication is that this 'way of life' is the key cause of poverty, and therefore it is people's own fault if they are poor. This view developed particularly in the United States, but has now been applied to Britain and is associated with new right thinkers. In Britain, Saunders (1990) argues that there are four key features that distinguish members of the underclass: (1) they suffer multiple deprivation, (2) they are socially marginalised, (3) they are almost entirely dependent on state welfare, and (4) they have a culture of resigned fatalism. It is perhaps the last two of these points that are most clearly identifiable as elements of the cultural approach to the underclass. In some ways these ideas are a development of the culture of poverty thesis first identified by Lewis (1968) in his work in Mexico. The key difference seems to be that while Lewis identified what he and the poor themselves saw as some positive aspects of this culture, the culture of the underclass is invariably seen as entirely negative. At the centre of this is the concept of the dependency culture, the idea that people become dependent on state welfare handouts in a similar way to drug dependency, and this dependency is seen as an entirely bad thing, fitting in with the new right critique of the welfare state.

In the United States, the cultural version of the underclass thesis was most clearly developed by Murray (1984), who argued that the growth of state welfare programmes to combat poverty had led to more poverty rather than less. According to Murray, access to welfare money allowed people to engage in types of behaviour that were destructive, notably having children outside marriage.

In contrast the structural view of the underclass stresses structural barriers in society that keep people in poverty. For instance one such barrier for ethnic minorities is the existence of racism. Since this is not the fault of the ethnic minorities, the structural view tends not to blame the victim but finds the cause of poverty in the structures of society. By implication, attempts to eradicate poverty also require structural change, and therefore some government action at the very least. This approach to the underclass is associated particularly with Weberian writers. For instance it is used to describe the situation of ethnic minorities in the employment and housing markets in Rex and Tomlinson's (1979) study of Birmingham.

Cultural approaches to the underclass, which in relation to the United States are largely debates about race (see Chapter 9), have been criticised by those who argue that the position of poor American blacks cannot be separated from the experience of the black middle class. It is not possible to view the black middle class as an underclass, and since they have enjoyed relative success the argument that black people are poor because they have a different culture is undermined by the very existence of a black middle class. Wilson (1987) has criticised such cultural accounts by arguing that it is structural factors, notably the changing jobs market and the decline of low-skill manufacturing jobs, that are responsible for the creation of a black underclass. Mann (1995), as well as identifying the two distinct theoretical conceptions of the term underclass, also identifies a third group who object to any use of the term. This group consists of more radical sociologists, including Marxist sociologists.

Ruth Lister (1991) provided a summary of the objections to the term in an article in the *Social Studies Review*. She points out that the term is used to cover a diverse group of people who have little in common but their reliance on some sort of welfare benefit. Hence the concept provides no explanation of why people are poor since it covers a multititude of living arrangements. Secondly, she argues that the concept is tinged with a view of the poor as a disease or threat to social order, and therefore encourages a pathological view of the poorest members of society. Crucially, this is seen as a resurrection of the Victorian distinction between the deserving and the undeserving poor, a distinction made not on the basis of need but on morality.

In relation to the cultural version of the underclass thesis, Gallie (1994) investigated whether the unemployed and those on benefits did (as cultural underclass theory suggests) hold distinctive views compared with the rest of the population, but he could find no evidence that such a distinction actually exists. This is important, since Pilkington (1992) argues that even some structural versions of the underclass thesis seem to be in danger of taking on board some elements of the notion of the dependency culture.

Instead of using the term 'underclass', some – mainly European – social democratic thinkers contend that the poor should be described as 'socially excluded'. This view does not concentrate on the behaviour of the poor, but on the rights and entitlements that all citizens should have, and builds on the work on citizenship undertaken by T. H. Marshall (1963).

Exam question

The following exam question is taken from the InterBoard Syllabus Summer 1996 examination.

ITEM E

The decline of class?

Gordon Marshall et al. have conveniently summarised the alleged 'decline of class' in Britain in the following way. The first factor is the restructuring of capital and labour. The decline of manufacturing industry and the rise of service industries have led to the numerical decline of the manual or traditional working class. Capitalists are considered to have used the changing economic situation to reassert control over labour. Secondly, a greater variety of social, cultural and political differences and identities are considered to occur within the major class groups than in the past. Thirdly, instrumental collectivism means that workers in a particular industry are members of a union to pursue their own sectional interests rather than the interests of the working class as a whole. Fourthly, individuals and families are seen as becoming home-centred and privatised, enjoying relatively affluent consumer lifestyles. Finally, due to these developments, issues of inequality is either obscured or seen as less important.

(Source: Adapted from O' Donnell (1992) A New Introduction to Sociology, 3rd edn, Nelson.)

ITEM F

Social class of all persons in employment, 1971–91 (per cent)

	1971	1981	1991
Professional and managerial	22	26	33
Clerical	21	23	23
Foremen and skilled manual	28	25	22
Semi and unskilled manual	29	26	22

(Source: Calculated from Censuses of Population 1971, 1981 and 1991.)

Questions

(a) Briefly outline in your own words what is meant by 'instrumental collectivism' in Item E. (*3 marks*)

(b) In your own words briefly describe how Item E suggests 'the restructuring of capital and labour ' has affected the working class. (*5 marks*)

(c) Summarise the changes in the social class structure shown in Item F (*6 marks*)

(d) Outline and critically assess the view that class remains the most significant aspect of social inequality in the UK (*16 marks*)

4 Theories of class inequality

By the end of this chapter you should:

- be aware of a wide range of sociological theories on class inequality;
- be able to distinguish between three broad approaches to the explanation of class inequality: meritocracy models, structural theories and class formation approaches;
- have a critical understanding of the strengths and weaknesses of each approach;
- be aware of the variety of theories contained within each approach;
- have practised structured exam questions.

Introduction

Class inequalities were the first inequalities sociologists turned their attention to. The origins of the subject lie in the industrial revolution, a revolution that changed the economic and social structure of society. Early theories reflected the dominance of functionalism and talk of meritocracy. These were superseded by more structural theories based on the work of Marx and Weber, and while these are still important today, another trend is discernable. Structural theories sometimes tend to portray people as powerless puppets at the mercy of forces beyond their control, but in more recent years emphasis has being placed on how people actively construct social classes, reflecting a greater interest in class consciousness and subjective factors that can be contrasted with debates on the construction of social class schemas.

This chapter will outline in broad terms the three following approaches to class inequality:

- Meritocracy models of class inequality.
- Class as a key structural basis of inequality.
- Class formation approaches.

Meritocracy models of class inequality

'Meritocracy' means rule by those with merit, and suggests that in a society where talents are unequally distributed it is rational for those with the most talent to occupy the more important positions.

Exercise 4.1

 Suggest a number of possible indicators that someone has merit and ways we might seek to measure this.

It follows that these people must be encouraged to develop their talents to the full. This means they must be provided with a financial incentive to do so: in simple terms, they must be provided with the prospect of jobs that will bring them sufficiently high incomes to compensate for the extra time spent in education.

The key implication of this is that a society will have a degree of inequality, and those who advocate meritocracy (principally the functionalists and the new right) argue that such inequality is acceptable as long as society is truly meritocratic and that inequalities in society are a reflection of unequal talents. Insofar as this is the case, then inequality is a positive thing.

We can divide the meritocratic approach to inequality into the following theories:

- Functionalist theories of inequality.
- New right theories of inequality.
- New left realist theories of citizenship and inequality.
- Neofunctionalist theories of inequality.

1. Functionalist theories of inequality

Functionalists argue that inequality is functional for society since it ensures that those who exhibit the most potential talent are encouraged to develop this talent through lengthy spells in education and training, with the promise of higher incomes when they qualify. In order to ensure that society's functional prerequisites are properly met, society must ensure that people fully utilise their talents (Davis and Moore, 1945). Inequalities arise from the different values that society places on various roles by consensually agreed norms and values.

Exercise 4.2

Provide your own definition of the terms 'norms' and 'values'.

Inequalities therefore reflect differences in talent and the different values that society places on certain roles. Since there are so many roles in the contemporary world, inequality is an inevitable part of modern society (Parsons, 1951, 1977). Since functionalists believe that the appointment of people to various positions should be based on merit, they see this inequality as legitimate. In other words, they argue that there is equality of opportunity to find your place in a society that offers different levels of reward.

Exercise 4.3

[a] Complete the table below by adding your own examples of seven jobs that require talent and three that do not. For all ten, list the educational or other qualifications needed to do the jobs and then suggest the level of pay you think such jobs attract. The first two job examples have been provided.

Job	Skills required	Annual salary	
FE Lecturer	PGCE or equivalent	£14,334	London
Typist	Word Processing 45 wpm	£12,200	London

You can check the accuracy of your estimate of the salary paid for these jobs by looking at the latest copy of the *New Earnings Survey*, which should be available at your local reference library if not in your school/college library.

When confronted with the question of inequality, functionalist sociologists characteristically declare it to be functional for society since it ensures that those with talents develop them, being willing to go through the sacrifice of spending years in education since they will eventually reap their reward in the form of higher salaries (Davis and Moore, 1945). Davis and Moore also argue that since there is societal consensus on the relative merit of certain jobs and therefore the salaries they command, inequality does not cause conflict but is seen as legitimate by all. Inequality is an accepted part of society.

The key problem with the functionalist view is its tautological nature. When asked to provide evidence of why some occupations are more functionally important than others and therefore deserve higher wages, the response is that they are more important because they are paid more. This becomes a completely circular argument. In an attempt to avoid this, Davis and Moore tried to argue that there are other ways of considering functional importance, but if there are jobs of high functional importance to which only low rewards are attached, this undermines functionalism as a theory of inequality.

Functionalism is nonetheless important, since its essentially individualist liberal view of society (meaning that society is composed of individuals who are basically good and get along with each other) has been taken over and developed by new right sociologists. The latter have reopened the debate about the extent to which inequality is a good thing rather than a bad thing, and also the extent to which it can be explained on the basis of an unequal distribution of individual talent rather than on the basis of structural barriers in society – for example class background or being a woman rather than a man – which create inequality regardless of individual talent.

Exercise 4.4

Reread the above section and summarise the strengths and weakness of the functionalist theory of inequality. A few pointers have been provided to help you.

Strengths

- The theory allows inequality to be linked to talent, which is unequally distributed in society.

Weaknesses

- It assumes there is consensus about the relative merit of jobs, whereas the relative social prestige attached to some jobs and the financial rewards associated with them do not always seem to be a matter of consensus.
- It rests on the assumption that there are no structural barriers to those with talent.

2. New right theories of inequality

At the most simple level, those in the new right think that the free market should be the key distributional mechanism in society. They therefore reject an active state role in the economy, which was the basis of the consensus in political economy circles from the end of the Second World War until the early 1970s. The 'active state' notion was exemplified by the Beveridge Report (1942) and the creation of the welfare state, as well as Keynesian economic policy, which advocated an active role for government in managing the economy.

Exercise 4.5

1. What is meant by the welfare state?

2. Beveridge identified five evils that the welfare state should tackle. We have listed these below, along with their contemporary solution in terms of welfare institutions. Your task is to provide a description of the services offered by each of these institutions.

The five evils	Contemporary institutions	Services provided
Idleness (unemployment)	Job centres	
Squalor (bad housing)	Local authority housing	
Ignorance (poor education)	Schools, colleges universities	
Disease (bad health)	National Health Service	
Want (poverty)	Social security Local authority Social services	

The new right receive consideration not only because of their prominence in global economic and social policy in the 1980s and 1990s, but also because of the very radical nature of some of their arguments.

The New Right believe in inequality (or at least income inequality) and see it as a necessary spur to economic growth and therefore rising living standards: 'we should be wary of assuming that inequality is necessarily immoral or socially damaging, for there are strong arguments to suggest that inequality is to some extent the price we pay for an expansion of a society's resources' (Saunders, 1990, p. 51).

Saunders (1995b) argues that capitalism based on private property, the pursuit of profit and inequality generated through the market is a 'growth machine'. He points to the massive rise in productivity under capitalism, citing the fivefold growth in output per person in Britain between 1871 and 1989, the elevenfold rise in output per person in the United States since the 1870s and the 25-fold rise in output per person in Japan since the 1870s. This has provided the basis for rising living standards and is the result of capitalism in operation. The key reason for this is that the free market possesses, via the system of price signals that lie at its heart, an information system that is not capable of being bettered. The market provides accurate information about the wishes and desires of consumers, and this allows producers to produce what is really wanted. In short, the market works by providing accurate information on the value that society places on certain commodities. The state cannot provide such a sophisticated information system and therefore any attempt to interfere with the market leads to a mismatch between what is wanted and what is produced, which in turn leads to shortages and unhappiness.

However the new right do endorse equality in another sense. They argue that we should all be equal before the law, meaning that contracts entered into can be enforced and the market can operate. However any further incursion into the lives of citizens undermines their personal freedom or liberty and should therefore be opposed. Nozick (1974) sees equality as the equal right to own property, and justice as recognition of people's legitimate right to own property, when such property has been justly acquired. This of course does not mean that everyone should own the same amount of property, and any attempt by the state to ensure such an outcome should be regarded as unjust since it would involve denying people's just right of personal ownership.

One problem with this is that much property has been distributed as the spoils of war and much has been acquired by virtue of conquering or taking from others. Nozick argues that in such cases the original owners should be entitled to compensation (a principle that underlies the compensation given to previous owners of property in former East Germany), but Saunders (1995b) has pointed out that this could undermine all present-day property ownership. He therefore argues that although Nozick is opposed to the idea of the redistribution of property, his proposal would, if implemented, lead in such a direction.

Exercise 4.6

Reread the above section and outline the strengths and weaknesses of the new right theory of class inequality. A few pointers have been provided to help you along.

Strengths

- The theory was clearly very popular in the 1980s and part of the 1990s with the dominance of free-market economics and the electoral success of new right politicians in that period.
- Capitalism has produced economic growth.

Weaknesses

- The theory provides no real answer to instances of market failure, and no real notion of what to do with the victims of free-market competition.
- Free-market economies with a large degree of inequality may have slower economic growth than societies with less inequality.

3. New left realist theories of citizenship and inequality

Critics of the new right suggest that there is no evidence to support their claim that free market capitalism provides the best possible basis for rising living standards. They argue instead that as inequality has become more widespread, economic performance has fallen and therefore there have been no gains to offset the problems caused by greater inequality. According to Glyn and Miliband (1994), annual economic growth in Britain from 1979 (when the first Thatcher government came to power) to the early 1990s was only 1.6 per cent on average, which was worse than the 1.9 per cent achieved in the 1970s by Labour governments not committed to the free market. It could be argued that this was not due to new right policies but simply reflected the poorer economic performance everywhere, regardless of whether free market economics were applied or not. However in answer to this point, Glyn and Miliband assert that those societies which experienced the greatest economic growth in the 1980s were those which were the most equal in terms of income distribution.

One particularly influential critique of new right thinking and policy was written by Will Hutton, the editor of the *Observer* (Hutton, 1996). He argues that the key problem of new right thinking is that it is based on untenable theoretical assumptions. For example free market economics assumes that we will decide how to spend our money by comparing the relative prices of two goods of equal quality. While this may sound fine in theory, it is actually impossible. If you check the price of a tin of peas in Tesco and then go to Sainsburys and find the same article cheaper, this is absolutely no proof that Sainsburys' peas are cheaper since it is possible that the price in Tesco might have changed in the meantime. Unless you spend all your time checking and no time buying you cannot make decisions based on price. The flaw in new right thinking is that it is based on a model that assumes that time does not exist, and therefore the world holds still while you search around for the cheapest goods. This has no correspondence with reality. It is not simply that the application of free market economics is flawed and therefore unprovable, but that the central theory underlying the idea that the free market is superior is merely stated not proved, and Hutton does not accept that this statement is true.

Consequently he argues that inequality, which is a necessary part of free market economics and has risen to new heights in the 1990s, is not the price we have to pay for greater efficiency but a very negative thing: 'a system which degrades the environment, excludes millions from secure employment or causes social disintegration is not efficient in the broader sense of being sustainable' (ibid., p. xxi). In Hutton's view, new right policies have led to the creation of a 30/30/40 society, where social inequality is greater than ever and societal institutions are breaking down. Britain seems to be trapped in a low-wage, low-skill, low-investment economy and the free market, left to itself, will do little to rectify this.

The reason for this is the centrality of the financial sector in the British economy and the importance placed on making large profits quickly. According to Hutton, this leads managers to boost profits by cutting jobs. Therefore profits do not result from enterprise and risk-taking but from the hiring and firing of workers. Job insecurity does not create economic benefits and Hutton shows that economic growth since 1979 has been lower than at any other time since the Second World War.

The solution to this, according to Hutton, is to develop a 'stakeholder society', where companies are required to recognise that their responsibilities extend beyond their shareholders and where the prominence given to finance capital is eroded. This effectively means some kind of welfare state, and is certainly a view that would be rejected by the new right but endorsed by most centre-left commentators. In relation to inequality therefore, the welfare state understood in terms of citizenship has assumed centre-stage. While it is clear that some early observers of the welfare state saw it as a possible way of eroding capitalism and bringing in some form of socialism by parliamentary means, the current debate is about how to create a welfare state that incorporates some of the positive aspects of the free-market decision-making mechanism.

Exercise 4.7

From the discussion above and other sources, identify arguments for and against the welfare state.

It is clear, however, that even this fairly minimal amount of social engineering would be totally rejected by the new right, for whom the welfare state can be nothing other than a bad thing. In the words of Marsland (1996):

> How dare we in Britain chide the peoples of the former communist empire for their dilatory movement towards the conditions of a market society and democratic freedom when we ourselves continue to exclude from the market the whole of the welfare sphere – one-half at least of economic transactions, involving many of the most important services people need. The necessity of rolling back the state and liberating individual initiative is at least as imperative in Britain or the United States or France as it is in Russia or Romania or Khazakstan. . . .
>
> Socialism has failed, and is being replaced. The Welfare State has failed at least as badly. We must set about replacing it with institutions more appropriate to a free people. We must liberate welfare from the shackles of the state, and provide for ourselves a system of welfare which liberates from the cramping oppression of the Nanny state our natural capacity for responsible autonomy (Marsland, 1996, pp. xi, 3).

Exercise 4.8

Using the ideas of Hutton and Marsland outlined on pages 53–4, answer the following:

1. Why does Hutton think that his proposal might be criticised as 'the nationalisation of inequality'?

2. What solution does Marsland offer to the need for welfare provision?

3. Draw up a table to show the contrasts between these two approaches, and any similarities you can think of.

Exercise 4.9

Draw up a table that outlines the strengths and weaknesses of the new left realist theories of class inequality. This time you are not provided with any material to help you out.

4. Neofunctionalist theories of inequality

Neofunctionalists accept that there were some problems with Talcott Parsons' (1937, 1951) formulations, most notably that his stress on value consensus tended to underplay the existence of conflict in society. He also tended to view human activity as largely determined by the social system, providing a picture of society that is similar to a puppet theatre, where people's actions are effectively constrained by long-standing social structures, notably the cultural value system.

Alexander (1985, 1990) and Munch (1987) argue that there is a need to integrate an adequate theory of social action into sociological theory, but unlike ethnomethodologists and phenomenologists they retain the idea that there is a social reality that constrains the actions of individuals. According to Alexander (1985), it is only by understanding this that we can obtain a theory of society that explains social order, rather than assuming that society is inherently random and unpredictable. For Munch (1987), the changes in the social system, notably that of the law, show that a system logic is operating, which he argues arises from the increasing complexity of society.

Both these authors draw heavily on the writing of Durkheim (1893) and Parsons (1937,1951) to stress that society exists as a reality in its own right and cannot be understood merely as a collection of small group interactions; and that this normative system of society does not simply arise from economic calculations of individual gain. It is in this respect that neofunctionalism diverges from the new right (Saunders, 1990,1995b; Marsland, 1996). While both Alexander and Munch see capitalism as broadly meritocratic and therefore consider that some degree of inequality is necessary for the development of individual talent, the new right emphasise that the justification of this is purely individual self-interest which they see as the key basis of a successful society, while neofunctionalists argue that it is not possible to explain society on this basis and suggest that economic inequalities are somehow linked to social values.

These differences are significant in contemporary terms in the following way. New Right theorists would follow Adam Smith (1776) in suggesting that society is based on contracts between individuals on the basis of pure self-interest, but which collectively add up to a prosperous and dynamic society. Neofunctionalists would see the social value system (the set of norms and values that people share, which means they do not exist as isolated individuals) as more important and would argue that it is not possible to envisage society simply as a collection of self-interested individuals. Moral and normative regulation is required as well. In this respect some neofunctionalist arguments bear a similarity to some forms of contemporary social democratic thinking, ranging from ethical socialism (Dennis and Erdos, 1992) to communitarianism (Etzioni, 1995) and radical versions of Durkheimian theory (Hirst, 1990; Pearce, 1989). While it is important to stress the main difference between these approaches and functionalism, namely the social democratic thinkers' acceptance that there can be genuine conflicts in society, they do share its emphasis on morality and societal regulation. It is certainly arguable that New Labour owes more to functionalism than to Marxism.

Exercise 4.10

 Use your knowledge of the policies of the present Labour government to identify any elements of their proposals that have a link with functionalist and neofunctionalist ideas.

Summary of the meritocratic approaches

While neofunctionalism is arguably associated with the centre-left in political terms, and this is one form of resurgent Durkheimian sociology among left-wing sociologists, it is clear that the defence of inequality has been much more powerfully articulated by the new right

Exercise 4.11

Reread the previous section and draw up a list of the strengths and weaknesses of the neofunctionalist theories of class inequality. A few pointers are provided to help you out.

Strengths

- Neofunctionalism accepts the criticisms that have been made of the original functionalist theories.
- It does allow for a notion of active human agency in society.

Weaknesses

- The moral theories that underpin neofunctionalism are not necessarily accepted by all, and are not necessarily the same in all versions of the theory.

Exercise 4.12

 Using the information you gathered for Exercises on the strengths and weaknesses of each of the individual theories in section 4.11, write an overall evaluation of the meritocracy-based theories of class inequality. Remember to add a concluding section on what you think of this approach.

Class as a key structural basis of inequality

While there are variations within the meritocracy approach, particularly with regard to the question of whether the free market broadly operates on meritocratic lines (the new right), or whether a just and meritocratic society needs the market to be supplemented by a moral order (neofunctionalists) or a notion of citizenship (the Durkheimian influenced social-democratic tradition), all seem to emphasise that it is possible to arrive at a meritocratic order within capitalism. This would be rejected by Marxist sociologists, who consider that class inequality and the exploitation of one class by another is inherent in capitalism. They would also reject any suggestion that it is possible to effect reforms (either institutional or moral) to lessen the inequality produced by capitalism. This is squarely based on Marx's analysis of the structure of capitalism and the way in which inequality is created through its actions.

This section considers the development of Marxist theories of class inequality and some of the arguments that have developed out of this.

1. Marxist analysis

The key difference between Marxist conceptions of class and other sociological approaches is that for Marxists class is a relational concept. Class is determined by an individual's place in society and therefore in relation to society. As such, inequality of income and wealth, as a commonsense indicator of the arrival of and boundary between social classes is rejected by Marxists. Inequality is the result rather than the cause of social classes. Inequality results from socially determined class structures that arise in particular historical circumstances.

Schemas such as the registrar-general's social class classification do nothing more than describe the result of the established class structure. They are not able to provide an explanation of why things should be as they are or how they might change. It is this dynamic, relational aspect of the theory of social classes that is Marx's unique and fundamental contribution to social analysis.

Central questions for Marxist analysis: the middle class

It is often said that for Marx there were only two classes in society, namely the proletariat and the bourgeoisie. Hence some have argued that Marx's analysis was flawed because of the existence and growth of the middle class or classes.

This argument is an oversimplification and it is quite clear that Marx recognised the existence of more than two classes in society. The *Communist Manifesto* is often seen as the basis of the assertion that there are only two classes. However as Hal Draper (1978) has shown, this was largely due to the revisions made to the English translation of this work five years after Marx's death. Also, as Stuart Hall (1977) has pointed out, the *Communist Manifesto* contains reference to and discussion of classes such as the lower middle class, the small manufacturer, the shopkeeper, the artisan, the peasant and the dangerous class – the social scum. Marx was acknowledging the existence and growth of a middle class when he argued the need to take into account 'the growing number of the middle classes, those who stand between the workman on the one hand and the capitalist and the landlord on the other' (Marx, 1975, p. 573).

In spite of this it is still claimed that Marx denied the existence of classes other than the proletariat and the bourgeoisie. It is true that he argued that some classes were more fundamental than others, and it is quite certain that he saw the fundamental conflict as that between the proletariat and the bourgeoisie because in the course of the development of capitalism the intermediary classes would somehow disintegrate, disappear or be incorporated into the proletariat. It is the latter prediction that is seen as dealing the decisive blow against the usefulness of Marxist theory. Therefore, although it is wide of the mark to say that Marxism is outdated because of the rise of the middle class, for some it is true that – contrary to Marx's prediction of class polarisation – the middle class have come to constitute a specific group with distinct economic interests.

Anthony Giddens (1980) is the most notable exponent of the latter view, though it is clear that the concept of the service class (as advocated by John Goldthorpe, see page 35) does suggest that professional and managerial groups constitute a stable collectivity. On the other hand the idea of a single middle class has been criticised by Roberts *et al.* (1977) and Savage *et al.* (1992), and therefore the question of whether Marx was right to argue that intermediary groups form a stratum rather than a class is very much an ongoing subject of debate. The existence of a middle class or classes does undermine the idea of polarisation, and furthermore the embourgeoisement argument suggests that the reverse of the process predicted by Marx is taking place, that is, instead of the middle class merging into the working class, some elements of the working class are merging into the middle class. On the other hand the theory of proletarianisation (a latter-day version of Marx's theory, based explicitly on volume 1 of *Capital*) argues that a process of deskilling is taking place, with the result that clerical and professional workers are finding themselves in a similar situation to the working class. What is common to all these arguments is a consideration of the direction of change and whether the middle class are a temporary or permanent element in society.

Such discussions are not helped by the use of class schemas such as the registrar general's scale to illustrate their arguments. It should be remembered that the distinction between manual and non-manual labour is not a fundamental division according to Marxist theory, yet it is precisely this division that is used to identify the middle class. The weakness of such approaches is underlined by Westergaard and Resler (1975), who point out that the term middle class is one of 'startling elasticity' and is used to describe all those who are not manual workers. The important point is that the bourgeoisie or upper class are obscured in this. This highlights the fundamental problem of evaluating Marxist theory using statistics derived from non-theoretical analyses of social class, based solely on occupation. All those without an occupation disappear. As feminist sociologists correctly point out, this makes many women (for example full-time housewives) invisible in class analysis, but it also renders the bourgeoisie invisible as well.

As such, one point that might be made about theories that stress the importance of a middle class is that nothing they say can have any consequence on Marx's theories of the class structure since they derive from a conception of class that is fundamentally at odds with Marx's one. This is rather like saying that since IBM software does not generally run on Apple Macintoshs this proves that Apple Macintoshs do not work.

When faced with two contradictory theories we should consider which of them best describes reality. Here there is some evidence that the middle class do present a problem for Marxist theory. Quite simply, there is a lot of evidence to show that in a number of respects, most notably in their political orientations, there is a middle class or classes who behave in fundamentally different ways from the working class. As a result a number of differing solutions to the 'problem of the middle class' have been formulated, all of which provide greater sophistication to Marxist class analysis. These are considered on pages 38–41, in particular the works of Nicos Poulantzas, Erik Olin Wright and Mike Savage *et al*.

Exercise 4.13

Read the following lists of the strengths and weaknesses of Marxist class theory and then reread the above section on Marxist approaches.

1. Add to, amend or delete from the lists in line with what you see as the strengths and weaknesses, of the approaches.

2. Rearrrange your amended lists into an evaluative paragraph remembering to add your own concluding thoughts.

Strengths of Marxist class analysis

- It is a relational theory that stresses the importance of considering how classes develop historically and relate to each other dynamically.
- It considers both the static class structure and the more dynamic element of class formation.
- The theory of inequality has probably had the most impact on the world we live in.
- Sociologists working in the Marxist tradition have been and continue to be at the forefront of sociological research on inequality.
- It is an all-encompassing theory of society showing the economic and social relationships between its constituent parts.

Weaknesses of Marxist class analysis

- The marginality of the middle class occurs because of the assumptions and concepts upon which the theory is built, namely that there are only two fundamental antagonistic classes in society. The rise of the middle class might be used to argue that these assumptions and concepts are false.
- The definition of production is open to the criticism made mainly by feminist sociologists that this only applies to paid work, and thus unpaid domestic work by women is excluded. As a result, Marxism is unable fully to explain inequality that arises from relations that are not centred on the wage relationship.
- The fracturing of Marxism into many warring factions undermines its claim to provide an overall theory.
- The development of the argument that social, political and cultural factors have relative autonomy from the economic sphere is an admission that Marx's attempt to explain the whole of society from the economic base is untenable.

2. 3. Weberian approaches to social stratification

Most of the contemporary debates on social class concern the relative usefulness of the schemas drawn up by Karl Marx and Max Weber. For instance the work of John Goldthorpe (1987) is largely based on a neo-Weberian format while Erik Olin Wright (1985) has produced the most noteworthy neo-Marxist classification. Therefore in order to understand these contemporary debates it is important to consider the similarities and differences between Marx's and Weber's approach to social class.

Max Weber (1921) argued that all forms of inequality are based on some form of power and in this sense he was taking up the ideas of Friedrich Nietzsche (1969), who emphasised the all-embracing nature of power in society. However Weber argued that such power may appear in a number of different forms, of which the most important are class, status and party. This provides the first important difference from Marx, who emphasised class above all else. For Weber, therefore, class and economic power were merely one example of power, whereas Marx believed that ultimately all forms of power have economic origins.

It is important to emphasise that while this has often led to Marx being accused of economic determinism, this is generally a result of misinterpreting what Marx actually said and the criticism could be more fairly levelled at the kind of Marxism that was predominant in Germany in Weber's time, which was indeed crudely economically determinist. This was the Marxism of the Second International and Edward Bernstein (1899) and has little to do with contemporary Marxism. Lenin and the Bolsheviks consciously split from such an interpretation of Marxism by forming the Third International. As such the actual difference between Marx and Weber may not be as great as is often portrayed and may rest instead on Weber's distaste for the crudity of Second International Marxism, a distaste shared by contemporary Marxists.

Nonetheless, it is clear that even if we consider Marxism as based on Marx rather than Bernstein there are still important differences with Weber. Marx and Weber both used the term class, but they meant very different things by it. Weber was concerned to develop a comprehensive notion of class and therefore did not accept the distinction between objective and subjective notions of class, as for example in the Marxist distinction between a 'class in itself' and a 'class for itself'. Here Marx distinguished between those who are in the same class because they share the same objective place in the sphere of production – that is all proletarians or all members of the bourgeoisie – and the fact that this will not automatically lead them to feel a shared identity with the other members of the same 'class in itself'. It is the presence of such a shared feeling and class consciousness that characterises a 'class for itself'. For Weber, a group who shares an identity and therefore acts in community is better understood as a status group. 'A class is not a community, in the sense of a self-aware group with a clear identity. A class is a possible, and perhaps frequent, basis for communal or collective action but is not in itself a community and does not automatically become one' (Hamilton and Hirszowicz, 1993, p. 11).

Class is therefore more limited in Weberian theory than in Marxism.

The second major difference is that while Marx talked of class in relational terms (classes defined according to their relation to the means of production), Weber saw class in terms of similarity of life-chances brought about by a similar market position (income and other benefits such as working condition and similar skills and qualifications.) At the risk of simplifying this somewhat, what he meant is that classes are composed of people with similar incomes, skills and qualifications and therefore similar life experiences in relation to a number of factors.

While Weber agreed with Marx that the ownership or non-ownership of property is the fundamental determinant of class, he argued that such a view ignores the possible divisions between different types of property owners such as a factory owner and a farmer. He also argued that there are divisions among non-owners based on the level of skill they need to do their jobs. As a result, the binary class system developed by Marx was further subdivided by Weber into a multitude of possible classes. The fact that members of a class do not need to feel any identity of interest with people in the same class means that such a categorisation is based purely on an assessment of skill, and as such the potential number of classes is enormous. Giddens makes this point when he says that 'although Weber employs for some purposes a dichotomous model which in certain general respects resembles that of Marx, his viewpoint strongly emphasises a pluralistic conception of classes' (Giddens, 1973, p. 42). Classes are defined purely in terms of the market place and essentially on the basis of how much people are paid on the basis of their skills.

A continuing subject of debate in sociology is whether our place in society is determined by who are parents are (an ascriptive system) or by our individual talents (an achievement system). Weber's notion of class focuses purely on inequalities that arise in an achievement system, and his notion of status is there to cover inequalities generated by access to the market place being restricted by factors in people's backgrounds such as ethnic origin, social background or gender. Since no system exists where people's place in society is based only on achievement, no pure class system exists.

Class always interacts with status categories to determine individual life-chances. Hamilton and Hirszowicz (1993) argue that this creates problems since if status is to do with your background and if most of the contemporary capitalist class inherited property at some time in the past, then the capitalist class is really a status group and should be distinguished from self-made capitalists. This cuts across Weber's acceptance that ownership and non-ownership of property is a class issue. While people's background does affect their place in society (for example the Duke of Westminster, the richest man in England, inherited his wealth) the division in Weberian thought between class as a consequence of present market position and status as an effect of background does sometimes serve to obscure the link.

It is for this reason that a number of contemporary thinkers, notably Rosemary Crompton (1993), have argued that stratification theory needs to achieve a synthesis between class-based notions of inequality and status-based notions of inequality. According to Parkin (1971, 1979) much of the confusion created in neo-Weberian circles is due to a tendency to counterpose class and status in a way that is contrary to Weber's views. He argues that this often derives from examples showing that people with high-status jobs often earn less than people in low-status jobs, and such examples are attempts to show that class and status cut across each other. In Parkin's view they show nothing of the kind since income is not equal to class and it is important to remember that Weber talked about 'life chances' not income when he referred to market position, and this involves elements such as job security and fringe benefits as well as basic income. Parkin therefore argues that a correct interpretation of Weber would show that the notions of class and status are more linked than is often assumed and that the alternative 'multi-dimensional approach has led to the trivialisation of Weber's ideas, in particular through exaggerated claims regarding the functional independence of different aspects of inequality such as class and status' (Parkin, 1971, p. 18).

Weber argued that the position of workers in the workplace, which is the central element of Marx's theory of capitalism, is only one aspect of the way workers suffer as a result of the existence of other spheres of power in society. They face expropriation in all spheres due to the rise of bureaucracy and rationality, which has led to the separation of ownership and control in all modern institutions. Here we come to Weber's central concern, namely the growth of bureaucratic and rational forms of authority based on clear principles and that treat everyone equally and impersonally. These are an advance on traditional forms of authority, which worked on the basis of favouritism.

Nonetheless modern bureaucracies could become an 'iron cage' that stifles individuality and creates a highly regimented and impersonal society. It is essentially this insight into the 'dark side' of modernity that has inspired the growth of postmodern theories, which reject rationality on grounds similar to those expressed by Weber. For Weber, class relations are embedded in and part of the overall power relations of modern society: 'whereas Marx's abstract model of capitalist development proceeds from the "economic" to the "political", Weber's model is derived from the opposite process of reasoning, using the "political" as a framework for understanding the "economic"' (Giddens, 1973, p. 47).

It could be argued that this emphasis on political power reflects the situation in Germany in Weber's time, with the importance of Bismarck and the level of control he exerted from a political position. As a result, Weber's analysis generalised from the specific and not entirely representative case of Germany in the late nineteenth century. The same point might be made about Marx's reliance on the French Revolution and British capitalism as models from which to generalise.

When he came to look at how people act together Weber distinguished between *class* and *social class*. Class based on market position is a purely economic entity, but social class comprises groups of classes who are linked by their similar chance of mobility. He identified four main social classes: (1) the working class (manual workers), (2) the petty bourgeoisie, (3) white-collar workers and technicians and (4) those privileged though property or educational qualifications. It can be seen that the most important difference is the emphasis Weber placed on groups that today are conventionally thought of as middle class and his assertion that such occupations would grow with the increasing importance of bureaucracy in society.

Contemporary debates on class draw on this both in terms of the distinction Weber made between manual workers and white-collar workers, and the notion of a privileged group based on educational qualifications. It is this which Giddens (1973) sees as the key basis of the 'new middle class' and it is also central to Goldthorpe's (1982) notion of the 'service class'. Both broadly accept Weber's notion that such groups will rise in importance in society, and as a result they reject (as did Weber) Marx's theory of class polarisation. The size, extent and significance of the middle class is therefore the terrain upon which neo-Marxist and neo-Weberian accounts are tested in the contemporary debate, which will be examined later (see pp. 67–73 Chapter 5). This central debate on the middle class concerns the importance of social mobility as the basis for the formation or non-formation of stable social classes in the Weberian tradition. This can be seen, for example, in Frank Parkin's (1971) adoption of the notion of social closure with regard to the formation of social classes.

Exercise 4.14

Drawing on the previous section and material from elsewhere, complete the following table on the similarities and differences between Marx's and Weber's th2eories of social class.

Similarities	Differences
Both saw class as an important form of social inequality	Weber saw social class as an example of unequal power relations in society, whereas Marx saw it as the predominant form of inequality
Both saw class as related to economic sphere	Marx developed a model with two fundamental social classes while Weber's model implies a multitude of social classes

3. Feminism and inequality

Feminist sociologists have criticised the earlier views on inequality as 'malestream' (see Abbott and Wallace, 1997).

Firstly, if people's position in the class structure is defined by their role in the sphere of production, what about women who are full-time housewives? They stand outside the class system in a direct sense, yet it would be absurd to say that such women do not experience inequality. Feminists have argued that a more adequate theory of stratification needs to consider the way in which inequalities arise other than on the basis of class. In this respect, radical feminists consider that gender divisions and sexual oppression are more important than class differences. They argue that such inequalities arise not from capitalism but from a system of patriarchy, meaning rule by males. Males everywhere oppress women and one important facet of this is that women have less income and wealth than men. Radical feminists tend to stress the way in which men physically oppress women through violence and rape, and also through a system of laws that have made property ownership by women much less likely. According to Delphy (1984 and Leonard, 1992), as a result of patriarchy we should see women as a separate class from men.

A second factor in feminist theories is that the exclusive focus on the workplace ignores the way in which gender divisions in the rest of society influence and constrain the way women participate in the sphere of paid employment. This is most obvious in the case of childcare. Radical feminists argue that it is in this reproductive sphere of society that the ultimate basis for inequality lies, rather than in the productive sphere as most theories of stratification suggest. The assumption that women will bear the primary responsibility for childcare clearly affects the length of time they spend in paid work and whether it is part time or full time. All of this has an effect on the types of job that women can take on and therefore the income they receive. The fact that domestic labour is unpaid also means that women are economically dependent on males, further reinforcing male power over women. An adequate theory of income inequality needs to take into account the gender assumptions operating in all spheres of society and the effect these have on women's access to financial resources.

Marxist and socialist feminists have tried to construct a theory that shows how gender and indeed ethnic inequalities interact with class inequalities by placing limitations on women's participation in paid employment. The result is that women are restricted to a secondary labour market consisting of mainly part-time, lower-paid jobs with less security and less chance of promotion (Walby, 1990; Bradley, 1996).

Critics of feminist analysis suggest that while it points to the importance of gender inequalities, it tends to break down because of differences among women themselves, for example a division between white and black women, causing splits in the feminist movement. This leads one to question whether gender is any more capable of providing a full explanation of income inequality than any other concept.

Westergaard (1995) has argued that class inequality remains fundamental since in the 1980s there was increasing inequality in income distribution but the difference in income distribution between men and women became narrower. Therefore gender cannot explain the overall trend in the 1980s, leading to a reassertion of the primary importance of class analysis.

Exercise 4.15

[i][a] Draw up a table of the ways in which feminism is similar to Marxism and the ways in which it is different. Add a further column outlining the similarities and differences between the feminist and Weberian theories of class inequality.

Exercise 4.16

[a][e] Conduct your own evaluation of structural theories of class inequality. First compile a list of the strengths and weaknesses of the Weberian and feminist theories of class inequality and then, using your list and the material from the earlier exercise on Marxist theories of inequality, write two evaluative paragraphs on the overall structural approach to theories of class inequality. Don't forget to include your own conclusion.

4. From class structure to class formation

One major problem with Marxist analysis is that the working class have not seemed overly keen to take on the role Marx assigned to them. The main explanation of this is that some form of ideological brainwashing has been inflicted on the workers by the capitalists. In order to explain the failure of workers to overthrow capitalism in Western Europe, Marxists came to concentrate not simply on the direct repression of attempts at revolution (centred on the police and the army) but also on the way that capitalism as a system influences the workers' ideas, leading them to think of capitalism as natural.

Althusser (1971) distinguishes between the repressive state apparatus, meaning the police, the army and the courts, which exercise coercive power, and the ideological state apparatus, which manipulates people's beliefs and thoughts. The implication is that the fight against capitalism must include ideological struggle as well as economic and political actions and struggles. The ideological state apparatus perpetuate the ideology of capitalism and causes the workers to remain docile. Ultimately the structural bias in this explanation leads to the conclusion that it is impossible for people to affect history. They are simply passive reflections of the deep structures of society.

Some Marxists were therefore asserting that people could not change history, in contradiction to Marx's notion that this can indeed happen. As a result the structuralist Marxist view of history has been challenged by a number of Marxist writers, notably E. P. Thompson (1968, 1978), who wanted to reinsert into Marxist analysis a concern with the way individuals and social classes struggle to change history. Thompson is famous for his survey of the development of the English working class and constantly stresses their activism. He places much greater emphasis on how classes come to be formed and recognise themselves as such, and this has become the basis of a third approach to the consideration of class inequality, namely that concerned with class formation.

Class formation approaches

Recent debates on class have included the question of whether or not class is a useful concept, the general approach that should be taken when conducting class analysis, and the theoretical and methodological implications of these.

Conventionally class analysis has been based on employment groupings and the implication of being placed in a particular grouping in terms of income, education and health. This analysis, which is generally based on official statistics of one sort or another, has been criticised as being both static and theoretically uninformed. This does not however prevent it from being a fruitful line of inquiry into social inequality, and as Crompton (1993) points out, such information is often the only material available.

The last twenty years have also seen the emergence and consolidation of theoretically derived models of the class structure. These have been used both to analyse the importance of class in people's lives and to test the relative usefulness of the theoretical work of Marx and Weber on social class. This approach is best exemplified by large-scale quantitative social surveys, often employing sophisticated statistical techniques. The most important examples of this type of work include Goldthorpe (1987), Wright (1985) and Marshall *et al.* (1988).

Marshall *et al.* set out to test the relative usefulness of the class structure models developed by Goldthorpe and Wright and to consider the relative importance of social class and other inequalities in contemporary Britain. Their survey revealed that Goldthorpe's picture of the class structure is more useful than Wright's, and that social class is still an important feature of inequality in our society, contrary to the arguments of those who assert that class is dead. They found a large feeling of injustice among all social classes about the present distribution of income and wealth and a sense of social class being important, although not perhaps a sufficient degree of class consciousness to merit the use of the Marxist term 'class for itself'. The study is important in that it provides a relatively up-to-date testing of the ideas of the two most prominent advocates of the study of social class through quantitative models of the class structure, namely Goldthorpe and Wright.

One criticism of the approach is that, while it can provide information on the broad class structure, it only gives a picture of isolated individuals due to the inability of the methodological techniques to examine social relationships in any detail. As a result, emphasis has began to be placed on the process of class formation: the way in which particular individuals or occupational groupings come to have a collective identity and therefore become a social class. It is argued that the most appropriate way of studying this process is through case studies, since they can consider in depth the formation of relationships and provide a dynamic picture of the formation and changing nature of class groupings. The case-study approach has a long history in stratification research, most notably that by Goldthorpe *et al.* (1968), but in terms of class formation it can be specifically seen in the recent work of Abercrombie and Urry (1983) and Savage *et al.* (1992).

Exercise 4.17

Using the information provided in the above section and material from other textbooks, list the advantages and disadvantages of social surveys and case studies as techniques with which to consider class and other social inequalities. You should come to your own conclusion as to which of these two techniques you prefer.

In some ways, the distinction between the large-scale social survey and the case-study approach correspond to the distinction between structure and action, a long-standing dualism in sociology. Sociologists who favour a more structural approach (primarily functionalists and Marxists) have tended to see individuals as largely shaped and determined by the preexisting social structure, sometimes almost totally so. Conversely the social action tradition in sociology (primarily symbolic interactionism and phenomenology, both of which were influenced by Max Weber's work) have tended to emphasise the way in which human actors working in social groups construct society.

Giddens' (1984) theory of structuration, which attempts to overcome this distinction, is a possible third approach to contemporary stratification analysis. He argues that the perennial division between structure and action can be resolved by understanding that the social structure has a dual nature, that is, it does constrain our actions but it also enables them as well. This duality of structure allows Giddens to establish a clear link between the ideas of social structure and social action. Structures such as school rules are the basis of the larger structures of society and the important thing to realise is that all these are created by human action. Giddens argues that we cannot see humans as puppets that are wholly determined by structures but rather as knowledgeable agents who are able to take action, and also to consider whether that action is attaining the desired goals and hence to modify that action if necessary. Humans are, to use his phrase, 'reflexive agents'. It is through the process of reflexive action that the structures of society are reproduced to create the next generation of human agents.

Giddens' theory of structuration provides the theoretical basis of an attempt to go beyond the structure–action division, which has been a central element of sociology since its inception. However, little empirical work has been based on the concept because of the difficulty of operationalising it for research purposes. One possible example of the sort of work that the concept has produced, a work that is cited very favourably by Giddens, is Paul Willis's (1977) study of a male subculture and its role in the reproduction of the labour structure. However some have argued that the distinction between structure and action is an actual distinction in the world and therefore any attempt to overcome it does not represent an advance of sociological understanding but a divergence between theory and reality.

A distinct but related debate broadens the question of what is meant by class and therefore class analysis, by arguing that the link between occupation and class is a limited notion of class that reflects the productivist bias of the early sociologists, that is, the sphere of production and work is seen as more important than any other aspect of society. This argument can be linked to debates about postmodernity and the possible existence of other bases of identity (see Chapters 5, 6, 8 and 10). However while some advocates of this approach argue that it necessitates the abandonment of the notion of class, others argue that it simply requires a modification of the concept of class to free it from its productivist bias. Much of the inspiration for this approach comes from the work of Pierre Bourdieu (1984, 1990).

Exercise 4.18

[i] Place the following methodological terms and authors in the correct box in the chart below on the basis of your reading of the above section:

- Abercrombie and Warde
- Crompton
- Marshall *et al.*
- Goldthorpe
- Wright
- Case Study
- social survey

Approach adopted	Class structure to class formation	Class formation to class structure
Methodology		
Examples		

Class structure and class formation in class analysis

In reality, class theorists tend to consider both class structure and class formation. However the direction and emphasis of their analyses differ and also cut across the Marx–Weber dividing line, which is often seen as the crucial division in class analysis. A summary of the different emphases on class analysis provided by these concepts is given by Savage *et al.* (1992, p. 226):

> If class structure refers to the system of positions in the division of labour, class formation, on the other hand, tends to refer to the way in which these groups of people who occupy a common place in the social division of labour may form as a social collectivity on the basis of these positions.

1. Weberian analysis

Weber is famous for his insistence on the need for sociologists to consider how purposive social activity contributes to the make-up of society. This has become known as the social action approach. As a result, one would expect Weberian-oriented writers to be concerned with the extent to which classes become socially conscious actors, or in pure Weberian terms, the extent to which economic classes become active status groups.

The most important way that class formation has been analysed within the Weberian tradition is through the study of social mobility and the process of social closure. Goldthorpe (1987) has emphasised the importance of class cohesion to the growth of class consciousness (the feeling of being aligned with others). He uses the extent of self-recruitment (that is, the proportion of a class who are born into that class) as a measure of class cohesion, and also the actions of political parties in mobilising class groups. Parkin (1971) has used the notion of social closure to suggest that the boundaries between various classes cannot be constructed in the abstract from some occupational schema, but instead reflect the shifting boundaries established by processes of social closure and social usurpation (when those excluded try to get in).

Looking at class analysis in this way is far removed from a simple correlation exercise between occupational background and some other variable such as educational qualifications or health. It pushes the emphasis away from attempts to draw up such schemas and towards a consideration of the way in which people construct classes through their social actions.

Despite this, Goldthorpe in particular is open to the criticism that he starts by constructing a social class structure and only then considers how people experience social mobility, thereby commenting on class formation. However studies of social mobility inevitably have to make comparisons based on the occupational position of people at a given time and therefore inevitably freeze this process of class formation into a static class structure. Marshall *et al.* (1988) feel that as a result, approaches such as Goldthorpe's unduly limit class analysis and its ability to comment on class formation. Parkin, on the other hand, has been criticised precisely because his overall emphasis on class formation tends to suggest that the class structure is in constant flux, thereby preventing any picture of the class structure from being produced.

While Weberian writers have tried to include an emphasis on social action, the most successful class analysis in this tradition – the work of John Goldthorpe and others at Nuffield College, Oxford – has tended to be led by constructions of class structure and only afterwards by a consideration of class formation.

Within the broad Weberian tradition, a more qualitative, historically based approach can be found in the work of Michael Mann (1986, 1993), whose detailed history of society from the beginning of time is an ongoing project that presents a picture of the dynamics of class and other power relations. Greater stress has been placed on class formation in the work of Fiona Devine (1992), who conducted a qualitative retesting of Goldthorpe and Lockwood's 1968 study.

Exercise 4.19

Listed below are one strength and one weakness of this approach. Reread the section above and add to the lists.

Strengths

- It recognises the importance of human action in the construction of inequality.

Weaknesses

- Most empirical studies in this tradition have failed to include the notion of human action in their models.

2. Marxist approaches

Class structure and class formation are a consistent element of Marx's writings since it was his belief that the construction of a particular set of class relations (a class structure) had major implications for social change (through the process of class formation). If Marx himself wedded these two elements together, subsequent Marxist analysis led to divisions based on the relative emphasis to be placed on each element.

Structuralist Marxism, especially the work of Louis Althusser (1966, 1968, 1971) and Nicos Poulantzas (1975, 1978), has tended to dismiss the possibility that people can become conscious agents of social change. The work of Erik Olin Wright (1979, 1985, 1989, 1995, 1997) originates in structural Marxism and this may explain his tendency to place greater stress on class structures than on processes of historical class formation. His concept of contradictory class locations is an attempt to present a notion of class structure based on Marxist principles, and his work has also involved large-scale quantitative social surveys to test his schema empirically.

One of the critics of Althusserian Marxism was the British Marxist historian E. P. Thompson (1968, 1978), whose famous history of the working class in England is explicit in its adoption of a class-formation approach: 'the working class did not rise like the sun at an appointed time. It was present at its own making' (Thompson, 1963, p. 9). This work is just one in a long tradition of analysis developed by members of the British Communist Party's historian group including Rodney Hilton (1978) and Eric Hobsbawm (1962, 1977, 1987, 1994). They tend to emphasise the humanism (an emphasis on people as active and stressing human values) in Marx rather than the economic determinist elements that are emphasised in structural Marxism. Such an emphasis underlies much of Western Marxism, for example the work of Antonio Gramsci (1971), whose concept of hegemony stresses the construction of consent and domination.

It is this approach that is favoured by Savage *et al.* (1992), who argue that the middle classes are social classes because they are cohesive social groups. They utilise the notion of the possession of assets as a basis for exploitation, using the ideas of Erik Olin Wright (1985, 1989), but adding the notion of cultural assets derived from the work of Pierre Bourdieu (1984, 1990). On this basis they proceed to examine the effect of differences in these assets and the dynamic interaction between them for the formation and cohesion of the service class and various sections within it, such as professionals and managers. However, despite this emphasis, the fact that their work rests on secondary analysis of published statistics forces them to use class structure statistics derived from sources that do not share their theoretical orientation. This highlights the difficulty of testing theories derived from the class formation approach and is linked to the problems of the case study method, which is the preferred tool of this kind of approach.

Exercise 4.20

1. Write your own list of the strengths and weaknesses of this set of Marxist theories.

2. Using the knowledge you have gained from the exercise on Weberian approaches and the material in this section, write your own evaluative paragraph on the class formation approach, plus your own conclusion about its usefulness.

Class analysis: theory and methods

This debate highlights the fact that divisions between sociologists in the field of class analysis do not simply occur because of differing sociological perspectives, but also because of differing theoretical approaches to the structure and action division within sociology generally and, linked to this, differing methodological preferences. This illustrates that the big debates such as structure versus action and quantitative versus qualitative are not simply relevant to theory and methods but are real issues that impact on the work of sociologists in all fields, and certainly in the area of class analysis.

Exercise 4.21

[a] 1. With reference to the above section on methodology and its link to class analysis, answer the following questions, which are designed to elicit information about the class structure using only closed questions:

   (a) Do you think of yourself as belonging to any particular class?

   (b) Do you think class inequality is inevitable?

[a] 2. Construct an informal interview schedule to consider issues of class formation. Here you need to consider the subjective notions of identity and the effect of these on inequality and class formation.

3. Structuration theory: solving the conundrum?

The most famous attempt to resolve the structure–action dichotomy was undertaken by Anthony Giddens (1984), who developed the concept of structuration to show how the notions of structure and action are inextricably linked. Therefore in class analysis, class structure and class formation need to be considered together as partners in a dynamic relationship. Giddens first developed the notion of the structuration of social classes in his book *The Class Structure of the Advanced Societies* (1980), but the theory was developed into a more general theory of society in *The Constitution of Society* (1984). At the heart of this work is Giddens' own reworking of the notion of social structure. Conventionally, perhaps best expounded by Durkheim, the notion of social structure has been seen as a constraint on the behaviour of individuals. However Giddens argues that 'all structural properties of social systems are enabling as well as constraining' (Giddens, 1984, p. 177). For example the rules of a school do in some sense constrain individual action, but they also enable the school to function. In other words, they enable social systems to operate.

Here it is important to point to the very different meaning of social structure adopted by Giddens. While most sociologists use the term to refer to large-scale, relatively long-lasting institutions such as the family, Giddens uses the term 'social system' for this level of analysis and 'social structure' for the set of rules and resources that people use. For Giddens, therefore, the social structure rooted in social practices that create order in the social system. This notion of social structure is much closer to the idea of social action than in more conventional structural accounts of the impact of social structures. This is because the rules and resources that comprise social practices are made and used by human agents, leading to the conclusion that social structures are created by and enable the actions of human agents. This Giddens describes as 'duality of structure'. Structures are created by the actions of knowledgeable human agents and this moves us far away from the 'puppet theatre' presented by more structurally inclined sociologists, where humans are seen as having no real choice and their lives are determined for them by structural forces beyond their control. In effect Giddens is asking who makes these structures, and how they might enable humans to act.

Exercise 4.22

a 1. Suggest ways in which the structure (that is, rules and resources) of your school or college may be enabling as well as constraining.

a 2. Give your own examples of other structures that may be enabling as well as constraining.

Language, because it has a set of rules for grammar, punctuation and so on, effectively constrains us to communicate in certain ways. However as Giddens points out, it also enables communication to take place since it creates a shared meaning, and it is also amenable to modification by the actions of human agents. Giddens therefore rejects the notion of structures as a constraint on the lives of individuals since he argues these constraints only really exist bearing in mind the choices that individuals make. Marx argued that propertyless labourers have no choice but to sell their labour power, but Giddens comments that 'there is only one feasible option, given that the worker has the motivation to wish to survive' (Giddens, 1984, p. 177). He goes on to argue that this situation is also enabling since it allows the worker to earn a living. The notion of choice, in this context the choice of whether to survive or die, rather blunts the notion of structures as a total constraint and maximises the notion of choices made by knowledgeable agents.

Giddens' work is an example of the move away from structural-oriented sociology towards an attempt to explain structures as the product of human action. This trend can be seen in a number of streams of sociology. Firstly, there has been the growth of rational-choice models, which stress the need to start with individual actions to explain societies. Since these are derived from the same theoretical origin as free market economics they have become popular as the hegemony of the market has grown in the 1980s and 1990s. Secondly we have the philosophical movement of post-structuralism, which in the form of postmodernist analysis has also undermined attempts to talk about structures and led to a debate about fragmentation and diversity. For instance an investigation of consumption patterns may reveal a multitude of lifestyles that can be supported with the same level of income. This type of analysis places much less emphasis on common positions in the production process, which underlies class analysis, and instead concentrates on a multitude and diversity of individual lifestyles. In many ways this has led to a reinvigorated pluralist analysis, with emphasis on the multitude of ways of living and expressing identity.

This is linked to the third sociological stream, namely that of Weber in the footsteps of Nietzsche (1969). The Weberian preference for methodological individualism, allied with the resurgence of liberalism with the rise of the new right, has returned the centre of gravity to microsociology, or at least macrosociology (sociology that speaks in terms of societies and global forces) rooted in micro foundations.

This was perhaps last seen in sociology in the late 1960s with the emergence of ethnomethodology and phenomenology, which emphasise the social constructedness of social life and the fact that rules, regulations and ways of living need to be explained in terms of the way in which individuals and small social groups try to construct meaning out of the situations in which they find themselves. This was popular until structuralist analysis took over in the mid 1970s. The key element of structuralist analysis is the denial that humans can have an impact on society, since they are seen simply as bearers of structures.

Giddens, however, is not without his critics. A major criticism of his theory is that he has not really achieved a synthesis of structure and action since the meaning he has given to the term structure is very different from its traditional meaning. The term structure in sociology has conventionally been used to describe something that is formed before an individual comes into being, and thus provides the framework into she or he is thrust, and will continue to exist after she or he is dead. Giddens uses the monetary system as an example of this.

The problem with this notion of structure is that it covers a wide variety of things. A school can be described as a structure, as can an education system, but so too can an industrial society or capitalism. So are we talking about institutions when we talk of structures or are we talking about global systems such as capitalism?

If we take structures to be institutions, then Giddens' notion that structures are the creation of human action and are enabling as well as constraining makes sense. Change in this institutional structural layer can take place without change at the level of the entire social system. Giddens' structuration theory is therefore a sophisticated form of reformism (the belief that society can be gradually changed, as opposed to theories, primarily Marxist, that stress the need for revolution). By concentrating on structures that are relatively easy to change he appears to merge structure and action, but this ignores the overlaying structure of capitalism within which both his structures and actors exist and which Marxists would argue would have a determining effect on both.

As such the theory has been criticised for not really overcoming the problem of the relationship between structure and action, but merely conflating the two, and as a result losing the ability to consider the relative importance of action and structure (or freedom and constraint) in any particular social circumstance. For instance Margaret Archer (1988) argues that one of the problems with structuration theory is that it depicts society as continually in motion, with everything always in progress, and therefore it is never possible to look at something as the product of other things (see also Best, 1997). In a later book she argues that Giddens' theory views every aspect of structure as being dependent on human action, and therefore any real notion of structural constraint is missing from the account (Archer, 1995). A similar point is made by Derek Layder: 'there is a case to be made that Giddens underplays the objective force of structural constraints insofar as he suggests that they only exist in the reasons and motivations of actors' (Layder, 1995, p. 145).

While it is true that Giddens' structuration theory has been the most influential attempt to move beyond the structure – action division in sociology, and as such has prompted a lot of debate about the process of class formation and the effect of this on the class structure, this theory is not accepted by all. It is important to state that the attempt to move from static measures of the class structure to an analysis based on class formation underlines the way that class analysis has moved on since the 1970s, and that there is now a serious concern to avoid both purely action-oriented theories (best seen in 'symbolic interactionism') and notions of society purely as a structural constraint (best seen in structural Marxism), but the critical comments on Giddens' work show that this key debate is still continuing.

Exercise 4.23

 As a summary for your notes, copy out the table below and complete it with the help of the relevant sections of this chapter and other sources.

Perspective	Summary of views on inequality	Examples
Functionalism		
New Right		Saunders (1990) Saunders (1995) Marsland (1988) Marsland (1996)
Marxism	Believes that inequality arises as a result of the exploitation of one class by another: the rich get rich as the poor get poor Inequality arises from processes which occur in the workplace	
Weberianism		Goldthorpe (1980)
Feminism		

Exam question

This comprises part of the AEB's November 1995 examination. Here we also reproduce the mark scheme and an actual answer written in exam conditions.

Use the mark scheme to provide marks and comments as appropriate in relation to the answer provided.

Item A

Functionalists tend not to talk of class as such but of stratification. By this, they mean any system of ordering by which society is broken down into layers or strata. This may be in terms of fairly rigid 'class', 'caste', 'gender' or 'racial' differences, or it may be in terms of an occupational hierarchy. Talcott Parsons, for example, argues that it is the commonly held values within a society that guide the way people are ranked into different strata. So, those people who perform well in terms of society's criteria will be highly ranked. This assumes that there is a set of shared values and that the inevitable ranking and differences in material reward that result from them are reasonable and just.

(Source: L. Harvey and M. MacDonald, Doing Sociology, Macmillan, 1993.)

Questions

(a) According to functionalists (Item A), what determines the ranking of individuals in society? *(1 mark)*
Commonly held values or the equivalent form of words

(b) Item A outlines a functionalist theory of stratification. With reference to this and alternative theories, assess the usefulness of the functionalist theory in explaining the stratification system of industrial societies. *(8 marks)*

Mark scheme

0: No relevant points

1–3: Answers will tend to be descriptive, with some misunderstandings in evidence. Reference to alternative theories may be thin and unfocused. As a consequence, evaluation will be unconvincing and simplistic. Irrelevant reference to non-industrial socities may also creep in.

4–6: The functionalist position will be well understood, with supporting evidence applied to support points made. Alternative approaches will also be described and understood, though evaluation will likely exist as juxtaposition of theories rather than explicitly.

7–8: There will be a good understanding of all the positions laid out, which will be used to answer the question set and not just laid out side to side. As such, evaluation will be addressed explicitly and not just taken for granted, with an attempt to specifically address the question as set.

Student answer

(a) According to functionalists the ranking of individuals in society is determined by, the way people perform in relation to society's values. Those that have the ability to perform well are ranked highly.

Mark: 1
Comment: for you to complete

(b) Functionalist theory is based on the idea that everyone has a function to perform to a greater or lesser extent in society, and the basis of the theory is that everyone shares a set of values in a particular society and the rewards obtained from excelling at these values is recognised by society to be right and just. Marxists thoroughly reject this view and argue that stratification systems in industrial societies are based on class and economic power. Industrialists, Marxists assert, own the means of production, e.g. factories, raw goods and other forms of capital, and the superstructure of society, e.g. legal institutions, financial institutions, and the Government endorses and supports the industrialists' interests.

The working classes, Marxists argue, have only their labour power to sell and are very unlikely, no matter how diligent and successful they are in their jobs, to be rewarded appropriately (as functionalists would assert) as the industrialists' main concern would be maximisation of profits.

Functionalists do not seem to take account of a person's social background, e.g. class and race, and others such as Bowles and Gintis would say that due to the hidden curriculum in schools these social groups may be at a permanent skills disadvantage in industrial society. The hidden curriculum supports the middle class values which society endeavours to aspire to. Functionalists would dispute these objections and argue that everyone in society has an equal opportunity to succeed and fulfil the functionally important roles in industrial society if they have the ability, ambition and education to do so. If a person does suceed they are rewarded accordingly both in status and financially. An argument which is used to dispute this view is how the functionally important roles are decided and indeed who decides this, for example a dustman and a doctor are both important to society.

Another disadvantage of the functionalist theory of industrial society is that no account is taken of ethnic and other groups which make up an industrial society. Functionalists would assert that the commonly held values should be shared by the whole of society.

Marks: For you to complete. First of all try to work out which band on the mark scheme you think the answer fits and then which level within that band.

Comments: For you to complete

5 The end of social class?

By the end of this chapter you should:

- be aware of the debate on the continued usefulness and relevance of the concept of class;
- have a critical awareness of the debate on the alleged death of class;
- be familiar with the debate on social mobility and understand the sociological significance of social mobility;
- be aware of the criticisms of social mobility studies;
- have practised structured exam questions.

Introduction

Social class was one of the formative concepts in sociology and until the 1970s was central to the understanding of inequality. This reflects its importance in Weberian, functionalist and particularly Marxist theories.

However since the 1980s the concept of class has been under attack. This has taken a number of forms, but three arguments are predominant: (1) that the concept of class is limited since it only relates to the sphere of production; (2) that people do not actually see social class as central to their identity and therefore it is not the basis of social mobilisation; and (3) that the inequalities to which class analysis refers in fact no longer exist. In this chapter all three arguments will be examined in turn.

Class as biased towards production relations

It has been argued that the concept of class, centred on the world of work, is not able to explain inequalities that arise from relationships that are not exclusively based in the arena of work. Feminist sociologists argue that theories that centre on the sphere of production are gender-blind and similar criticisms have been made about its ability to explain inequalities based on race and ethnicity. While this debate has led to the rise of other theories of inequality, such critiques have not claimed that class differences are unimportant, only that a consideration of class inequalities has to be put alongside explanations of other inequalities.

Various neo-Marxist writers have attempted to analyse the way in which these diverse forms of inequality interrelate, and non-Marxist theorists have also attempted to see how such inequalities operate together. For instance dual-systems theory (see Chapter 7), developed by feminists, attempts to explain the way in which capitalism (as understood by Marxists) and patriarchy (as described by radical feminists) are both systems that seek to oppress women. Class is not denied in these accounts, but it is now just one concept with which to explain inequality. This argument rejecting the primacy of class inequalities is used by feminist sociologists and many post-Marxist writers on race and ethnicity. It is partly inspired by a rejection of Marxism as economistic, which also spurred the growth of post-modernism. The notion of diversity and difference in postmodernist writing provide the basis for an examination of the many dimensions of inequality, and the postmodernist hostility to all-encompassing theories reinforces this.

The lack of mobilisation around class

The second attack on the concept of class also does not deny that objective differences in income and life-chances exist, but rejects the idea that people who face similar objective situations will act together. This criticism is aimed at the Marxist theory of class, which holds that workers exploited by capitalism will in time recognise this and act collectively to overthrow capitalism. The main problem with this is that workers have not acted in this way – the revolution has not come to Western Europe. This does not mean that people are happy with their lives or that inequalities have been eradicated, merely that people have not responded to inequality in the way suggested by this interpretation of Marx.

Instead it is suggested that things other than social class are better indicators of how people behave and what they believe, for example patterns of consumption. This sort of analysis is present in some recent Weberian writings and also in postmodernism, since postmodernists argue that consumption is now more important than production.

A recent example of a postmodernist argument that combines the essentials of the first two critiques of class analysis outlined here is the work of Malcolm Waters who seeks to outline 'the patterns of inequality that sociology needs to theorize, assuming that class is dead' (Waters, 1997, p. 23). He argues that the problem with class-based analysis is that (1) it is economistic, by which he means that it views economic and productive relations as predominant in society; (2) it entails the notion of 'groupness', meaning that classes are more than simply statistical aggregates but represent real potential cleavages in society; (3) it includes the notion that there is a link between membership of a particular class and the behaviour and culture of individuals within that class; and (4) that classes are important actors in social transformation.

Waters goes on to argue that the study of inequality needs to take into account factors that cannot be explained on the basis of class analysis, as he outlines it. Essentially these are (1) the existence of power and domination, particularly through the action of the state, and the fact that not all power is economically based; (2) the existence of ascribed status memberships, notably those of gender and ethnicity; and (3) conventional status divisions based on lifestyles and values. This is an attempt to provide a contemporary version of Weber's notion of inequality based not solely on class but on the trilogy of class, status and power. However by arguing that class is dead, Waters moves beyond Weber and into the realm of postmodernism.

He provides a periodisation of history that, he argues, points to the changing way in which the stratified order has manifested itself. Firstly he defines what he calls the economic class society – a period roughly covering the nineteenth century in Britain. This, he argues, is the model of society that best approximates the general model of class analysis. In other words, in this particular period of history property relations were predominant and the groups that developed on this basis were both closed and often acted together, particularly with the rise of the militant working-class movement.

Secondly, he argues that there was a period of organised class society, which covered the first 75 years of the twentieth century and was characterised by the overall importance of the state and the political arena in the exercise of power. A state-based elite was able to dominate the subordinated masses, while the sharp dividing line between the propertied and non-propertied classes of the earlier period began to break down. Class conflict became more fragmented, but insofar as it did exist, it was institutionalised through such bodies as the state, political parties, the trade unions and the welfare state.

His third period, from 1975 to the present, he calls the status-conventional society, where inequality exists in the cultural sphere of society and status groups have developed around lifestlyes and value commitments. Intelligence and market attributes have become more important than material property, and with the onset of globalisation the state is no longer able to organise class conflict in a national setting. Politically this period is characterised by partisan and class dealignment, with voters choosing how to vote on issues and divisions other than class.

Waters is influenced by Bell's postindustrial society thesis, the work of Lash and Urry and theories of globalisation and postmodernisation. This leads to a vision of contemporary society as based upon the primacy of cultural phenomena, ways of life, information exchange and values, which have become more important than material issues; and fragmentation whereby classes consist of continually shifting and unstable identifications, where the economic location of individuals is no longer a very good indicator of their subjective feelings or behaviour, and where choices about subjective identity are continually being made.

Waters argues that just as Marx and Weber avoided categorising the classes that emerged under capitalism as new forms of the feudal stratification system based on estates, so too must sociology avoid categorising these new forms of statuses in a post-class society on the now outmoded model of classes:

> If class then is a traditionalistic remnant in a postmodernizing world, the question remains of whether sociology can continue to make a central theoretical contribution if it abandons the concept of 'class' on which it relied for a hundred years. The answer is that it indeed must abandon its insistence on the centrality of class if it is to survive (Waters, 1997, p. 37).

Clearly the question of whether cultural identity or material inequality are the most important bases for stratification and identity is a central aspect of the argument about the validity and usefulness of the postmodern world view.

Marxist sociologists such as Westergaard (1995) and Wright (1997) continue to argue that class is important, but do not insist that it is the only form of inequality. They assert that there is a need to distinguish between the notion of exploitation (taking the value of someone else's labour power), which is central to Marxist analysis, and the concept of oppression (all other forms of power relations that create inequalities). While it is possible, though unlikely, that we could arrive at a non-oppressive form of capitalism where there is no inequality based on gender or ethnicity, it is not possible to eliminate exploitation under capitalism since it is this very exploitation upon which capitalism relies.

Importantly therefore, there is a crucial difference between class analysis and other analysis of inequality, namely that class analysis, at least in its Marxist form, has provided an analytical model of the dynamic nature of exploitation under capitalism and the way that in order for capitalism to survive it is necessary to create class divisions. A similar point is made by Pollert (1996) in relation to the fact that the concept of patriarchy fails to provide an analytical notion of the way that gender inequalities are created. A similar criticism can be made of the model outlined by Waters. If we accept his argument that status divisions originating in culturally fluid identities are now the key basis of the stratification system, there does not seem to be any full explanation of how and why this operates. By placing emphasis on the way that subjective identities are chosen, he tends to downplay considerably the importance of structural inequalities that act to constrain choices individuals and groups make. Finally Waters's model does appear to utilise Weberian concepts, but reverses the historical pattern outlined by Weber, who saw history moving from the primacy of inequality based on status divisions to the primacy of inequality based on class divisions. Waters's model appears to suggest historical progression going the opposite way.

Weberians have been more able to take on board postmodernist views, largely because of the importance of power (from Nietzsche) in both Weber and postmodernism. Marxists share no such common heritage and are opposed to the notion of postmodernism, as well as concerned to see the continued importance of production, economic and class inequalities in contemporary society.

The demise of class?

The third criticism of class argues that class inequalities have been eradicated and that Britain is now a meritocracy, where individuals' place in society does not depend on what their fathers did (that is, their class of origin) but on their own skills and talents. The central premise here is that the structural barriers that used to limit people from a working-class background have been removed and their life-chances depend solely on them as individuals. It is this issue that was the original spur to studies of social mobility, which sought to examine the relative importance of background and individual talent in establishing a person's place in society. The view that Britain had become a meritocracy was voiced by John Major when he asserted that we now live in a 'classless society', and the idea has been sociologically developed in the work of new right sociologists such as David Marsland (1996) and Peter Saunders (1990, 1995a, 1995b).

Studies of social mobility

One of the original motives for studying social mobility (movement from one's class of origin) was to guage the extent to which inequality depends on individual ability rather than family background. This was expressed in the notion explored and developed by early functionalist sociology that a key difference between industrial society and preindustrial society was that people's position in industrial society rested on achievement (generally considered in terms of educational qualifications) rather than ascription (meaning who their parents were). If this were the case, talented youngsters from poor backgrounds should be expected to move up the social class scale. Social mobility studies therefore offered a way to test the extent to which society was now meritocratic.

For Weberian sociologists there was a further reason. The formation of classes involved, for Weberians, the idea of social closure, that is, barriers set up to exclude people from certain privileges. The study of social mobility would reveal the existence or otherwise of such barriers. Weberians believed that such barriers led to the development of class solidarity and cohesion. It follows that if the barriers are removed and it becomes possible to engage in a high degree of social mobility, then the extent of class formation will be lower (Giddens, 1980). The study of social mobility therefore allows an insight into the process of class formation and class cohesion.

The first major study of social mobility in this country was undertaken by David Glass in 1949 (Glass, 1954). Using a seven-class schema (see Chapter 2) he compared the origins and current class position of 3497 males. Glass showed that while there was a degree of short-range mobility (moving up or down one or two classes) the extent of long-range mobility was very limited. For example he found that of all the sons whose fathers were in social class 7, none had risen to social class 1 and 27.4 per cent of them had remained in class 7. At the other end of the scale, of those sons with fathers in social class 1, 38.8 per cent had remained in social class 1, and only 1.5 per cent had moved into social class 7. Equally, of those sons in social class 7, 48.5 per cent had fathers in social class 1, while none had fathers in social class 7.

Because of the large numbers involved, and therefore the time and expense needed to conduct such studies, the next large-scale study of social mobility did not occur until 1972. This was a study of the social mobility experiences of 8575 males, conducted by John Goldthorpe and colleagues at Nuffield College, Oxford University (Goldthorpe, 1980). Although they did not use exactly the same class schema as the earlier study (the Hope–Goldthorpe scale was devised for this study; see Chapter 2), it was similar enough to allow judgement to be made of the extent to which patterns of social mobility had changed between 1949 and 1972.

The results of the 1972 survey showed that the extent of social mobility had changed. Goldthorpe and colleagues found that of all the sons whose fathers were in social class 7, 7.1 per cent had risen to social class 1 and 32.2 per cent had remained in class 7. At the other end of the scale, of those sons with fathers in social class 1, 45.7 per cent had remained in social class 1, and 6.5 per cent had moved into social class 7. Equally, of those sons in social class 7, 25.3 per cent had fathers in social class 1, while 12.1 per cent had fathers in social class 7.

Overall, the study found that there was a much greater degree of long-range social mobility than was the case when Glass conducted his study in 1949. On one level, this appears to suggest that ability and achievement are more important determinants of a person's ultimate social position, and therefore the theory that Britain was moving towards a meritocracy had something in it. However the authors were not convinced of this and argued that such measures only showed the amount of absolute social mobility. They stressed that changes in the class structure, in particular the growing number of non-manual jobs and the declining number of manual jobs (see Chapter 3), would inevitably lead to a degree of net upward mobility and that unless account was taken of this, social mobility statistics could not provide an accurate guide to the extent of upward mobility in British society. To take account of this and measure the extent to which home background still played a part in a person's final social position, they devised a measure known as relative social mobility. This measures the relative likelihood of people from various social class backgrounds ending up in particular social class positions. In order to investigate changes over time, those born in the period 1908–17 were compared with those born in 1938–47. The seven-class schema was compressed into the Goldthorpe three-class scheme (service class, intermediate class and working class).

The researchers found that for the early period the chance of ending up in the service class depended on the social class of the father: 55 per cent of those with fathers in the service class had remained in that class, while 25 per cent of those with fathers in the intermediate class and only 14 per cent of those with fathers in the working class had moved into the service class. Home background therefore produced an unequal ratio of 1:2:4 (meaning that a person born into the service class was four times more likely than someone born into the working class to end up in the service class). This became known as the 1:2:4 rule of relative hope (Kellner and Wilby, 1980).

These figures were compared with those for the later period, and it was found that the percentage chance of ending up in the service class in the later period still depended on the social class position of the father: 62 per cent of those with fathers in the service class compared with 30 per cent of those with fathers in the Intermediate class and only 18 per cent of those with fathers in the working class.

Exercise 5.1

The early period saw a ratio of 1:2:4 (14:25:55 per cent), showing the unequal chance of ending up in the service class in that period.

[i] 1. Using the statistics provided above, work out the ratio of the relative chance of people from various class backgrounds ending up in the service class in the later period.

[i][a] 2. On the basis of your answer to question 1, write a summary of the extent to which relative social mobility changed between the earlier and the later period.

[i][a][e] 3. Compare and contrast the picture provided of the extent of social mobility between 1949 and 1972 using absolute social mobility figures and relative social mobility figures.

In a later follow-up study using figures from the 1983 British Election Survey, Goldthorpe (1987) considered the extent of social mobility in a period characterised by economic recession, (1972–83). He found that the broad patterns discovered in the 1972 survey still held. Because of the continuing changes to the occupational structure, absolute mobility continued to increase, but relative mobility remained at the same unequal level.

An important area of study with regard to the opportunities afforded by the social structure was the education system. Any assertion that Britain was moving towards a meritocracy would need to show that able children from poor backgrounds could take full advantage of the education system. It is this question that lay at the heart of research by Halsey, Heath and Ridge (1980). Using data from the 1972 Oxford Mobility Survey they found that despite the introduction of the 1944 Education Act, which had made education free (see also Heaton and Lawson, 1996), not only had inequalities arising from social class background remained in terms of access to university education, but these inequalities had increased. Before the Act a boy from a service class background had been eight times more likely than a boy from a working class background to go to university; after the Act this figure had risen to 8.5. Their findings clearly contradicted the notion of Britain becoming a meritocracy.

Some years later Egerton and Halsey (1993), using a sample drawn from the General Household Surveys of 1985, 1986 and 1987, found that the relative advantages of those born into the service class remained, despite the large increase in higher education places.

An interesting study by Fiona Devine (1997) considers the reality of social class inequalities in the United States and Britain. She argues that there have long been stereotypical assumptions about both these societies, namely that Britain is a class-bound society and that the United States is a classless society. She believes that both these stereotypes are false and that the class structures of the two societies are remarkably similar, with considerable upward mobility in both societies, which means that people can and do escape their class of origin. However in both societies social class remains an important influence on people's life-chances. She concludes that Britain and the United States are neither entirely open nor entirely closed societies, and while they share a similar class structure due to a similarity of industrial and occupational change in the twentieth century (for instance the decline of manufacturing, the growth of low-level service sector jobs), these changes have occurred faster in the United States than in Britain. In relation to the impact of this on sociopolitical attitudes, she argues that:

> research in the 1970s and 1980s has shown that an identification
> with the working class remains strong among sizeable proportions

of the populations in both countries. In this respect, they are remarkably similar. However, class identification has not shaped sociopolitical attitudes and behaviour to the same degree in America as it has in Britain (Devine, 1997, p. 259).

Devine has also analysed the trends among the major classes in both countries. She argues that the wealthy in both countries have become more wealthy in the 1980s and 1990s, and that despite the alleged growth of globalisation there is little evidence of the emergence of a united transnational capitalist class.

The size of the middle class has increased in both countries, and although she identifies this grouping as a broadly conservative force in both countries, she argues that the public-sector professionals are in both cases more liberal on a range of social issues.

In relation to routine non-manual workers, she points to the importance of the growth of this sector for the employment of women, but disagrees with the argument that they have become proletarianised. Rather she argues that they identify more with the middle class than the working class.

Due to economic restructuring the size of the manual working class has declined in both countries and with it has come a decline in trade unionism. However Devine argues that this should not be taken as the end of notions of collective agency. Workers in both countries still largely identify with the notion of collectivism, that is, joining together to gain better living standards, and the working class in both countries remains culturally distinct.

In both countries there has also been a considerable growth in poverty in the last 20 years, with a poverty rate of around 20 per cent. This can be explained by structural changes, but the lack of a welfare state in the United States means that the depth of poverty there is greater.

Overall she concludes that 'Despite rapid economic, social and political change, social class is not dead. On the contrary, social class has also proved remarkably resilient over the twentieth century' (Devine, 1997, p. 264).

Support for the notion of Britain moving towards a meritocracy, in terms of both desirability and actuality, came from former Prime Minister John Major. His use of the term 'classless society' to describe Britain led to a resurgence of the debate on social mobility and equality of opportunity.

A second line of argument emerged with the reopening of the debate on how merit is measured. Because of concern about the extent to which IQ tests measured intelligence and the scandal surrounding the work of Cyril Burt, these tests had somewhat fallen into disrepute. This had been a contributory factor to the ending of the 11+ test and the introduction of comprehensive schools. These were never really accepted by Conservative politicians and the combination of their long period in office in the 1980s and 1990s and the interest shown by John Major in equality of opportunity led new right thinkers to question the exact meaning of equality of opportunity and the extent to which we had achieved this goal.

Peter Saunders (1995a) has launched a strong critique of the idea that structural barriers are still at the root of class inequalities in Britain. He argues that all studies of social mobility have shown a much higher degree social mobility in contemporary Britain than in the past, but that sociologists have resisted the conclusion that Britain is therefore a more open society by referring to relative social mobility. He stresses that this obscures the extent of social mobility and also that, insofar as there are differences in relative opportunities for mobility, these reflect differences in individual talent among social classes. He also argues that this evidence does not undermine the thesis that Britain is becoming a meritocracy.

Goldthorpe (1987) and Marshall *et al.* (1988) conclude that Britain is not a meritocracy because the chance of entering the service class is not equal for people of all origins and therefore background still has an effect. Saunders (1995a) argues that this contains an implausible criterion of social fairness, namely that there should be no link between people's class of origin and their ultimate class. This assumes that there are no differences in aptitude between the different classes and it is this assumption that Saunders rejects. He points out that there is little actual data on this, and that all previous social mobility studies have simply stated that there is no evidence of the existence of such differences and have not sought to provide it. He describes this as a long-running Hamlet in which the prince never appears.

What Saunders is referring to is the possibility that the differences in the relative chance of social mobility might reflect unequal abilities. If this is based on genetics, then we would expect successful middle-class parents to pass on their abilities to their offspring and a greater degree of social mobility among these offspring would therefore be expected. On this basis the most intelligent get on, and thus it might be possible to argue that Britain is a meritocracy after all.

It's top Marx in class poll

Karl Marx was right and every major political party and practically everyone in the media is wrong, say the vast majority of British voters.

Some 76 per cent of people believe there is a class struggle, according to a major Gallup opinion poll last week.

John Major talks about a 'classless society'. Tony Blair says, 'Class is no longer an accurate or helpful way to understand what needs to be done'. But more than three quarters of the people polled disagreed.

We are told that class used to be important in the 1950s and 1960s, but today everyone has abandoned it.

The reality is almost the opposite.

In 1964, when Gallup asked the same question, 48 per cent thought there was a class struggle. By 1974 that was up to 60 per cent. Today it is almost 80 per cent. Nor is this poll a one-off oddity. After John Major described himself as a 'one-nation Conservative' last October, Gallup found just 11 per cent thought Britain was becoming more 'one nation', while 65 per cent thought it was becoming less.

In 1995 75 per cent of those polled thought Britain was divided into 'haves and have nots', up from 63 per cent a decade ago.

Politicans often claim to be following what the public wants. Let them take note of the sober conclusions from Gallup director Bob Wybrow: 'We've got this trend where more people believe there is a class struggle, that there are two nations, that the haves are gaining and that not everybody has a chance.'

The reason is simple – life for most of us is hard and insecure. But we can see a tiny minority of the rich and powerful living lives of luxury at our expense.

They try to make us work harder, hold down our pay or throw us on the dole if we don't make them enough profit.

As Gallup's Bob Wybrow says, 'What is conditioning people's attitude to the class struggle question is what is happening to them on a day to day basis, what is happening in thier lives'.

Even the *Financial Times* admitted last weekend that it is class which explains why

there is not a return of the 'feelgood factor' despite figures showing an increase in wealth.

Assets

The paper says, '72 per cent of net financial wealth is owned by only 25 per cent of the voters. This minority, which has not broadened during the Tory years, will account for most of the the increase in cash and securities. For the rest the big swings in assets may seem as remote as the weather.'

Practically everyone in the bus queue or supermarket checkout lane knows there's a class struggle in Britain.

It is only the bosses (in public), the smoothly suited politicans, the media pundits and the 'modernisers' who persuade themselves it has gone away.

A writer in the impeccably pro-Blair *New Statesman* magazine says. 'There is now no political machinery to reflect this stubborn view about the continuing class struggle.'

Real socialists have to fight hard to make sure we continue to build one.

(Source: Socialist Worker, 31 August 1996.)

ITEM A   *Exercise 5.2*

1. Read Item A and summarise the criticisms the article makes of the notion that Britain is a classless society.

2. Using the material in this section, suggest how Peter Saunders would reply to the arguments put forward in Item A.

For Saunders (1995a) the evidence that talents are unequally distributed and that the cause of this unequal distribution is to some extent genetic is compelling. He points out that Halsey *et al.* (1980) estimate that the average IQ is 109 for the service class, 102 for the intermediate class and 98 for the working class. On this basis he argues that 69 per cent of the advantage service class children have in gaining grammar school places, and 55 per cent of the disadvantage faced by working-class children in this respect, can be explained by the differences in their average IQs. He therefore argues that genetic and moral differences, which have been ignored by researchers, might actually play a role in social mobility.

Furthermore, it is possible to construct a model of what society would look like if it were perfectly meritocratic, based on Saunders' assumptions about the differential IQ of social classes and the extent to which this is passed on from parent to child. He argues that what we would see would be virtually identical to the figures produced by Goldthorpe (1987): 'What happened to the ten thousand men interviewed on the Nuffield project is almost precisely what we would have expected to happen had they and their fathers been recruited to their class positions on the basis of their intellectual abilities' (Saunders, 1995). Such an analysis reduces the advantage enjoyed by service class origins from a factor of 4:1 to 1.4:1.

While Saunders accepts that social background is still important in relation to elite occupations, he argues that the rest of British society might be a meritocracy. This cannot be proved because of the absence of IQ data, but according to Saunders it is precisely this absence in the work of sociologists such as Goldthorpe and Marshall that makes it unable to be seen as a refutation of the meritocracy thesis. Hence the strength of Saunders' argument is that it demonstrates that the assumptions upon which comments on relative social mobility have been based are essentially made in the absence of any IQ data.

However the weakness of his approach is that he assumes that such measures are a valid measure of intelligence, but the most likely reason why IQ figures have not been collected is that most sociologists reject them as an accurate measure of intelligence because IQ tests measure just one type of ability and not general intelligence, as is claimed. Furthermore the notion of a general intelligence level is flawed since there are a multitude of different types of aptitude, skill and intelligence and someone who scores highly in one area may not necessarily score highly in other areas. This means that IQ tests are a very crude measure of ability and do not offer an assessment of general intelligence.

More controversially, it is argued that the data that led to the adoption of IQ tests, based on the work of psychologist Cyril Burt, was actually fraudulent. There are two reasons for this: (1) it is suggested that the degree of agreement shown by Burt's original figures was a statistical impossibility, and (2) the two female research assistants that Burt said had worked with him have never been traced.

In the 1980s there was a renewed debate about this and a campaign to reinstate Burt, at a time when there was a political desire for a return to selective education on the part of new right thinkers and governments. The British Psychological Society announced in 1992 that it no longer believes Burt's work was fraudulent (Bates, 1992). This has of course sparked off controversy, but has also led to further debate on the biological basis of inequality in which new right sociologists were prominent. For example, Peter Saunders believes that there is compelling evidence to support the view that genetic factors play an important part in intelligence, and the work of Herrnstein and Murray (1994) in the United States is based on a similar acceptance of the importance of genetic factors in intelligence.

Social mobility studies–what about women?

Another controversy has arisen from the data on social mobility in Britain. Both Glass (1954) and Goldthorpe (1987) used male-only samples. Since we know that gender inequalities exist, it is reasonable to assume that the social mobility patterns of females might be different from those of males, and therefore statements about British social mobility on the basis of exclusively male samples might be somewhat misleading. Abbott and Wallace (1997, p. 62) make the following point: 'Analysis of female social mobility suggests that patterns of intergenerational and intragenerational social mobility are very different from those of men. This is perhaps not surprising, given that the female occupational distribution is very different from that of males.'

A major study of the class system that did include figures for both male and female social mobility was the Essex Class Project (Marshall *et al.*, 1988). They found that there are fewer opportunities for women to enter the service class, and since the expansion of this is a key source of mobility opportunities for men, such an absence produces a position where the daughters of service-class men, unlike their sons, are likely to experience downward mobility. It is also the case that if women move into manual occupations they are much more likely to be doing semi-skilled or unskilled work rather than skilled manual work, which is dominated by men.

Abbott and Wallace (1997, p. 65) make the following point about the overall mobility opportunities for men and women: 'Long-range social mobility is also more common among men than women: 21 per cent of men from working-class origins are in Class I or II occupations, but only 15 per cent of women. Whatever their origins, women are much more likely than men to finish up in Class III.' The reason for this is the effect of labour market segmentation, meaning that the kind of jobs that women do and the opportunities that are available to them for promotion are clearly very different from those available to men. Even if they come from exactly the same background, these labour market differences will contribute to the reproduction of gender inequalities.

Therefore it is clearly not possible to make statements about social mobility on the basis of exclusively male samples, since this assumes that the social mobility experiences of men and women are similar, and this is not so.

Link Exercise 5.1

*i**a*** Using the material on labour market segmentation in Chapters 6 and 7, write a summary of how this contributes to the differential patterns of social mobility for men and women, as outlined above.

Exam question

This is part of the AEB's June 1995 question. Again the mark scheme is provided and an actual student answer. Here we have not provided the mark and your task is to suggest what mark you think is appropriate for the answer on the basis of the mark scheme. You will find that when there are bands suggested in the mark scheme, you should first decide which band the answer fits into and then decide where within that band the mark should be set. You should provide comments to justify the marks you give.

ITEM B

At the root of our confusion about class is our equation of class with money. As we have become more prosperous, as the working classes got their washing machines in the sixties and videos in the eighties, old class allegiances have faded. Everyone moved on up. We may have not gone fully into Europe, but Europe has got fully into us. Cap-puccino, fresh pasta and good wine are now available almost everywhere. We are all middle class now – or so the myth goes.

Clearly, class is no longer a fashionalbe concept, but the uncomfortable truth is that the gap between the classes is widening. We may be in danger of losing the statistics that show, time and time again, that mem-bers of the working class are far more likely to die of heart disease, lung cancer and strokes than the middle class. Or that babies born to middle-class parents have a better chance of survival than those born to working-class ones. For, in the end, class is not just a question of style or even lifestyle, but of life itself.

(Source: Suzanne Moore, 'The Ups and Downs of Them and Us', The Observer, 6 October 1991.)

A study of the middle class argues that 'decomposition' or to use the author's term, 'fragmentation' is occurring in this group. Roberts *et al.* examine the 'class images' of a wide range of white collar employees. They conclude that a variety of class images occur and that this is indicative of the fragmentation of the middle class into various strata. Accordingly, it is no longer accurate to talk of the middle class.

(Source: Adapted from M. O'Donnell, A New Introduction to Sociology, Nelson, 1992.)

Questions

(a) Apart from the ways mentioned in Item B, suggest one other way in which the working class may be disadvantaged compared to the middle class. *(1 mark)*

Mark scheme

Any reasonable disadvantage may score, as long as there is no reproduction from the Item. These might include references to education, housing, employment, etc.

(b) How far does sociological evidence support the view that the 'gap between the classes is widening' (Item B)? *(7 marks)*

Mark scheme

0: No relevant points.

1–2: Answers are likely to consist of prosaic accounts of the gap between rich and poor, often expressed in an assertive way and lapsing into commonsense at times.

3–5: Candidates in this band will be aware of a range of evidence concerning the gap, and there will be a concentration, though not necessarily balanced, of the case both for and against widening. Evidence cited will be used directly to answer the question. Evaluation will be either one-sided, or by juxtaposition of positions.

6–7: Responses will be more balanced, acknowledging the case for the narrowing of the gap as well as its widening. Evidence will be well applied and focused. Evaluation should be explicit and candidates should come to a conclusion about the issue, which emerges from the body of the responses.

Question

(c) To what extent do sociologists agree that the modern class structure is fragmented (Item C)? Refer to the Items and other sources in your answer. *(8 marks)*

Mark scheme

0: No relevant points.

1–3: Candidates here will offer simplistic accounts of the modern class structure, perhaps asserting its obvious fragmentation, though in a descriptive way, with little supporting evidence applied. As such, evaluation will be limited or non-existant.

4–6: Answers will be more balanced, examining the case for and against fragmentation, though not necessarily equally. Studies which are used will be focused on the issue and applied in some measure. Evaluation may appear as juxtaposition or through the opposition of different approaches, rather than explicitly.

7–8: There will be a balanced consideration of the case for and against fragmentation, with any information interpreted and applied in a focused way. As a consequence, evaluation will be appropriate and stemming from the body of the response. It will likely appear in a separately drawn part of the answer.

Student answer

Use the mark scheme to provide marks and comments in relation to the answers provided.

(a) The working class lack resources for educational equipment compared with the middle class, so are disadvantaged.

Mark: for you to complete

Comment: for you to complete

(b) According to Item B, 'the gap between the classes is widening'. Marx predicted that as the bourgeoisie get richer due to an increase in surplus value, the poor are getting poorer and the division between the two is increasing. Butler and Rose believed that embourgeoisement was occuring. This means that people were becoming middle-class. They believed that the top, the more affluent working class were losing their working class identities, lifestyles

---

and values and were becoming middle class by supporting the Conservative Party. McMilland pointed out that the income gap between classes was decreasing and middle-class goods were becoming more affordable. There was also an increase in educational opportunities and an increase in geographical mobility so there was movement from the North to more prosperous areas. However, other sociologists such as Goldthorpe and Lockwood disagreed. They studied Luton which they believed was most likely to be experienceing embourgeoisement and expected to find similar wages, promotional prospects, conditions etc. Instead they found that they lacked job security, were less likely to be promoted, there was no social mixing and they did have similar income but this was due to overtime, different shifts, conditions etc. Therefore, evidence suggests that the gap is not really widening but at the same time it is not really decreasing, and if it is, it is due to different conditions etc.

Mark: for you to complete
Comment: for you to complete

(c) Some sociologists have agreed that the modern class structure is fragmented. For example Item C points out that a study by Roberts *et al.* found that there was a range of white-collar workers and instead of talking about the middle class we should refer to it as the middle classes. Also, Item C suggests that the lower middle class and the upper working class can be thought of as from one stratum.

Sociologists such as Dahrendorf point to the decomposition of labour. He found that there were three types of working class: the unskilled, the semi-skilled and the skilled. There is also a division between the middle classes. There is an upper middle, middle middle and lower middle.

Some refer to the middle class as the traditional one which consists of the legal and medical profession and the new middle class which involves clerical workers, teachers and journalists. Lockwood also believes that there is an intermediate stratum – the new middle class – and this is supported by Marshall *et al.* However, Marxists would criticise the view that the structure is fragmented, believing that eventually there will form two major classes: the proletariat and the bourgeoisie. Weber on the other hand points out four classes: the propertied upper class, the propertyless white-collar workers, the petty bourgeoisie and finally the manual working class. However there is more evidence to suggest that there is a fragmenting class structure.

Mark: for you to complete
Comment: for you to complete

6 Gender and inequality

By the end of this chapter you should:
- be familiar with recent empirical material and indicators of the various aspects of gender inequality;
- understand the nature of the debate on the changing nature of women's involvement in paid employment;
- be aware of the debate on the role of the family in the oppression of women;
- have a critical understanding of the variety of feminist views on the sociology of gender inequality;
- have practised structured exam questions yourself.

Introduction

Gender inequality is an important aspect of society and sociology. The rise of feminism as a political movement and sociological approach led to much greater emphasis on gender inequality in the sociological literature from the late 1970s onwards.

There are a number of aspects to gender inequality and this section will consider recent empirical material in relation to some of these. We shall first look at the sphere of paid employment. Here both the level of pay and the type of job done are structured by gender.

Secondly, we shall look at gender inequalities in the domestic sphere, in particular at the way socially constructed assumptions about behaviour affect roles inside the home, and how such assumptions affect women's participation in paid employment.

A third aspect is the extent to which the oppression of women takes a directly physical form, such as physical and sexual violence, which affects their feelings of well-being in society and which some feminists see as the ultimate basis of male oppression of females.

Women and paid employment

Sociological evidence shows that gender has an effect on people's place in the paid employment sector. This manifests itself in a number of ways, including whether or not a person is involved in paid employment, the type of job held, the level of job held and the level of pay obtained.

With regard to involvement in paid employment, government statistics on this are published in the Labour Force Survey, where the population is divided into various employment categories and figures are quoted for unemployment (on the International Labour Organisation, ILO, basis: see Madry and Kirby, 1996) and the economically inactive (including the retired, those who are sick and housewives). This categorisation has been subject to criticism, most notably because while the unemployed are categorised as economically active (since in order to be classed as unemployed they need to be seeking work), housewives are not. This reflects the fact that economic activity is defined as doing paid work or looking for it. This restricts the definition of work to paid employment, which has been the subject of criticism by some sociologists (see Deem, 1988).

The statistics in Item A include some people who are classified as employed but are unpaid, namely people working in family businesses who receive no direct remuneration. This category does not extend to those permanently engaged in housework. However these figures do provide some indication of the extent of gender differences in involvement in paid employment.

ITEM A

Labour Force Survey on economic activity (000s)

	Employees	Self-emp.	On training schemes	Unpaid family workers	Unemp.	Econ. inactive	% Employ.
Males							
Autumn 94	11 306	2470	192	44	1667	5837	65.1
Winter 94	11 328	2478	189	41	1584	5917	65.1
Spring 95	11 401	2471	171	40	1574	5902	65.3
Summer 95	11 446	2448	161	44	1572	5908	65.3
Autumn 95	11 455	2460	156	42	1551	5939	65.3
% Change	1.3	−0.4	−18.0	−4.5	−6.9	1.7	
Females							
Autumn 94	10 280	806	97	98	863	10 663	49.4
Winter 94	10 359	807	91	88	820	10 650	49.7
Spring 95	10 346	793	91	93	858	10 641	49.6
Summer 95	10 442	796	95	81	842	10 575	49.9
Autumn 95	10 471	792	87	88	847	10 558	50.0
% Change	1.8	−1.7	−10.3	−10.2	−1.8	−0.9	

(Source: Economic Trends, April 1996, London, HMSO.)

Exercise 6.1

Study Item A and answer the following questions:

i 1. Identify one type of employment activity in which men outnumbered women in autumn 1995 and one in which women outnumbered men in autumn 1995.

i 2. Identify the percentage change in the number of males categorised as employees during the period covered in the table. Identify the equivalent figure for females during the same period. Which sex experienced the highest percentage rise in the category of employee over the period quoted?

i 3. Which sex experienced the highest percentage fall in the unemployed category during the period in question?

i 4. What percentage of the total adult male population were in employment in autumn 1995?

i 5. What percentage of the total adult female population were in employment in autumn 1995?

i 6. Using the statistics in Item A, summarise the gender differences in economic activity.

a *e* 7. Why might sociologists not wish to rely exclusively on sources such as Item A when considering gender differences in relation to work?

1. Gender differences in paid employment

Exercise 6.2

a Jot down as many examples as you can of jobs that have traditionally been seen as 'female'.

While the figures in Item A can be used to show that gender is an important structural division in relation to economic activity, they tell us little about the type of work people do. For example a City stockbroker on £140 000 per year and a schoolteacher on £15 000 per year would both show up in the employee category, but clearly these two people would have very different life-chances and we therefore need to break down the notion of employment further in order to investigate which types of job men and women do.

When considering this issue, sociologists refer to the segregation of the labour market. Horizontal segregation refers to the sector in which people work, for example coal mining or hairdressing. We can investigate this to see the extent to which men and women do different jobs. Research by the Equal Opportunities Commission (quoted in COI, 1996) revealed that job segregation is still widespread, with women concentrated in the clerical and administrative sector while men predominate in skilled manual work, senior professional and technical work.

There is also vertical segregation, which relates to the designated level of particular jobs. For instance one civil servant might be a clerical officer and another a permanent secretary, and while both are described as civil servants they are at different levels and as a result have very different levels of pay. Likewise professional and managerial workers tend to earn more than unskilled manual workers. In the 1980s Beechey (1986) found that women held only 9 per cent of managerial jobs. More recent EOC research (COI, 1996) shows that managerial staff are still overwhelmingly male and over 50 per cent of workplaces still employ only male managers. We shall therefore consider the extent to which women occupy jobs that tend to be less well-paid than those occupied by men (Items B to E).

Horizontal segregation

ITEM B

Employment by sector in Britain, spring 1995 (thousands, not seasonally adjusted)

	Men	Women	Total	% women
Agriculture and fishing	362	136	498	27.3
Energy and water supply	264	63	327	19.3
Manufacturing	3 467	1 346	4 813	28.0
Construction	1 604	174	1 778	9.8
Services	8 252	9 565	17 817	53.7
All employees and self-employed	14 028	11 321	23 350	44.7

(Source: Labour Force Survey data, quoted in COI, 1996, table 9, p. 48.)

Exercise 6.3

Study Item B and answer the following questions:

1. Identify the sectors where women make up the highest and lowest percentages of the workforce.

2. Suggest reasons for the low participation of women in the energy and water supply sector.

3. To what extent does this table support the notion that there is considerable horizontal segregation in employment?

Proportion of men and women (aged over 16) in selected occupations, (per cent) 1985

	Men	Women
Construction, mining and related	99.5	0.5
Processing, making, repairing and related (metals and electrical)	96.4	3.6
Transport operation, materials moving and related	96.4	3.6
Professional and related in science, engineering and technology	93.3	6.7
Farming, fishing and related	83.1	16.9
Professional and related supplying management and administration	77.1	22.9
Managerial	74.9	25.1
Professional and related in education, welfare and health	34.8	65.2
Clerical and related	22.8	77.2
Catering, cleaning, hairdressing and other personal services	20.8	79.2

(Source: Labour Force Survey 1985, quoted in Bradley, 1989, table 1.1a, p. 13.)

Exercise 6.4

Study Item C and answer the following questions:

i 1. Identify the two occupations with the most gender segregation and the two occupations with the least.

a 2. Using the information in Item C and other sources on the changing composition of the occupational arena, consider the extent to which such changes will affect the level of horizontal segregation in the future.

Vertical segregation

Women in the Civil Service by grade level

	1984		1994	
	Number	Per cent	Number	Per cent
Grade 1	0	0.0	2	5.7
Grade 2	5	3.7	9	7.4
Grade 3	25	4.7	48	10.1
Grade 4	11	3.4	35	9.4
Grade 5	173	6.6	379	13.3
Grade 6	380	7.7	674	13.2
Grade 7	956	7.3	3 464	19.4
Senior executive officer	1 390	6.4	3 623	15.0
Higher executive officer	6 867	14.0	17 554	22.3
Executive officer	36 788	29.0	54 650	46.6
Administrative officer	108 111	61.5	117 728	68.8
Administrative assistant	86 193	79.2	61 800	70.4
Other	22	–	270	–
Total	240 919	47.7	260 236	51.3

(Source: Equal Opportunities Division, Cabinet Office statistics, quoted in COI, 1996, table 11, p. 59.)

Exercise 6.5

Study Item D and answer the following questions:

a   1. Which grade had a lower percentage of women in 1994 than in 1984?

i a   2. How might this table illustrate the notion of vertical segregation in the job market?

i   3. What trend in gender imbalance is illustrated by this table?

ITEM E

Socioeconomic groups by sex, 1981 and 1991 (per cent)

	1981		1991	
Socioeconomic group	**Men**	**Women**	**Men**	**Women**
Employers and managers	78	22	69	31
Professional	89	11	83	17
Ancillary	44	56	41	59
Supervisory non-manual	52	48	40	60
Junior non-manual	29	71	24	76
Personal service workers	13	87	18	82
Skilled manual	90	10	90	10
Semi-skilled manual	68	32	61	39
Unskilled manual	58	42	41	59
All employees	61	39	55	45

(Sources: Walby, 1990, for 1981 figures, Census 1991 for 1991 figures. Office for National Statistics © Crown Copyright.)

Exercise 6.6

Study Item E and answer the following questions:

i   1. In which socioeconomic group did the proportion of women decline between 1981 and 1991?

i   2. How many socioeconomic groups had a majority of men in (a) 1981 and (b) 1991?

i   3. Write a 100-word summary of the changes revealed by these statistics.

i   4. Which two socioeconomic groups had the greatest amount of gender imbalance in 1991.

2. Debates on the divisions in paid employment

Traditionally there have been two broad positions in sociology to explain gender differences in paid employment. The first, which is largely associated with Weberian sociologists (Barron and Norris, 1976; Rubery, 1980), is the dual labour market theory. According to this theory there are two distinct job markets: the primary and the secondary. The primary sector is characterised by permanent, secure, well-paid jobs and the secondary sector by temporary or insecure and/or poorly paid jobs. The theory suggests that women and men are involved in different job markets and women are much more likely to be consigned to the secondary job market, with worse conditions in terms of job security, pay and promotion prospects. Barron and Norris explain this in terms of women's lower levels of training and trade union involvement, but Rubery argues it is more to do with exclusionary practices (meaning barriers that exclude women from certain occupations) by male workers who wish to keep the best jobs for themselves.

Bradley (1989) contends that the problem with this approach is that it is unable to explain inequalities between men and women who work in the same sector. This is a problem, since many women work in the primary sector, in nursing and teaching for example, and some men work in the secondary labour market.

The second broad approach, associated with Marxist writers such as Braverman (1974) and Beechey (1977), argues that women in the labour market can best be described as a reserve army of labour. This idea derives from Marx, who argued that capitalism always requires a reserve army of unemployed people to ensure that those in work keep their wage demands down and remain in fear for their jobs. It is suggested that women have come to be an important part of this reserve army, allowing the workforce to be increased in times of economic expansion and also quickly reduced in times of recession.

According to Braverman, at the same time as the service sector was expanding the jobs within it were being deskilled, and women came to fill these jobs as other sources of new labour dried up as a result of the falling birth rate and restrictions on immigration. Beechey suggests that the fact that these jobs are done by women might provide a more accurate explanation of the low pay associated with them rather than a decline in skill levels. She argues that women can provide a reserve army of labour because their domestic obligations mean that they are much more likely to accept part-time work than men, making them more desirable to employers seeking a flexible workforce. This notion of flexibility is seen as an important characteristic of what some have described as the emergence of a post-Fordist society.

However critics of this argument point out that if women employees were on average cheaper than men it would make more sense for employers to dispense with the most expensive employees in times of recession, and this would mean that men's jobs would be more insecure than women's.

These explanations concern vertical rather than horizontal segregation. The extent to which women do different jobs from men is not really explained by these theories, particularly the reserve army theory, which sees women as substituting for men in certain circumstances. The known facts about horizontal segregation suggest they do not.

Hakim (1980) has argued that the extent of horizontal and vertical segregation between men and women has changed little this century. This situation is sometimes referred to as industrial apartheid, keeping men and women in very different roles and levels in the workplace. For instance Martin and Roberts (1984), in their survey of workplaces, found that 63 per cent of women worked only with other women, while 81 per cent of the husbands of these women worked only with other men.

It is argued that this represents a change from previous centuries when women were not involved in paid employment at all, but this is open to dispute. According to Hakim (1995), there was little or no change in female participation rates in paid employment between 1851 and the late 1950s, and no change in female full-time work rates from 1841 until 1993. She considers that the increase in the economic activity rate (having paid employment or looking for it) of women from 47 per cent in 1961 to 53 per cent in 1995 (COI, 1996) can be explained by the substitution of women working part time for women working full time. This coincides with a substitution of married women for single women in the work place, as it is now much more likely that married women will have paid employment compared with just after the Second World War. This reflects the ending of the marriage bar, which prevented married women from working and was effective until the late 1940s, or until 1963 in the case of the Post Office. The full-time employment rates for women only started to increase in the late 1980s. Hakim therefore argues that stability not change has characterised female employment patterns until very recently.

This view has been challenged by Ginn *et al.* (1996) who assert that it is more appropriate to consider the proportion of women in employment. On this basis, although two women working part time may work the same number of hours as a full-time worker (the basis of Hakim's claim of stability) Ginn *et al.* argue that this makes an important difference to these women's lives. So if we look at the proportion of women who are economically active, this does show an increase. More and more women are entering paid employment, though the total number of hours worked by women will not show substantial increase due to the rise of part-time work.

Exercise 6.7

[a] In groups, brainstorm the reasons why many women work part time and why they are more likely to do so than men.

The reasons for the increase in part-time work are also subject to debate. According to Hakim (1995), women choose to work part time because they are less oriented towards work than towards their families. She further argues this is a matter of choice and not because of a lack of childcare facilities. Conversely Ginn *et al.* (1996) contend that there is no evidence that part-time workers are less attached to their jobs than full-time workers. Rather it is precisely the lack of childcare facilities that forces women into 'choosing' part-time employment, along with the continuation of the patriarchal attitude that it is women not men who should change their employment pattern to look after children.

Bradley (1989) has pointed out that women with equal qualifications to men (in medicine and education) fall behind men in terms of pay and promotion even when working full time. Choice about how to work cannot therefore provide a full explanation since there is inequality even when people have similar qualifications and job commitment.

This debate is about the extent to which the differences between men's and women's involvement in paid employment can be explained on the basis of cultural or structural factors. Structural factors are those things that are beyond the bounds of any individual or group to change easily within their lifetime. Cultural arguments tend to emphasise lifestyle choices and other factors that can be changed by individuals or groups. In essence, this debate revolves around the extent to which women's situation is a reflection of the choices they make or is due to structural factors beyond their control.

Exercise 6.8

i a 1. Re-read pages 102–5 and divide the reasons cited for gender divisions in paid employent into those that emphasise cultural factors and those that emphasise structural factors.

e 2. Which approach do you find most convincing?

Women and the domestic arena

One of the Oakley's aims in her 1974 book on housework was to show that it was very similar to paid work and it was therefore wrong to define work solely in terms of paid employment. That such work is unpaid and is largely done by women is an important factor in the oppression of women in society. The expectation that women will see this as their prime responsibility inhibits their involvement in paid employment and causes many to be economically dependent on men.

Oakley's study also undermined the notion of the family as a consensual unit with equality between its members – the vision presented by functionalist-inspired accounts of the family, such as that by Wilmott and Young (1973). Surveys since that time have consistently shown that women undertake the majority of work around the house even when they have a full-time job. There is evidence of a small increase in male contributions when women are involved in paid employment (Warde, 1990). Pahl (1989) and Morris (1993) have shown that there are some instances where women have gained a greater say in family finances, particularly when the male is unemployed. Pahl (1989) points out that in such cases women often manage the finances in order to provide goods for their husbands or children, but they often go without themselves in the process. Wheelock (1990) studied households where the male was unemployed and the wife had paid employment. Wheelock found that while the men did become more involved in domestic work, this varied in line with the number of hours of paid employment the women had and the women retained primary responsibility for the core household tasks.

Exercise 6.9

Time use diaries

Give two copies of the following table (one for the male, one for the female) to a number of households that contain an adult male, an adult female and at least one child under the age of 11. Ask them to complete the table by inserting the relevant details for one week, and then to return the completed diaries to you.

Parent/Guardian male or female: Age:	Hours worked in paid employment for one week	Time spent on domestic tasks for one week		Time spent on childcare tasks for one week	
		Task	Time	Task	Time

Once you have collected your data you should compare your findings with those of other sociology students in the class and summarise your overall findings.

1. Explaining the domestic division of labour

Radical feminist writers see the household as the central oppressive institution where women are exploited by men. They argue that the household, which is concerned with reproduction, is a more fundamental arena than work and the sphere of production, which is seen as the key arena by Marxist sociologists. All men are viewed as oppressors of women, but this has been criticised as a form of biological reductionism since the basis for such oppression is the biological fact that only women can bear children, and it is this that makes them dependent on men (Firestone, 1972). Marxists argue that this situation originally arose because of the desire by some men to ensure that the economic surplus they built up stayed in the family, thus requiring the imposition of monogamy (only one sexual partner) on females. The oppression of women in the home is seen as the result of the rise of class society. It follows that socialism, by ending class society, can end women's oppression in this arena. The debate on this subject between Marxist and radical feminists continued throughout most of the 1970s and early 1980s.

Over time the Marxist analysis of the family has moved away from consideration of the economic aspect of household production to the ideologies surrounding the construction of masculine and feminine roles (Barrett, 1980). A continuing focus on the material aspects of household production can be found in the work of Christine Delphy (1984; and with Leonard, 1992). She argues that the work done by women in the home is expropriated by men (meaning that it is men who mainly benefit from the work of women in the household) and that this is the basis of women's exploitation in the home. Her point is that this exploitation should be attributed to men and patriarchy, rather than capitalism. She argues that there are two distinct modes of production: the capitalist mode, where workers are exploited, and the domestic mode, where women are exploited by men.

Alternatively Hartmann (1981, 1982) suggests that it is women's weak position in the labour market that causes their dependence on the men in their households. This analysis seeks to provide a link between the domestic arena and the production arena and is an example of dual-sytems theory, which seeks to show how the two systems of capitalism and patriarchy coexist. This approach can also be seen in the work of Walby (1990) and Bradley (1996).

Exercise 6.10

[i] [a] Use the information on pages 97–107 to complete the table below on the reasons for job segregation in paid employment.

Explaining job segregation

Key factor	Explanation	Examples
Employers' attitudes and actions	Some employers simply discriminate and prefer male employees. More recently, the demand for a flexible labour force has led to the creation of poorly paid part-time jobs, largely filled by women	Becker, 1957
Action by male workers and trade unions to exclude females	Males keep their privileges by excluding women. Being better-paid enables them to have control over women. They can do this because they are better organised	Hartmann, 1981

Ideologies of domesticity affecting women's work orientations	Women are brought up to feel that the home is more important. This leads them either to be full-time housewives or to seek paid employment that fits in with domestic responsibilities.	
Domestic labour responsibilities		
Women have less human capital		
Sexual harassment		
State legislation limited women's involvement in work		Walby, 1990

2. Violence against women

The second aspect of the oppression of women relates to the physical and sexual violence suffered by women at the hands of men. It is this that has been central to radical feminist analyses of female oppression.

Feminist writers point out that such violence is widespread and can not be explained on the basis that some men suffer psychological problems. The extent of the problem is quite startling in terms of the human misery and suffering that the relevant statistics portray.

As Walby (1990) points out, many incidents of rape and indecent assault are not reported to the police and so the official figures are quite clearly an underestimate. On the basis of the findings of the British Crime Survey, only 11 per cent of such attacks are reported to the police. The official figures for 1987 were 2471 rapes and 13 340 indecent assaults (Walby, 1990).

Walby also quotes the findings of a survey in the United States conducted by Russell (1984): 44 per cent of the women surveyed had been subjected to rape or attempted rape at some point in their lives and of these assaults only 6 per cent were committed by a stranger. Twenty-one per cent of those who had been married had been assaulted by their husband; 28 per cent of the women had experienced sexual abuse by the age of 14 and 38 per cent by the age of 18. Walby makes the point that comparable figures are not available for Britain simply because no money has been made available for research. The state's response to such violence is criticised as inadequate, though this again leads to a debate as to whether greater powers for the police are a good thing for women, which rather depends on whether you view the police and the state more generally as able to act justly or simply as a tool of repression.

Hanmer and Saunders (1984) argue that male violence against women is a systematic form of social control of women by men. They also point out that much of this violence is considered a private domestic matter and has led to the police being reluctant to intervene. This means that the state and state authorities are complicit in such acts. Brownmiller (1976) has made a similar point about the way rape and the threat of rape is used by all men to keep all women under a form of social control. MacKinnon (1982) discusses the way the state permits the use of women in pornography. She argues that since this leads to sexual violence against women, women should be able to claim compensation from the producers of pornography. This view has been criticised as favouring censorship and therefore siding with the neoconservative wing of the new right. It has also led to debates about whether women want to use some form of pornography themselves as an expression of sexuality, or whether such a view of sexuality is a purely a male preserve that women want nothing to do with.

Socialist feminists have argued that there is a class dimension to this in that violence against women results from economic stress suffered by men and therefore only some men are violent (Wilson, 1983).

The issue of class has also been raised in relation to child abuse, the extent of which is considerably greater than previously thought. An NSPCC survey found that one in six people had been abused as a child. There were complaints to the Advertising Standards Authority about the accuracy of this claim, but the claim was upheld. Radical feminists have argued that child sexual abuse is committed almost exclusively by males and there is no real evidence of difference by social class. They therefore stress that it is the result of male power and not class factors. Socialist feminists have pointed out that if we consider overall abuse, including the physical abuse of children, women are involved almost as much as men. According to Renvoize (1978), this can be explained by the fact that it is usually women who are expected to look after children, and German (1988, 1989) cites statistics produced by the NSPCC that show that abuse is more common among housewives or unemployed women than among men, either in work or unemployed.

It is important to note that women should not simply be viewed as passive victims of this horrendous catalogue of violence, as they have been at the forefront of campaigns to change attitudes towards and laws on these forms of oppression. In 1992 this resulted in the overturning of the law that men could not be charged with the rape of their wives, because when women consented to marriage they consented to sex, a decree that dated back to 1736. Campaigns have also led to changes in the way rape and physical violence against women are dealt with by the courts.

Feminism and women's oppression

Feminism as a body of thought rests on the proposition that gender inequalities exist that result in women being oppressed. Both the nature of this oppression and its presumed agents can be identified but have led to serious debates and disagreements within feminism.

1. Liberal feminism and equal rights

Until well into the twentieth century women were systematically excluded from the rights enjoyed by men. Women did not gain the right to vote on an equal basis with men until 1928 in Britain and 1971 in Switzerland. Women were also formally excluded from higher education, and in Britain were not accepted as university students until 1877 (Perkin, 1993) – later in the case of Oxbridge, as women were not allowed full membership until 1920 (Oxford) and 1947 (Cambridge).

Women's response to this situation was to claim equal rights with men and this led to the rise of the first wave of feminists, the suffragette movement (which campaigned for women to get the vote) being the most prominent example in Britain.

This tradition has been called liberal feminism because it stressed that men and women should have equal rights within the law and should be treated as persons, not as men or women. It is this notion that lay behind the adoption of related legislation in Britain in the 1970s, notably the Equal Pay Act 1970 and the Sex Discrimination Act 1975. According to Phillips (1991, 1992), although liberal feminism has been criticised it did bring about reforms. (See also Phillips, 1993; and Barrett and Phillips, 1992.)

Exercise 6.11

Use a textbook to summarise the main aspects and provisions of the laws mentioned above and to evaluate how effective they have been.

The main limitations of this approach, which led to the development of both socialist feminism and radical feminism, was that while it stressed that men and women should have equal rights, its origins in liberal theory effectively meant that these rights would only apply to areas that were considered a matter of public concern (paid employment, education and so on) while leaving entirely untouched areas of concern within what was deemed as the private sphere. So, for example, the police might refuse to intervene when women were physically attacked by their husbands or lovers in the home, since it was deemed to be a private matter. The construction of separate private and public spheres is integral to liberalism, and since many of the problems women faced occurred in the private sphere, liberal feminism offered little help. Feminists have seen the very existence of this distinction as an important element of their oppression, and as a result have felt the need to go beyond the liberal notion of equal rights before the law (Pateman, 1988).

2. Marxist feminism and equality

In Britain in particular, many of the feminists of the second wave (which arose in the 1970s) first became involved in political activity through the Marxist and socialist movements. However they soon realised that these movements were not providing a full explanation of the position of women in society due to their emphasis on class. This spurred on these feminists to develop theories of gender inequality, but they remained largely influenced by Marxism and as such were critical of the liberal feminist approach to gender inequality.

They argued that although in many ways women were now treated equally under the law, this had not eliminated inequality between men and women, nor on its own could it. The explanation of this, according to Marxist feminists, lay in the nature of capitalist society and the particular way in which gender inequalities were constructed within it. This meant a focus on the notion that the divisions between men and women were used by capitalists to divide the working class. So women workers were defined as part of the reserve army of labour without paid employment, the existence of which was used to keep down the wages of those in work. But more importantly, a theory of the domestic sphere was integrated into this by arguing that the unpaid nature of housework and childcare, almost universally undertaken by women, was useful for capitalism since It meant that the labour force was reproduced very cheaply. This provided a theory that linked the position of women in the workplace with their position in the family, and therefore widened the scope of the theory of gender inequality. It has been argued that this is merely an example of bolting gender on to a class-based production-oriented theory, with the result that gender is always a subsidiary issue.

Since the agent of oppression here is capitalism, the logic of this theory is that working-class women have an interest in joining together with working-class men to fight for the overthrow of capitalism and the insitution of a socialist society that would not need to oppress women.

3. Radical feminism and patriarchy

The bolt-on nature of the theory of gender inequality that arose within the Marxist-feminist tradition was criticised by radical feminists, who argued that gender inequality is more fundamental than class inequality since gender inequality is an almost universal feature of human society while classes are not. As a result, gender inequality cannot be explained by reference to capitalism. It follows from this that the oppression of women will not automatically end with the overthrow of capitalism. Since socialism could not provide a solution the radical feminists did not agree with the solutions proposed by Marxist feminists.

Radical feminists argued that gender inequality had arisen from a different logic from that of capitalism, namely the system of patriarchy – the rule of males over females. Because patriarchy is a system in which all males oppress all females, collaboration with males in socialist organisations is not only pointless, but is also collaborating with the enemy. This led to calls for women-only organisations and the doctrine of 'separatism'.

One important contemporary debate has its origins in the ideas developed by radical feminists. As we have seen, one of the motivating forces behind the feminist movement was the achievement of equality with men. While there were debates about how equality was to be defined, which formed the basis of the arguments between liberal and Marxist feminists, some radical feminists insisted that equality should not be seen as the central aim of the feminist movement.

It is argued that the early emphasis on equality in liberal feminism tended to stress the public sphere and ignore the private sphere, the main domain in which women live their lives and suffer problems. The same line of criticism can be laid at the door of Marxist feminism since although they do talk about the family as a cheap form of reproducing labour power, the domestic sphere is only analysed as an adjunct to the production sphere. Secondly, in relation to both liberal and Marxist feminism, it can be argued that the stress on equality means that women are campaigning to gain equal access to a world whose structures have been devised by men. As an example, it might mean that a strategy of equality involves pushing for more female managers in industry. One problem with this is that if the characteristic required of managers remains the same, that is, the ability to operate in an authoritarian way and dictate to others, women would have to adopt this unpleasant characteristic in order to succeed.

Exercise 6.12

'Equal rights or liberal feminism may smooth over and deny class differences between women, but socialism smooths over conflicts between women and men' (Phillips, 1992, p. 213).

Read the above quotation and answer the following questions:

 1. Explain in no more than 60 words the problems with the various strands of feminism identified in the quotation.

 2. Name two variants of feminist theory not mentioned in the quotation.

 3. Compose a sentence to summarise the problems of these variants of feminism in the style of the quote above.

Exam question

The issue of gender inequality has been considered in a number of past exam questions. This section allows you to consider a real exam question and to apply the knowledge and understanding gained in this chapter towards answering the question.

Question a, b and c are taken from the AEB's June 1992 examination. This focuses on women and employment, but also provides links between gender inequality and class inequality. You will find that material contained in Chapters 2, 3 and 4 will also have a bearing on the questions.

ITEM F

Women to take half of all jobs 'by 2000'

Women are expected to make up more than half Britain's work-force by the turn of the century, according to a survey by the influential Henley Centre. At present, women account for one in three jobs, but their changing role in society, together with the restructuring of the family, means that there will be more female employees than male by the year 2000. Three quarters of all jobs created during the 1990's are expected to be filled by women. The proportion of women in full-time professional occupations or senior management will increase from its present 5 per cent.

The forecasting centre attributes the rise in female employment to the importance women now place on careers as well as the much larger numbers who delay having children or who return to work before their off-spring reach school age. Leading corporations, such as the High Street banks, are trying to make it easier for women to return to work after having children, and to encourage older women to work. 'Pressure is on single-parent women to work to provide for their family. Furthermore, divorce and illegitimate births are also set to rise significantly, adding still further to the disruption of the traditional family base', the report says.

(Source: Adapted from the Guardian, August 1989.)

A definition of underclass

Underclass: A term sometimes used for the poor who are also denied full participation in their societies. It may refer to workers who do the least desirable jobs and are denied the basic legal, political and social rights of the rest of the labour force. Illegal migrant labourers are the most cited example, but the term is sometimes extended to cover all or most of those in the 'secondary sector' of a 'dual' labour market. Alternatively, it may refer to particular groups whose poverty derives from their non-employment: the long-term unemployed, single-parent families, the elderly. Membership of these is often ascriptive: black or brown skin, females, the elderly.

Questions

(a) Suggest two ways in which leading corporations 'might make it easier for women to return to work' (Item F) *(2 marks)*

(b) What implications does the information contained in Item F have for sociological views of the class structure? *(6 marks)*

(c) Evaluate the usefulness of the concept 'underclass' (Item G) as a description of the position of women in the class structure. *(8 marks)*

Student answer

You should use the markscheme for the AEB's June 1992 examination (printed below) to mark your own answer and you should then read and comment upon the actual student answer provided below using the markscheme to do this.

Mark scheme: questions a and b

(a) Suggest two ways in which leading corporations 'might make it easier for women to return to work' (Item F) *(2 marks)*
Any two options might score a mark each, from provision of creches to the keeping of a job open while a woman takes pregnancy leave.

(b) What implications does the information contained in Item F have for sociological views of the class structure? *(6 marks)*
0: No relevant points

1–3: The answers in this band will sometimes touch upon relevant issues concerning the implications of an increase of women in the workforce for the class structure, but pertinent items may be hidden within more irrelevant material.

4–6: Candidates will offer a clear view of the implications for the class structure, perhaps concentrating on the head of household problem, the issue of mobility, their previous invisibility, cross-class families, etc. The answers should be well-structured, especially at the top of the band.

Mark scheme: question C

(c) Evaluate the usefulness of the concept of an 'underclass' (Item G) as a description of the position of women in the class structure. *(8 marks)*
0: No relevant points

1–2: The candidates here will only have a vague idea of the underclass with a consequently limited view of the usefulness of the concept.

3–5: In this band, candidates will have a clear view of the concept of the underclass and how it relates to women. The evaluation will be more explicit than the lower bands but may be based on a limited critique of the concept.

6–8: In responses which offer both positive and negative aspects of the concept of the underclass, there will be an explicit assessment of its usefulness as regards women. Analysis will be supported by appropriate evidence.

Student answer by candidate A

(a) Leading corporations might make it easier for women to return to work by (a) providing creche facilities (b) providing training programmes, to provide women who have been out of work on maternity leave the opportunity to 'catch up' on what they have missed, and keep up to date with advances in technology, etc., thereby encouraging women who leave to have children the chance to return.

Marks: 2

Comment: This answer does get full marks since the candidate does refer to two distinct and relevant changes which might be made. However the candidate then goes on to elaborate in a way which is not necessary for 2 marks. It is also the case that the candidate effectively rewrites out the question twice within the answer, once at the begining and once at the end. In a time-constrained atmosphere (which an exam is) you should ensure you get maximum marks for such questions, but you should also ensure that you do not misallocate time by providing over-elaborate answers to questions for few marks.

(b) If women are going to 'represent half of the British workforce by the turn of the century', then classification scales, such as the Hall–Jones scale, or the Registrar-General's Classification will have to make room for women to be classified on their own, not on their husband's occupation or status. If there is to be a growing number of single-parent women then women must be given a class of their own in order to accurately reflect the class structure of Britain.

Women in the work-force will have implications on the theories of proletarianisation and embourgeoisement. Women are cheap labour to companies, and the growing numbers of women, particularly in clerical white-collar work (i.e. secretaries) has decreased the wage and market value of this type of occupation, so diminishing the gap between the market value of white collar and blue collar work. This would give support to the idea that the middle class are becoming proletarianised. This feature of class structure, however, gives weight to the theory of re-structuring as outlined by Steven Lukes, who saw that increased mechanisation and the growing numbers of women in the class structure would lead to an undermining of the traditional significance of class solidarity, and give rise to a new division of society based on consumption. Women in the class structure may mean an increasingly 'fragmented' structure (Goldthorpe and Lockwood *et al.*) which means that society can no longer be as clearly seen in terms of upper, middle and lower classes.

Mark: 5

Comment: This answer does clearly focus on the issue of women and the class structure tackling the issues of the way class is defined and the implications of the change for the male head of household model, as well as going on to link the issue of women and employment to the debate about proletarianisation and embourgeoisement and therefore to the changing class structure.

While this is well done by and large, there are some areas where elaboration is not as full as might be expected if the candidate was to achive maximum marks.

(c) The concept of an 'underclass' as a description of the position of women in the class structure is useful because as Item G states those belonging to an underclass often do the 'least desirable jobs' and this is often the case for women. Women often do the 'least desirable jobs' because as Graham Allen describes, housewifes work is often tedious and monotonous. Women also heavily dominate shop-work, nursing, teaching and clerical work and often do not gain promotion to higher, more desirable jobs.

The term 'underclass' is also useful to describe the position of women in the class structure because they are often 'denied the basic legal, political and social rights of the rest of the labour force'. For example even though the Sex Discrimination Act has been introduced women are still discriminated against at work.

Item G suggests that an underclass is also 'extended to cover all or most of those in the 'secondary sector' of a 'dual' labour market'. The Dual labour Market theory is a fairly Weberian theory and it claims that the primary sector is well-paid, stable and promotion prospects are good whilst the secondary sector is less well paid, unstable and promotion prospects are not good. It is also claimed that the secondary sector is largely dominated by women. The reasons for this are that recruitment is often done internally, within the firm. Therefore women are often discriminated against because they are thought to be unreliable workers. This theory also suggests that women do not gain promotion because one requirement is continual years of service. Therefore women who have taken time off to have children are immediately disadvantaged.

The term underclass is also useful because women at home could be classed as in 'non-employment' therefore they are often ignored. The fact that the social class of women is ignored is illustrated by the fact that they are ommitted from social mobility studies and are often placed in a class according to their husband or father's occupation. Therefore women do appear to be an underclass.

The term is also useful because single-parent families are most often headed by women and poverty due to being elderly is also more of a problem for women because they tend to live longer than men.

Also, because membership of an underclass is often ascribed, women would find it difficult to get out of it.

Marks: 5

Comments: For you to complete using the mark scheme and the mark given.

7 Theories of gender inequality

By the end of this chapter you should:

- be aware of a wide range of sociological theories on gender inequality;
- be able to distinguish between three broad approaches to the question of gender inequality, namely sex and gender socialisation models, structural theories of patriarchy and sex and gender formation approaches;
- have a critical understanding of the strengths and weaknesses of each approach;
- be aware of the variety of theories contained within each broad approach;
- have practised structured exam questions.

Introduction

There are biological variations in human physiology, and one of these is the difference between men and women. The origins of the sociology of gender lie in a challenge to biological theories of inequality. The link between biology and differential treatment, which was seen as the key explanation of why women were treated differently and the fact that this differential treatment often meant unequal treatment, with women treated as second-class citizens, has been questioned. The term gender was developed to suggest that the social roles allocated to individuals identified as biologically male or female are not natural in any way but socially constructed. The extent to which biology constrains us to act in certain ways is seen as extremely limited and certainly can not explain all aspects of differential treatment and inequality.

In attempting to explain inequalities based on such constructed notions of gender, early theorists focused on the socialisation process whereby children learn to act in certain gendered ways. However this approach tended to focus on attitudes and did not offer a developed notion of how such attitudes are embedded in the structure of society, which serves to reinforce such attitudes. The problem is therefore more than simply a matter of trying to change attitudes.

The central concept developed to explain the structural nature of the oppression of women is that of patriarchy, meaning the systematic power of males over females. This concept was developed in radical feminist theory, which focuses on male power in the form of male violence and control over women's bodies. Marxist feminists, on the other hand, explain the structured inequality faced by women by refering to the needs of capitalism.

One problem with explanations based on patriarchy is the tendency to assume that all women face the same form of oppression since patriarchy is conceived of as a universal phenomenon. The fact that middle-class women may experience gender inequality differently from working-class women, or black women differently from white women, has led to concern that the category 'woman' is insufficient to describe the variations in experiences of inequality, and to a desire to understand the differences between women in diverse situations. This approach has been influenced by postmodernist notions that reject all-embracing explanations. Finally the approach dismisses the division between sex and gender since it rejects the idea that clear biological differences (sex) can be distinguished from gender. Such an approach may be called 'sex and gender formation'.

This chapter will consider the various theories that have sought to explain gender inequality:

- Biological theories of sexual inequality.
- The sociology of gender.
- Power and the structures of inequality: patriarchy and/or capitalism.
- Sex and gender formation

Biological theories of sexual inequality

The basic biological argument rests upon the proposition that the hormones that differentiate the two sexes are responsible for their different behaviours in society. For example it is argued that the greater aggression exhibited by males, and which can be seen as the basis of their dominance over females, results from male hormones such as testosterone and androgen. Goy and Phoenix (1971) conducted experiments on female rhesus monkeys and observed increased aggression among monkeys injected with testosterone before birth. Goldberg (1979) argues that testosterone is responsible for male dominance and this explains the existence of male dominance in every society. The two main criticisms of this theory are (1) it is mainly based on experiments on laboratory animals, and as such the findings are not applicable to humans in non-laboratory (that is, real life) situations; and (2) the studies correlate aggression with male hormones and suggest that it is the hormones that cause the aggressive behaviour.

However it is possible that the opposite is true, that is, it is male dominance that causes the production of higher hormone levels. This is the suggestion of Oakley (1972), and the implication of this argument is that changing social conditions can lead to a change in biological make-up.

A second biologically based argument centres on genetics, evolution and reproduction. This is most famously found in sociobiological theses such as that by Wilson (1975), who explains male promiscuity as a rational attempt to maximise the number of offspring they produce. The work of Tiger and Fox (1972) can also be seen as an example of this. They argue that although culture can affect behaviour (thus avoiding a totally biologically determinist position), genes provide a strong predisposition to behave in certain ways. They also argue that hormonal and genetic differences can explain the preponderance of males in positions of power, such as in politics. Barash (1979) suggests that the differences he identifies have important implications. Because men discharge millions of sperm every time they ejaculate and continue to produce an unlimited stock, while women release only one egg at a time and have a limited, non-renewable supply, women try to ensure the continuation of their genes by seeking out high-quality men and investing a lot of energy in producing and rearing a small number of offspring. Men on the other hand try to ensure the continuation of their genetic line by producing as many offspring as possible. This may involve sexual relationships with many women. Hence the theory seeks to explain gender differences in terms of sexual behaviour patterns and the greater identification of females with their offspring due to the limited number they can produce. It seeks to explain the greater role of women in childcare as ultimately biologically based.

Two variations of this theme have been developed. The first is that women are more concerned to get married and produce children because they know they are up against the 'biological clock', while men are not. The studies claim that women who delay having children in order to build up their careers might as a result find themselves unable to conceive. Claims about biology are therefore mixed in with negative assessments of the effect of the changing status of women in society.

In 1982 Schwartz and Mayaux argued that women over 30 have a 40 per cent change of being infertile, and this led to a whole ream of books that popularised the notion of the 'biological clock'. McKaughan (1987) and others have argued that the cause of the problem of infertility is that women, influenced by the women's movement, have put their personal needs first and are now paying the price. Some propose that the likelihood of suffering fertility problems is exacerbated by changes in social behaviour. Others suggest that professional women are more likely to suffer miscarriages (see Norwood, 1985).

Faludi (1992) argues that there is very little evidence to back up all this concern about infertility. She points to studies showing that professional women have the lowest miscarriage rate (Norwood, 1985) and that fewer women over 35 give birth to Down's Syndrome children than women under 35. She also points to statistics from the US National Center for Health showing that American women over 32 only face a 13 per cent chance of being infertile, and that overall the infertility rate fell between the 1960s and the 1980s. So there is no evidence to support the scare stories that have been produced, stories that Faludi sees as part of a male backlash whose intent is to get women back into the home by arguing that they have to choose between having a career and having children. The focus on infertility has presumed it to be a problem for women and ignores the possibility that it might be males who are becoming less fertile. It is therefore a political issue and not a medical problem, and this can be seen in cutbacks in NHS funding for infertility treatment.

Concern about the falling birthrate has also led to a resurgence of eugenic pronouncements. Herrnstein (1989) argues that the fall-off in the birth rate is highest among 'brighter' women because they are chasing careers and this will result in a decline in the 'quality' of the gene pool, as only 'less intelligent' women will continue to have babies. The future of America is seen as being under threat and career women are a crucial component of this. However all this is based on the assumption that intelligence is genetically inherited, and the key criticism of this approach is that it cannot be substantiated by scientific data (see Fraser, 1995) or any other supporting evidence (Faludi, 1992).

More common are theories that avoid absolute genetic determinism but still suggest that there is a clear link between biological difference and gender inequality. The most notable examples of such theories are those which suggest that work is apportioned in ways that are ultimately explained in terms of biological difference (Murdock, 1949). Thus men who are stronger monopolise warrior positions and long-distance hunting, while women engage in activities such as gathering fruit and nuts and cultivating vegetables, since they spend much of their adult life pregnant and need to avoid travelling too far so that they can reach home quickly to give birth. Since the children are also at home, it is natural that the main burden of looking after them should fall on women.

Such theories have been undermined by recent anthropological research, which suggests that a clear sexual division of labour cannot be found in all societies, and therefore something other than biology is needed to explain the division. Secondly, the relative unimportance of hunting and gathering in late-industrial society means that these activities cannot serve as the basis of an explanation of gender inequalities today. If this was all there was to it, gender inequality would have disappeared with the arrival of industrial society, but it did not.

In biological terms the differences between men and women seem fairly clear, summarised basically by Gittins (1985) as only women can conceive and suckle babies, while only men can impregnate. It might also be said that men are usually physically stronger (Stroller, 1968). However both these authors insist that these differences can in no way explain the inequalities that arise. Being biologically female does not explain why women earn less or are expected to look after the children. This needs to be explained in terms of the social construction of roles and identities linked in some way to biological entity, that is, the construction of masculinity and femininity.

Hence the inequalities between men and women cannot be explained solely by biological difference. Two important implications of this are that, firstly, gender inequality is an important area for sociologists to study, and secondly, since social relationships can change while biology largely cannot, socially based theories of gender inequality present the possibility of ending such inequalities. This view is supported by a number of biologists who reject the determinism of biologically based theories and attempt to point to the important influence of the environment (see Rose *et al.*, 1984)

Kessler and McKenna (1978) have even insisted that the biological categories used to explain inequalities, namely 'male' and 'female', are themselves social constructions, since there are societies where a third sex, the berdache, are recognised. They argue that the notion that there are only two sexes and that each individual is either one or the other is a result of the unwillingness of scientists to see these categories as other than polar opposites. Male and female as opposite categories with no other possibilities are therefore social constructions.

Exercise 7.1

i *a* Reread the above section and compile a list of the strengths and weaknesses of the biological approach to the explanation of gender inequalities. A couple of points have been provided to help you.

Weaknesses

- Biological views tend to imply that all men and all women act in a uniform way, a view that is contradicted by the evidence. This suggests that factors other than biology affect the way we act.
- Much of the information upon which these theories are constructed has come from experiments on animals, and may bear no relation to human behaviour.

The sociology of gender

Sociologists have conventionally distinguished between the terms 'sex' and 'gender' to highlight the point that inequality and oppression arise from decisions about the social roles of men and women and not directly from the biological differences between them. Gender is about the social constructions placed upon identified sex differences. It is important to be aware of this fundamental distinction and the reason behind it, namely the notion that it is society not biology that is the basis of men's and women's destiny. Such a view does not deny that biological differences exist, merely that they cannot explain the inequalities that result from these differences by reference to biology alone.

Ann Oakley (1972) argues that the notion that inequalities are natural and stem from biological difference cannot be sustained. Her main evidence for this is the variability of the sexual division of labour. She uses evidence gathered by George Peter Murdock (1949) to point out that there are societies where there is no apparent sexual division of labour, for example among the Mbuti Pygmies. There are plenty of examples of jobs that biologically-based theories see as natural women's work, such as cooking, are in fact shared activities. Since the biological distinctions in these societies are the same as elsewhere, biology cannot explain these diverging patterns, so they must be culturally produced. In other words, human beings construct the notion of masculine and feminine and construct a sexual division of labour on this basis. However the way in which this operates in different societies varies. Oakley's work is still considered important for the way in which it destroyed the notion of biological determinism in relation to the social position of men and women. In doing so, it opened up for sociological exploration a whole new field of how different roles are constructed, and this is the basis of sociology of gender.

In her explanation of inequality Oakley (1972, 1974) focuses squarely on socialisation process. She argues that during the socialisation process (the way in which people are brought up and introduced to behavioural norms and values) parents treat boys and girls differently and as a result young children develop either 'masculinity' or 'femininity'. These are learned social traits that are constantly reproduced through the socialisation process, and not biological realities. The implication of this is that changes in the socialisation process would allow society to dispense with the notion of masculinity and femininity. This would allow children to develop all sides of their personality, together with a wide range of skills previously designated masculine or feminine. Gender roles would be overcome, and in the process the assumption that there are fundamental differences between men and women would also be overcome.

Oakley's analysis therefore focuses on attitudes and stereotypes as the basis for the gendering of society. Her emphasis on socialisation was the starting point for an analysis of gender inequalities via the concepts of masculinity and femininity, which are not automatically linked to the biological concepts of male and female. It is argued that through the process of socialisation, identities are formed that provide the basis for later inequalities and that such inequality is perpetuated through the ongoing process of socialisation. Such theories have particularly looked at the family, but also at education and the media as complicit in the construction of notions of masculinity and femininity (Newson and Newson, 1963; Sharpe, 1976; Tuchman *et al.*, 1978; Deem, 1980; Sarsby, 1983; Kelly, 1985).

Exercise 7.2

[i][a] Listed below are adjectives that are commonly used to describe people. For each one, suggest whether it is mainly used in relation to males, mainly in relation to females or in relation to both.

• aggressive	• dainty	• emotional	• caring	• catty
• ruthless	• sensitive	• insensitive	• sloppy	• ambitious

Since socialisation is the earliest process children go through and is largely conducted within the family (primary socialisation) this has prompted a focus on the family. This is seen as the place where masculinity and femininity are constructed and reproduced, and the roles and behavioural traits associated with them are viewed as central to explaining the reproduction of gender inequalities.

Masculinity is associated with an active, lively or aggressive attitude towards life and femininity with passivity and gentleness. Boys are therefore taught to be assertive and girls to be passive, and this feeds through into employment with males being more likely to obtain jobs requiring leadership abilities – jobs that are also more highly paid.

The socialisation approach considers how this process is extended to institutions other than the family, for example the mass media have been shown to present gendered images. Tuchman (1978) has demonstrated that adverts contain fewer women than men, and when women are shown they are cast in stereotypical roles based on sexual attractiveness or the position of wife and mother. Studies of education have highlighted the differential treatment given to boys and girls because of preconceived notions of masculinity and femininity. For instance Stanworth (1983), in her study of A level classes, found that both male and female teachers operate on the basis of gendered expectations and that much more attention is given to male pupils. This, combined with the fact that girls underestimate their ability while boys overestimate theirs, shows the impact of wider socialisation and the continuation of differential socialisation patterns in education. The point is that such gender constructions are so deeply embedded in the institutions of society that they are very difficult to break down.

Exercise 7.3

The media are one of the most important contributors to gender stereotyping. Read a textbook on the method known as content analysis and then use this method to conduct an analysis of a variety of media sources and books used in your own education.

Evaluating the sociology of gender approach

The strength of this approach is that it undermines biologically based theories that see gender inequality as the natural result of biological difference. As such, it allows the possibility of change and therefore the creation of a society where gender is no longer an important reason for inequality.

However the approach also has weaknesses. Walby (1990) points to the following:

- The notions of masculinity and femininity used in socialisation accounts are relatively fixed.
- The question of power is underdeveloped in these accounts. While they can show that masculinity and femininity are socially constructed and lead to great differences, this by itself cannot explain why men dominate and women are oppressed.
- Such studies tend to assume that people passively accept the identities imposed on them in the various stages of the socialisation process.
- While socialisation theory explains the existence of gendered identities (masculine and feminine) it gives no explanation of the origin of these identities, or why they are constructed in the way they are.
- The concentration on socialisation leads to an emphasis on institutions that are central to that process, notably the family and the education system, but relatively little on the gendered aspects of other areas of social life, for example paid employment.

Such concerns have led into attempts to discover the origin of ideas of gender inequality in terms of social structure rather than concentrating on the socialisation of individuals.

This in turn has led to the development of perspectives that stress the gendered nature of language and all social structure being consequent upon that (Spender and Spender, 1983; Spender 1980) as well as more psychoanalytic perspectives based on the notion of the unconscious as a transmitter of relatively permanent social structures (Mitchell, 1971) (see pages 137–9).

Reread the previous section and write an evaluative summary of the sociology of gender approach. First construct a list of its strengths and weaknesses and then use this to write an evaluative paragraph, ending with your own conclusion about the usefulness of the approach. A few hints are provided here.

Strengths

- The approach rests on a clear distinction being drawn between sex and gender. It therefore bases inequality squarely on social not biological factors.
- It implies that gender inequalities can be removed.

Weaknesses

- The approach is very weak in its consideration of a structural basis for gender inequality and focuses mainly on process of socialisation.

Power and the structures of inequality: patriarchy and capitalism

Kate Millett (1970) uses the concept of patriarchy to highlight the way that men exert control over women in the social context, since all the structures of power in society are in the hands of men. This is seen as true of all societies:

> Our society, like all other historical civilisations, is a patriarchy. The fact is evident at once if one recalls that the military, industry, technology, universities, science, political office, and finance – in short, every avenue of power within the society, including the coercive force of the police, is entirely in male hands (Millet, 1970).

This leads to an important question. Would patriarchy be undermined if women somehow came to hold these positions of power, or would they merely be administering a still patriarchal system? Is it personnel or structures that make the state and society patriarchal? This is a similar question to the one posed in the debate between Miliband (1973) and Poulantzas (1973) over the state. It has important implications since in the 1990s some women are moving into top positions, and your view on the system of patriarchy will affect your evaluation of the likely consequences of this.

Finch and Groves (1983) have argued that material and structural factors are at the root of women's choices in the context of marriage. Their analysis of housework and domestic labour considered the ways in which women are incorporated into their husband's work, for example entertaining clients. The analysis provides a link between the domestic realm and the paid employment arena, because Finch and Groves contend that women marry not only a man, but also his work. They reject arguments that rely simply on socialisation theory to explain why women continue to consent to such a situation since this portrays women as ignorant of what is happening to them. Instead they propose that marriage needs to be understood as the route taken by many women in the absence of viable alternatives. They also argue that since women do become involved in their husband's work, it is difficult for them to withdraw from their marriage without facing financial hardship.

Patriarchy as a concept links the inequalities between men and women to a power structure, in this case the power of men over women. It stresses the fact that sexual inequality needs to be considered as an independent aspect of society. It rejects Marxist approaches not only because they ignore or downplay the analysis of gender inequality as an independent form of inequality, but also because patriarchy as a concept stresses the universal nature of the oppression of women in all societies, and does not see this as something that can be overcome purely by the abolition of capitalism (Alexander and Taylor, 1980). Patriarchy provides the theoretical basis for the women's liberation movement, since it outlines the way all men oppress all women, thus showing that women have a common interest and need to organise separately from men.

The origins of the women's liberation movement lie in the involvement of women in the civil rights movement in the United States, which sought to gain basic civil rights (such as the right to vote) for black Americans. The development of the civil rights movement led in the direction of black nationalism, that is, the idea that black people must organise separately from white people. This rested on the proposition that all white people are racist. White women therefore faced hostility but also learned about the idea of separatism. When applied to the question of gender inequalities, this led naturally to the position where all men were seen as sexist and women needed to organise separately to combat this.

The radical feminism of the time combined the emphasis on sexism as rooted in the power structures of society (patriarchy) with the idea of separatism. Gender, not class was seen as the key division in society and the implications of this were spelled out by Millet (1970):

> class differences are not important – it is for women to see how they are subjected as a whole that is crucial. In the home the social function and psychic identity of women as a group is found ... the position of women as women takes precedence: oppressed whatever their particular circumstances. Hence the importance of feminist consciousness in any revolution.

The desire for separatism was enhanced by the disgraceful treatment many women met in the ranks of supposedly socialist movements in the United States and Britain. At an anti-Vietnam war demonstration in Washington in 1969, women speakers were heckled by men shouting 'Take her off the stage and fuck her', and at a conference on new politics in 1967, Shulamith Firestone was stopped from speaking by a chair who stated: 'Cool down, little girl, we have more important things to talk about than women's problems' (quoted in Cliff, 1984).

Firestone was the author of one of the most important radical feminist texts, The *Dialectic of Sex* (1972). In this book she mimicked the structure of Marx's writings but argued that the real basis of society was not the process of production, as Marx argued, but the process of reproduction. This led the analysis of gender inequality towards consideration of the family as the key institution of reproduction and as the arena for interpersonal relations between men and women. Since Firestone sees this as the real basis of society, she proposes that gender divisions are more fundamental than other inequalities, primarily those of class.

Firestone argues that women were sexually oppressed by men prior to the emergence of class societies and therefore sexual oppression will not be eliminated by the emergence of a classless society, as argued by Marxists and Marxist feminists. Equality can only be achieved through the elimination of the constraints imposed by biological difference, notably when women are freed from the biological constraint of pregnancy and motherhood. She therefore views the development of birth control as a move in the right direction, but as women still have to endure pregnancy in order to reproduce she stresses the need for new reproductive technologies that will allow reproduction to take place outside the womb. This would mean that women would no longer be dependent on men since the period when they were unable to work would be minimised or even eliminated.

The emphasis on sexual reproduction and sexual relations formed the basis of the well-known argument that the 'personal is political'. What this means is that the most personal of relationships are bound up in unequal power relations that leave women dependent on men. This idea shifted the notion of politics away from an exclusive concern with the state and economic issues towards a consideration of the way that power underlies personal relationships. This led to growing concern about sexuality, sexual violence, physical oppression and the way individual men had power over individual women, and the way that this was sanctioned by the notion that what happened in the privacy of home was purely a private matter. These issues came to be of universal concern for all feminists but were particularly emphasised by radical feminists. Fighting this sort of oppression required going beyond changes to the law, as advocated by liberal feminists, it also meant rejecting the emphasis on workplace politics advocated by Marxism. Radical feminism grew up as the main opposition to liberal feminism in the United States, where the socialist tradition was weak, whereas in Britain the greater strength of the socialist movement led to the emergence of socialist and Marxist feminism. The division between the radical and socialist feminists was the source of many debates and splits within the British women's liberation movement.

Critics of Firestone and the radical feminist position argue that the theory is ultimately biologically determinist, since the biological facts of reproduction are at the heart of the theory. Versions of radical feminism tend towards the view that male actions such as sexual and physical violence towards women are linked to their biological make-up, notably the male hormone testosterone. The implication of this is that men can not be changed and therefore women can only avoid oppression by living totally separate from them. This ignores the distinction between biology and culture developed by gender sociologists, who have shown that the same biological make-up can result in very diverse ways of behaving in different societies. Firestone's optimistic vision of the use of reproductive technology has been criticised because the development and application of such technologies has remained in the hands of the male-dominated medical profession. Finally, the view that all women have a common interest ignores other social divisions between women that play an important part in the way family and reproduction are experienced by women.

The criticism that radical feminism is biologically determinist and holds an essentialist position on men and women (that is, it tends to see them both as homogeneous categories) has led Young (1980) to argue that there are two divergent trends within the feminist movement. The first, which she calls humanist feminism, bases itself on the achievement of equality between men and women. Since it is not argued that the biological differences between men and women will disappear, humanist feminism rests on the argument that these differences are not fundamental. The second strand that young identifies is gynocentric (woman-centred) feminism, which emphasises the difference between men and women and sees women as superior because of their biological make-up.

This division inside radical feminism has been summarised by Tuttle (1986) as follows:

Radical Feminist views of biology range along a continuum from the stance represented by Shulamith Firestone, that biology is a trap from which we can be freed by new reproductive technologies, to the glorification of all things female which postulates that there is a special wisdom available only to women through the physical experience of their bodies.

The most notable attempt to consider the oppression of women from a socialist-feminist perspective has come from Sheila Rowbotham (1981). She entirely rejects the concept of patriarchy precisely because it fails to consider the wide variety of situations women find themselves in and can only be applied to women at a level of generality that says nothing of any use when it comes to fighting inequality. Her analysis centres more on women as workers. Critics of this position argue that it tends to subsume the analysis of gender inequality under class categories, and since these were constructed with male workers in mind, such an approach risks being sex-blind. According to Smart (1984), whatever the problems with the concept of patriarchy, it should be retained since otherwise there might be a danger that the questioning of inequalities in gender relations will disappear with it.

Concerns of this type have led Marxist and socialist feminists to develop what has been called 'dual-systems' theory: that there are two independent but linked causes of the oppression of women, namely capitalism and patriarchy. Such an analysis is offered by a number of writers, such as Michèle Barrett (1980, 1984), Harriet Bradley (1989, 1996), Heidi Hartmann (1981) and Sylvia Walby (1986, 1990).

Hartmann (1981) sees Marxism and feminism as having had an unhappy marriage. She feels that Marxism is sex-blind, and feminism is therefore submerged under the larger struggle against exploitation by capitalists. The question of which is the more fundamental – class or gender – is a subject of continuing debate in Marxist and socialist feminist circles.

Dual-systems theory argues that an adequate analysis of inequality needs to consider both capitalism and patriarchy as structural elements. Sylvia Walby (1990) has provided the fullest expression of this idea. Walby is concerned with the point made by black feminists that the relationship between black women and black men is qualitatively different from the relationship between white women and white men. Therefore the concept of patriarchy and the understanding of what this means in terms of gender oppression has been developed by white feminists, and can not be applied to black women.

As a consequence Walby set out to outline her views on how the three systems of oppression (capitalism, patriarchy and racism) intersect each other to create concrete inequalities. With regard to patriarchy, she argues that there are six related social structures of patriarchy, but to some extent these are autonomous of each other. These six structures are:

- The patriarchal mode of production, meaning the way that women's labour is exploited within the household by male partners.
- Patriarchal relations in paid work, meaning the way in which labour segmentation excludes women from well-paid, high-status jobs.
- Patriarchal relations in the state, which refers to the way in which the operations of government and the law privilege men rather than women, for instance by placing a greater burden on women through the policy of care in the community, since this is often effectively

care by the family, or more properly, care by the women in the family.

- Male violence against women, in the form of rape, domestic violence and sexual assault.
- Patriarchal attitudes towards sexuality, meaning the double standard that men apply to women who are sexually active.
- Patriarchal relations within cultural institutions, which lead to the creation of masculine and feminine identities and involve the education and media structures of society.

Walby (1990) outlines in some detail the effects of these structures and the way they intersect with capitalism and racism. As such, it can be seen as the most sophisticated attempt to arrive at a dual-systems theory that utilises the concept of patriarchy, but there are nonetheless a number of problems with and criticisms of her approach.

In the 1970s Marxists were often criticised for seeming to say that the economic base of society has a determinate authority over other aspects of life. In order to combat this criticism, some Marxists (notably Althusser and Poulantzas) developed the idea that the structures of society are relatively autonomous from the economy, while still having some relationship to it. This concept of relative autonomy raised the question of just how much autonomy was implied and whether there could still be a relationship between the various structures of society.

Since Walby argues that the structures of patriarchy are relatively autonomous, her theory is open to the same question. Unless the links can be shown to exist, relative autonomy may give way to total autonomy and the whole notion of an overarching patriarchy will disappear. This has been part of the feminist debate for a long time, that is, whether or not the concept of patriarchy should be abandoned.

Acker (1989) argues that Walby's conception of patriarchy is overly influenced by Marxist concepts, particularly when she talks about paid employment. Acker sees this is the result of trying to start out from large-scale generalised theories using concepts such as patriarchy that are assumed to have some universal application. Instead there is a need to start with the specific ways in which gender and other inequalities are created, and only when this is understood should one use this understanding to develop more general theories. In essence, Acker is arguing that Walby starts from general, abstract concepts, but should start with concrete and specific instances of inequality and build up from them.

A second critique has come from those who argue that patriarchy cannot be viewed as an equivalent structure to capitalism, and therefore the attempt to devise a dual-system theory is misguided. The best example of this position is provided by Anna Pollert (1996). According to Pollert, the system developed by Walby has similarities with the Althusserian theories of the 1970s, in that it merges explanation with description and presents a circular form of explanation. Her argument is that while the concept of patriarchy can be used to *describe* the totality of the oppressive structures that women face, it is not an *explanatory* concept.

Patriarchy is defined as a system of social relations between men and women that enable men to dominate women. The problem with this is that the mechanism or way that men control women is only explained by itself, that is, by male control. This leads to the circular argument that the cause of male control is male control, or as Pollert puts it, 'The only explanation for men's alleged control over women's labour power lies in their acts of exclusion and control, which can only be explained by itself' (ibid., p. 642). She goes on to argue that this means there is a distinct analytical difference between the concepts of patriarchy and capitalism, so any attempt to combine the two to create a dual-system theory is flawed.

Her explanation is as follows. The key thing about the theory of capitalism is that it explains the dynamic of its reproduction within the theory itself. Capitalism needs to exploit workers, since without the surplus value that workers creates there can be no profit, and without profit there can be no capitalism. The exploitation of workers is therefore a necessary part of capitalism. The same is not true of the system of patriarchy and the oppression of women:

> There is no intrinsic motor or dynamic within 'patriarchy' which can explain its self-perpetuation. Capitalism, on the other hand, does have an internal dynamic ... Capitalists could not become 'good capitalists' by ceasing to exploit wage labour, they would cease to be capitalists and if they did it en-masse ... capitalism would disappear with it. By contrast, men can and do alter their gender as do women, and they can alter their material and ideological relationship into different sex-gender systems without social production grinding to a halt, or abolishing all gender relations and men and women ... The two sets of relationships – class and gender– are of a different analytical order (ibid., p. 643).

Pollert concludes that the analysis of the oppression of women should be undertaken on the basis of concrete human experiences. For this, the best method so far developed is that of historical materialism. This would allow an understanding of how gender and indeed 'race' are constructed as part of class relations.

This analysis is much more based on the legacy of Marxist analysis and historical materialism than some feminists might be willing to accept, but it is also clear that Pollert's argument represents a strong and clear case for seeing the two systems of patriarchy and capitalism as having different natures, and therefore it is not fruitful to try to combine them, as dual-systems theorists suggest.

Black feminism

For many black women, the feminism of the women's liberation movement did not speak directly of their experiences or the problems they faced. Just as the movement was sometimes criticised as being dominated by middle-class women, it was also criticised for being dominated by the experiences and thoughts of white women. This insight led to the growth of black feminism.

Gemma Tang Nain (1991) has provided an example of the problems black women face. It may well be, she argues, that individual black women are critical of the sexism of black men, but they, and this is a crucial difference from white women and their relations with white men, are also in sympathy with them since they too are the victims of racial discrimination. The feminist notion of a clear conflict between men and women does not seem to fit this picture.

Hazel Carby (1982) probably expresses this best by pointing out that black men do not and cannot have the same relation to oppressive capitalist and patriarchal structures as white men, due to the existence of racism, and therefore white women can in some instances be seen as the oppressors of black women. She specifically argues that the notion developed by white feminists that the source of the oppression of women is the family is not equally applicable to black women, since in times of slavery and colonial and imperialist oppression the family was a source of strength for black people. This means that the relationship between black women and black men within the family is different from that between white women and white men in the family structure. Hence 'women' as a group of people with a common interest are instead a group of diverse people with a great number of differences between them.

The complexities of black feminist identities are explored in the work of the leading black feminist in 1990s sociology, Heidi Safia Mirza (1997). Mirza points to the ambivalence of the debate about black identity since while the use of the term 'black' as a sign of political unity helped forge a strategic political position, at the same time people argued about who should or should not be called black and to which groups the term should apply.

In this context the development of black feminism was an attempt to announce a black identity, and to state the existence of and mark the presence of black women, as well as to create a space in which to talk.

The big problem here is the extent to which the unity this implies can coexist with the freedom to create a plurality of identities, or whether it will cause the fracturing of the black feminist movement in a similar way to that which split the white feminist movement. Identity points towards continual differentiation, but political strategy points to the need to gain maximum unity, and these forces tend to pull in opposite directions.

1. Write a paragraph summarising the usefulness of the concepts of patriarchy and capitalism in explaining gender inequality.

2. Reread your list of the strengths and weaknesses of the sociology of gender approach and make a list of the strengths and weaknesses of this approach for comparison.

3. Write a summary of the strong points of each approach and state which one you think offers the best explanation of gender inequality.

Sex and gender formation

In the 1970s and early 1980s there was a major debate between Marxist feminists and radical feminists about whether capitalism or patriarchy was the key structure underlying the oppression of women in society. This led to debates about the relative importance of paid employment and housework, and about the division of society into public and private spheres. Beechey (1987) argues that the Marxist theoretical framework was the main one upon which such theories were built, but it has since lost its dominance. As a result the gender debate has moved on to a new terrain, notably whether there are a multiplicity of divisions among women that cut across attempts to view society simply in terms of a duality between men and women. The crucial influences in this debate have been post-structuralism and postmodernism, with their emphasis on plurality and difference, but also developments in psychoanalysis and cultural theory. All of this has had a profound effect on the way gender is considered in sociology.

Many problems have arisen in connection with the usefulness of the two basic dualisms involved in the concept of gender. Firstly sociologists distinguished between sex (biology) and gender (culture) and out of this arose the second dualism, namely male/masculine and female/feminine. While at first sight this distinction might appear relatively clear-cut, some sociologists have pointed to difficulties. The first of these is that men and women are seen as distinctly homogeneous categories, as polar opposites. This notion has come increasingly into question. There are a number of examples of people whose biological status undermines the simple duality that is often assumed to be universal. Giddens (1993) refers to the condition known as testicular feminisation syndrome, whereby people of overtly female appearance are biologically unable to conceive and would be classified as male in the Olympics under the procedure for sex testing. If you ask yourself the question 'are such people male or female?', you will see that matters are not as simple as they appear. The answer is that they are whatever they are socialised as. They are usually identified as female since their physical appearance conforms to the popular conception of the female sex. However the point is that their behaviour is due to being socialised as a female, while it might be argued that they are not biologically female. This shows that socialisation not biology is the determinant of sex identity as well as gender identity. Ryan (1985) points to the case of twins who were born male but one of whom, because of medical problems, was surgically reconstructed as a female in terms of physical sex characteristics. During childhood the twins developed separate patterns of gender behaviour, suggesting the greater influence of culture than biology, although when informed of her history the female twin showed signs of insecurity. This is clearly understandable, but it is difficult to disentangle whether it was due to the revelation of the reconstruction or to the reconstruction itself. In other words, this in itself is not proof of biology outing itself in the end.

The second area of investigation is to question whether sex is biologically constructed, as is usually assumed. If the traditional distinction between sex and gender as being between the biological and the social is accepted, there is a suggestion that the two are linked in some way. Largely because it is relatively easy to identify whether someone is male or female, it is easy to adjust your behaviour. The behaviour may be socially constructed but it relies on correctly assessing the biological status of the person you are interacting with.

As a consequence, theories that distinguish between sex and gender do still leave the possibility of biological factors having some influence on the construction of inequality since although gender and sex are not identical they are linked.

Exercise 7.6

a e Write a definition of a man and a definition of a woman, then consider how valid these categories are in the light of the above discussion.

One response to this has been to question the biological underpinnings of gender by suggesting that no fixed biological entities can be identified and differentiated, as the notion of sex suggests. Instead it is argued that sex is a socially constructed phenomenon and therefore biology is firmly removed from any real role in the construction of inequalities.

The social construction of sex

Adoption of the term gender to denote the fact that the differential treatment of men and women in society can not be explained simply on the basis of their different biology (their sex) was an important starting point for the analysis of inequalities between men and women.

However the negative side of this distinction was that it gave too much room to considerations of biology by implying that sex is a purely biological category. This neat distinction has come under question by those who argue that we should consider the extent to which sex, as well as gender, is socially constructed.

Biological theories of inequality allow no distinction between sex and gender and argue that they correspond to each other and the causal element is biology. The sociology of gender counters that there is an important distinction between the two and that they do not correspond, in fact there are many variations in gender roles across societies. Inequality can not be explained by biology, only by the social connotations placed on biological differences.

The emphasis switched to culture from biology. However this distinction implicitly left sex to biology when arguing that gender (as distinct from sex) is a social construction. Proponents of sex and gender formation argue that while there is a distinction between the two they are interrelated and in a dynamic relationship with each other, and therefore sex should not be seen as a purely biological concept.

Morgan (1986) has pointed to the way in which biological 'facts' are actually socially constructed. He shows how the portrayal of sex differences in biology has changed over time, from women's position as the weaker sex being explained by the energy lost through processes such as menstruation and pregnancy, to the notion of hormones as the cause of sex differences. While these have both been accepted as 'facts', the changing nature of the explanations suggests that they are not facts, true for all time, but constructed in particular circumstances and open to change.

Hood-Williams (1996) suggests that while the distinction between sex and gender was important in undermining biological determinism as an explanation for the inequities between men and women, it has outgrown its usefulness because sex is just as much a social construction as gender. Hence we can no longer view sex as a biological constant in the way the distinction between sex and gender implied. To illustrate this, Hood-Williams looks at changes in our understanding of sex. Prior to the Enlightenment (an eighteenth-century movement that espoused a more scientific understanding of things), the human body was thought of in terms of a one-sex model in which women were an inferior version of the more perfect male (see Laqueur, 1990). The movement from a one-sex model to a two-sex model was not the result of greater understanding and scientific knowledge, but of a change of interpretation. In other words, knowledge of the biological entity (the body) did not automatically generate knowledge of the sexes. This only came from later interpretations of the body, and these have continued to change over time.

Hood-Williams (1996) considers the way in which bodies are sexed today on the basis of chromosomes, females having two X chromosomes (XX) and males an X and a Y (XY). The presence of a Y chromosome therefore signifies maleness. However he points to biologically acknowledged existence of XX males, which led to a whole field of research on chromosomal abnormalities, often linked to ideas about the causes of crime and deviance.

The point Hood-Williams concentrates on is the question of how XX individuals can be defined as male, if XY is a definition of maleness. If chromosomes determine sex, these individuals must be female. His conclusion is that if scientists are able to 'describe them as unusual men ... [this means] they must already know what it is to be a man before they can confirm it genetically'. In other words, it is likely they were defined as men on the basis of their external genitalia. This leads to the question of what defines sex: external genitalia or chromosomes. The fact that both are used as definitions shows the extent to which sex is a social construction. Biology and biological knowledge are therefore not invariable and both use other than strictly scientific criteria when categorising. Biology is rather more flexible and culture more constant than the old sex–gender distinction implies.

Postmodernism and difference

A second critique of the usefulness of the duality of sex and gender has come from writers influenced by postmodernism. They argue that the notion of gender subsumes a number of problems, crucially the assumption that it is possible to identify all women as distinct from men but having something in common with all other women.

Some writers stress that these concepts need to be examined in the light of postmodern notions of difference and the postmodernist wish to avoid any explanations that attempt to cover everything. They argue that all-embracing notions of gender inequality risk moving towards that. On the other hand Flax (1987) considers that feminist theory is compatible with postmodernist notions since it refuses to accept any fixed notion of gender relations and any suggestion that existing gender relations are natural.

Walby (1990) points out that Weber used the term patriarchy to refer specifically to rule by the head of household and therefore included the idea that older men dominated younger men. Radical feminists drew the focus of attention away from this and onto the area of how men dominate and oppress women. This example illustrates the point that undifferentiated use of terms such as 'men' may be problematic since it ignores inequalities between individual men. According to Walby, insofar as these inequalities are based on age and generation the attempt to include such factors in a theory of patriarchy leads to confusion. It highlights the way in which theories of inequality often privilege one form of inequality and tend to ignore other, potentially cross-cutting forms of inequality. In real life we live as individuals affected by all the potential structures of inequality. Walby herself points to the different manifestations of patriarchy arising out of the social structure and argues that patriarchy does not need to imply that all men oppress all women at all times. To do so is to focus on biology rather than social factors.

Criticisms: a realist approach to sex and gender

The attempt to remove the distinction between sex and gender, as seen in Hood-Williams (1996), has come under criticism for its implication that there is ultimately no distinction between the biological and the social, and that all aspects of gender relations are socially constructed.

Robert Willmott (1996) argues that there is a need to retain the distinction between sex and gender since they relate to two different levels: the biological and the social, which he argues are not reducible to one another. This is based on the realist argument that social life is layered and that each aspect of life must be analysed separately in order to investigate its relative importance in the overall dynamic of social life.

In Willmott's view, the idea of an unchanging biology is subject to criticism since there are a variety of hormonal conditions that cause an overlap between male and female, and this undermines the supposedly natural either/or way in which biology is presented to us. This does not mean that we need to abandon the distinction between sex and gender, but rather that we need to recognise that sex and gender (the biological and the social) interact. In order to discover the relative importance of each, we need to retain a notion of them as separate. In other words, we cannot remove the reality that there are human bodies and that biological differences do have an impact: 'Gender ideology clearly affected the interpretations of the discovery of hormones, but this in itself does not affect the reality of hormones! Importantly, there is a truth of the body, or rather bodies, human knowledge of which is fallibilistic' (ibid., p. 738).

We therefore need to recognise the reality of biology and the impact of this upon gender relations, but without the notion of a fixed biology. We need to consider the interplay between the biological and the social without collapsing one into the other. It is only by this method that we can recognise the reality of the limits of choice and constraints faced in gender relations.

This argument is based heavily on methodological arguments. In older sociology textbooks this is couched in terms of positivism versus phenomenology, that is, science versus social interpretation. Today such debates are more often between realism and post-structuralism. Realists are those contemporary sociologists who assert that there is a reality out there that we can attempt to understand through scientific enquiry, while post-structuralism argues that everything is a social construction, and hence there is no truth.

Postmodernism and feminism: towards post-feminism?

One of the problems that has emerged within the feminist movement is the question of women's relations with men in a perfect society. Early feminist formulations were based on the idea that women suffered inequality, and this implied that the desired end state was equality with men. This notion can be clearly seen in claims for equal pay and the outlawing of discrimination against women.

However a different emphasis has emerged as a result of discussions on the concept of equality. Equality implies that everyone should be treated the same, whereas some feminists (notably radical feminists) argue that men and women are fundamentally different and that feminism is about celebrating the positive qualities that women possess and opposing the negative qualities associated with men. Pursuing a strategy of equality would undermine this, and therefore some have suggested that equality in its basic sense cannot be the goal of the feminist movement. This idea of emphasising difference has been given a boost by the rise of postmodern ideas, to which the concept of difference is central.

The problematic nature of this debate was emphasised when two feminist thinkers ended up on opposite sides in a court case in the United States. Sears, a retail organisation, had been taken to court under equal opportunities legislation due to the underrepresentation of women in the firm's commission sales jobs. Sears' defence was based on the assertion that men and women are different, and that these differences are the result of long-standing cultural and social differences, including those relating to socialisation. This specifically meant that women were less interested in obtaining commission sales jobs, and therefore their underrepresentation was the result of these differences rather than any active sexual discrimination within the organisation. As a result Sears argued that the underrepresentation of women was outside its control, and won the case on this basis.

This is an example of the emphasis on difference leading to the undermining of laws that are designed to ensure equality. Since men and women are different we should not expect them to engage in actions in exactly the same way, which is the implicit basis of notions of equality. As Scott (1992, p. 260) comments, this produces a dilemma for feminists: 'If one opts for equality, one is forced to accept the notion that difference is antithetical to it. If one opts for difference, one admits that equality is unattainable.'

1. Evaluate the usefulness of the sex and gender formation approach to the explanation of gender inequalities.

2. Write a comparison of the three broad sociological approaches to gender inequality examined in this chapter, and conclude by saying which approach you prefer and why.

Exam questions

Questions a, b and c are from the AEB's November 1995 examination focused on the issue of gender inequalities, both in theoretical terms and in relation to the workplace. Reproduced below are these questions and the stimulus material relevant to them, along with the mark scheme for these questions and an actual answer provided by a student in that exam.

First consider the answer provided and complete the marks and comments in the space provided. Secondly, use material from this chapter and elsewhere (including Chapter 6) to try to write improved answers to these questions.

ITEM A

Some anthropologists have suggested that the biology of being male and female makes people take certain domestic roles. Thus, they argue, man has always been the hunter/breadwinner, because they have greater strength and speed, while women have always been the home-makers because they cannot move quickly during pregnancy, and, because they can breast-feed, nature has given women an instinct for the care of children. The close physical bond between mother and child makes the adult female role more expressive, while the males have kept a more instrumental role in gaining food and security from work.

(Source: Adapted from T. Lawson, 1986.)

The concept of a dual labour market emerged in the United States to account for 'a measured difference between the earnings of white male workers on the one hand and of female or black workers on the other'. White male workers, it was argued, were predominantly located in the primary market, while female and black workers were mainly found in the secondary market. Explanations for the emergence of such a dual labour market have, however, differed. If some writers highlight the role of technology in generating a dual labour market, others have emphasised the control exerted by employers or workers.

(Source: Adapted from A. Pilkington, Race Relations in Britain, UTP.)

Questions and markscheme

(a) What do sociologists mean by the expressive role (Item A)? *(1 mark)*
One mark available for an acceptable definition of expressive role

(b) With reference to Item A and elsewhere, outline and assess the argument that gender is socially constructed rather than biologically determined *(7 marks)*

(c) Using Item B and other sources, evaluate the idea of the dual labour market in explaining the position of either ethnic minorities or women. *(8 marks)*

Mark scheme: question b

0:    No relevant points

1–2: Candidates are likely to be unsure as to the difference between social construction and biological determinism, with the arguments confused. Points however will be made in passing, though as a consequence, assessment will be constrained. The application of information as description or reproduction predominates.

3–5: The candidates in this band are likely to provide unbalanced accounts, stressing one side of the debate at the expense of the other, or being uncritical in approach to a degree. Supporting evidence will be applied, but this may tend to provide description at times also. Candidates may not come to a specific conclusion but allow the opposition of ideas to substitute.

6–7: There should be a balanced consideration of both sides of the debate, with candidates providing appropriate support from the

Items and elsewhere. Evaluation is likely to be explicit, with candidates coming down on one side or the other, but with the conclusion emerging from the body of the response.

Mark scheme: question c

0   No relevant points

1–3   Candidates in this band may conflate material about ethnic minorities and women and be unsure about the meaning of the dual labour market. The answers may concentrate on the description of the position of their chosen social group rather than an examination of the dual labour market in relation to it. As such, assessment is likely to be limited.

4–6   Candidates will address both sides of the issue, appreciating the usefulness of the term and its limitations, maybe in an unbalanced way. The latter may appear as a consideration of alternative explanations. As such, evaluation is likely to be through the opposition of ideas rather than being explicitly done. Any information used will be applied rather than just described.

7–8   There should be a balanced consideration of the usefulness of the concept, with an acknowledgement of alternative explanations which might be applied. There should be a clear focus on one social group and material applied should reflect this. Assessment is therefore likely to be explicit, emerging from the body of the answer and perhaps contained in a separate part of the answer.

Student answer

> **(a)** Sociologists, when using the term 'expressive' role when describing the adult female mean that the role of women is to care for and nurture her family in her role as carer and homemaker.

Mark: 1

Comment: The answer does provide a definition and therefore gains the mark, although it is a bit long-winded for a one mark question and becomes a bit repetitive in part.

> **(b)** The theory that gender roles are determined by societies values rather than due to innate ability will be explored below. The most

important stage of an individual's life is primary socialization which normally takes place in the home initially but socialization is an ongoing life-long process. Western society, both in the home and at school, hold values which emphasize the different roles of men and women – men as the breadwinners and women as the home-makers. This in the toys a child plays with, e.g. a girls' pram and a boys' gun, and the subjects which prior to 1988 and the introduction of the National Curriculum, the different sexes took, e.g. home economics and history for girls and woodwork and physics for boys. History throughout the ages has nearly always portrayed women as the carers and it may be dangerous for some sociologists to insist that females have equal ability to men, as if their innate ability is not found to be so than women will always be portrayed as the weaker sex. Marxists and marxist feminists argue that gender is so-cially constructed for both men and women. Women are the slaves of 'wage slaves' and it is their duty to keep their husbands happy to enable them (the male 'wage-slaves') to work effectively for the industrialists. Feminists on the other hand disagree and assert that men in general view women as their property, through institutions such as marriage, for example.

Mark: 3

Comments: For you to complete

(c) The dual labour market is a system of primary and secondary employment, which can exist in one company. Company owners see women as only biding time until they get pregnant and leave. The employer is therefore loath to spend money on training courses for women if they are only going to leave soon after, and so women are given the menial, routine jobs which can easily be fitted with little training. The secondary market also suffer from lack of secu-rity, poor pay (which is acceptable as far as the employer is con-cerned in the case of women, as men are the main breadwinners), training, childcare provisions (as the women's place 'is in the home') and health and safety provisions. This attitude reinforces the tradi-tional and New Right theories that a woman's primary role is that of carer and homemaker. Even the unions are sometimes loath to take up a woman's concerns or complaints as they are still viewed as patriarchal institutions. In the event that a union does take up a woman's case and she wins, it can be years before the successful outcome becomes custom and practice.

Mark: For you to complete using markscheme above

Comment: For you to complete.

The following question is taken from the InterBoard Syllabus Summer 1996 examination. It covers the areas of both ethnic and gender inequality but particularly focuses on gender inequality. Use the material in this chapter and any other material you are familiar with to answer this question.

ITEM C

The Boys are Back in Town

A white male backlash apparently got under way this week in the United States. After 30 years of affirmative action in favour of women and minorities, men signalled their dissatisfaction. A campaign began in California to outlaw positive discrimination.

If Britain follows where America leads, what will this trend mean for men here? This country does not have the banks of laws and regulations that the US has. Yet some indicators demonstrate that, relatively speaking, men are not doing as well here as they once did. Men still earn more than women, but the gap has narrowed. Meanwhile the number of women in work has increased by 18 per cent since the late seventies

while male employment has fallen 7 per cent. Girls are overtaking boys at school. Research suggests that men still enjoy more leisure than women but the difference has diminished significantly. Could this provoke a British male counter-offensive?

The intellectual thought that might justify such a backlash is available. Thinkers such as Charles Murray argue that the best way to rescue the self-esteem of young men in the 'underclass', caught in crime and unemployment, would be to restore them as the bread-winners responsible for supporting wife and family.

But this is an absurd dream. Propping up the old male stereotype would require changes right through society. It would

mean diminishing the role of women in education and the labour market. Wage rates for women would have to be cut to render them incapable of supporting themselves and their children. Equality laws would have to be rolled back.

Men must reconcile themselves to the changed world they live in. Today men are expected to be totally committed to work, yet they are also told they should be full-time fathers. It is an impossible task. Women know this from the bitter experience of trying to fulfil twin roles. Only if men campaign for shorter hours, more flexible working and paternity leave will they be able to resolve such contradictions.

(Source: Adapted from the Opinion Column of the Independent, 14 January 1995.)

Questions

(a) Briefly explain and give two examples of what is meant by 'positive discrimination'. *(4 marks)*

(b) What do sociologists mean by an 'underclass'? *(6 marks)*

(c) Using the data in the passage, and any other evidence about the UK with which you are familiar, examine the view that, compared to women 'men are not doing as well here as they once did'. *(8 marks)*

(d) Outline and critically assess two sociological explanations of economic differences between men and women. *(12 marks)*

8 Ethnicity and inequality

By the end of this chapter you should:

- be familiar with recent empirical material and indicators of the various aspects of ethnic inequality in Britain;
- understand the nature of debates about the changing nature of immigration legislation and the impact of this on ethnic minorities;
- be aware of the impact of inequality in relation to employment and unemployment as it affects ethnic minorities;
- understand the continuing impact of racism and racial prejudice on the life chances and social situation of ethnic minorities in Britain;
- have practised structured exam questions.

Introduction

We need to know about the composition of those described as ethnic minorities in this country, since this is an area of ignorance that feeds some racist fears. There is another way in which the lives of ethnic minorities in this country are affected by such fears, that is, the changing controls on immigration into this country. The social context of ethnic minorities living in Britain is affected by politically motivated immigration changes and the moral panic that often surrounds them, which is sometimes made worse by the words and actions of some politicians and elements of the media. We therefore need to investigate the effect of immigration controls and the ideas and assumptions that lie behind them.

Once this issue has been looked at we can consider how inequality is experienced by ethnic groups. Here it is possible to distinguish two particular aspects of inequality. The first relates to paid employment. We shall look at the types of job undertaken by ethnic minorities and their levels of pay compared with the ethnic majority.

Finally, we shall consider the effects of racism on other aspects of the lives of ethnic and racial minorities, for example in terms of access to benefits and housing, and more directly in terms of racist attacks and the expression of racial prejudice.

Ethnic minorities in contemporary British society

Exercise 8.1

a 1. Ask a sample of your fellow students for their estimates of the proportion of ethnic minorities in the total population of Britain.

i 2. Are there any significant differences in the estimates given by (a) males, (b) females, (c) students of working-class origin, (d) students of middle-class origin, (e) members of the ethnic majority, (f) members of ethnic minorities?

i a e 3. Compare your overall findings with the actual figures by looking at the statistics from the 1991 census contained in this chapter. What conclusions do you draw from this comparison and from the exercise as a whole?

Ethnic minorities constitute 5.5 per cent of the British population (1991 Census) and consist of a multitude of different nationalities and ethnicities.

ITEM A

Ethnic minority groups as a percentage of each age group of the population

	Number in the total British population	% ethnic minorities
Under 16	11 152 000	8.2
Working age	33 907 000	4.9
State retirement age	9 925 000	1.0

(Source: Employment Gazette, February 1993, p. 26.)

The composition of the ethnic minority population of Britain has been largely determined by the boundaries of the old British Empire and the subsequent British Commonwealth, as it was from these countries that workers were recruited to resolve the British labour shortages of the 1950s. Ironically Enoch Powell, later famous for being a fierce opponent of immigration, was at the time a Conservative health minister who 'welcomed West Indian nurses to Britain' (Fryer, 1984, p. 373). The link between immigration and the economy can be seen in the fact that, during the depression in the interwar years, immigration to Britain fell steeply (Mason, 1995). Since the 1950s the composition of the ethnic minority population has been influenced by the gradual tightening of immigration controls, culminating in the 1981 British Nationality Act.

Immigration and inequality

Immigration policies are central to the structuring of opportunities for ethnic minorities in this country, and there have been many debates on the role of such policies in sustaining or fostering racist sentiments.

Immigration has largely been discussed in terms of black people, despite the fact that in recent years there have been greater numbers of white immigrants. This division between the Old Commonwealth (predominantly white, including Australia, Canada and South Africa) and the New Commonwealth (predominantly black) is central to the immigration debate, and discussions about immigration are in effect discussions about race and the desirability of black people living in this country. Mason (1995) shows that this situation derives from the 1968 Commonwealth Immigrants Act, which introduced a set of qualifications that prospective migrants needed to satisfy in order to qualify for the right to live in Britain. These rested on provable links to someone born, adopted or naturalised in Britain and came to be known as the principle of patriality. This qualification was much more easily met by people in the Old Commonwealth than those in the New Commonwealth.

The purpose of the 1968 Act was clear, as Mason points out: 'Although distinctions based on skin colour did not figure in the wording of the Act it is clear that the intention was indeed to differentiate between those whose skin colour was thought of as "white" and those whose skin colour was not' (Mason, 1995, p. 29). This law was the first example of a distinction being made between the right to hold a British passport and the right to live in Britain, a distinction further embedded in the 1981 British Nationality Act. This created a number of layers of British citizenship, not all of which involved the right to live in Britain. Although this technically brought the notion of citizenship into line with immigration law, the right to be a British citizen without the right to live in Britain must have seemed like a very empty right.

As Nanda (1988) points out, the 1981 British Nationality Act has made Britain unique in the world in being the only country to refuse entry to its own nationals. Her point is that Britain's immigration controls are based on the idea that black people are the source of racial conflict and therefore their numbers must be controlled. This affects all black people, including those living in Britain already, since it tends to label them as a potential problem. Conversely Alexander (1987) argues that an inspection of the history of Britain reveals the falsity of this argument. According to him, racism (mainly in the form of support for 'scientific' racism) reached its height between 1840 and 1918, which was also the period when the number of black people in Britain was very low: 'This would seem to disprove the widely held view that the numbers of immigrants and the level of racism are closely related' (ibid., p. 17).

Supporters of immigration control argue that it is only by controlling immigration that Britain can maintain a harmonious multiracial environment, though opponents argue that immigration controls are always exercised against black people. A further criticism is that the declared need to limit immigration tends to suggest that immigration is problematic. The fact that such sentiments exist can be seen in the following quotations:

People are really rather afraid that this country might be rather swamped by people with a different culture (Margaret Thatcher, 1978, quoted in Ohri, 1988, p. 14).

The main purpose of immigration policy . . . is a contribution to . . . peace and harmony . . . If we are to get progress in community relations, we must give reassurance to the people, who were already here before immigration, that this will be the end and that there will be no further large-scale immigration. Unless we can give that assurance we cannot effectively set about . . . improving community relations (Reginald Maudling, Home Secretary, 1971, quoted in Ohri, 1988, p. 14).

A contrasting view reflecting particularly on the experiences of Asian women, can be seen from the following quotation:

In Britain the most brutal and wide ranging racism which occurs day after day is not the work of fascist minority parties but of Her Majesty's Government (Amrit Wilson, 1978, p. 72).

The gradual tightening of immigration policy has reduced the level of immigration to this country. In 1976 80,750 were admitted for settlement in the UK, but by 1990 that had fallen to 52,400.

One of the problems with the statistics on immigration is that often the focus is only on immigration without a corresponding emphasis on emigration. They thus tend to encourage the false view that the UK is becoming more crowded which is itself likely to lead to racist sentiments. Between 1971 and 1983, more people left the UK than came in. Overall the population loss through net emigration totalled 465,000 and in 1988 there was a net outflow of 21,000. Britain is getting less crowded not more.

Ethnicity and employment

Access to the job market is crucial for income and therefore to many of life's important resources. In this respect ethnic minorities are disadvantaged compared with the ethnic majority population, but there are also important differences between the various minorities.

This disadvantage can be seen in the extent of unemployment. According to the 1982 PSI survey, at that time unemployment amongst

Bangladeshi women was 52 per cent compared with 10 per cent for white females. More recent figures from the Labour Force Survey show that in 1989 unemployment among ethnic minority males was 14 per cent compared with 9 per cent for whites. The equivalent figures for females were 13 per cent for ethnic minorities and 8 per cent for white women. Church and Summerfield (1996) provide figures relating to 1995, when white males had an unemployment rate of 8 per cent, while the rate for Pakistani/Bangladeshi men was 18 per cent and for black men 21 per cent. They also point to differences among ethnic groups and by gender in terms of the percentage who were economically active (having or seeking employment or self-employment). The figures for the economically active were 82 per cent for black Caribbean men and 70 per cent for black Caribbean women, compared with 66 per cent for Bangladeshi men and 20 per cent for Bangladeshi women.

Unemployment is particularly severe for young ethnic minority people. This is especially important since the young constitute a higher proportion of the ethnic minority population than is the case with the ethnic majority. For example Amin and Oppenheim (1992) report that in the late 1980s, when unemployment among whites aged 16–24 was 12 per cent, the equivalent figure for Afro-Caribbean youths was 25 per cent, for Indians 16 per cent and for Pakistani and Bangladeshis 27 per cent.

Sociological research has shown clear links between unemployment and poverty, ill-health and to some degree social isolation, so we can say that the ethnic minority population suffers a higher risk of these negative factors than the ethnic majority. One of the reasons for this is the greater concentration of ethnic minorities in manual jobs in manufacturing industry. These jobs are associated with a greater risk of unemployment, especially in the 1980s and 1990s, with the economic recessions of those periods.

This situation reflects the circumstances faced by the original migrants to this country and their place within the job market. Mason (1995, p. 24) notes that British workers were upwardly mobile due to the increase in skilled manual jobs and jobs in the service sector, and therefore the jobs available to immigrants were those which had been abandoned and were 'often dirty, poorly paid, and involved unsocial hours like nightshift working'. It is also the case that immigrants faced continuing disadvantage in the job market due to racial discrimination.

The early migrants' pattern of residential settlement and the fact that later migrants' entry to Britain was facilitated by earlier migrants means that the ethnic minority population is not equally distributed throughout the country. According to the 1991 census, 44.5 per cent of all ethnic minorities live in London, 14 per cent in the West Midlands, 8 per cent in the North West and 7 per cent in Yorkshire and

Humberside. Since these areas were among those worst hit by the recessions of the 1980s the job prospects of ethnic minorities today have been worsened by their geographical situation. Agitation by racist organisations such as the National Front and the British National Party has tended to be greater in such areas.

Within the overall category of 'ethnic minority' the pattern of joining others already here can be obscured, but if the figure is broken down into individual groups it can be seen that Afro-Caribbeans tend to be concentrated in London and the West Midlands, as do those of Indian descent, who are also present in substantial numbers in the East Midlands. Pakistanis tend to be concentrated in Yorkshire and Humberside and the North West, while Bangladeshis are concentrated in East London. These concentrations are overwhelmingly in urban areas, notably large cities such as Bradford, Manchester, Leicester, Birmingham and London.

Mason (1995) and Jones (1993) point to the importance of the differences in the age structure of the ethnic minority and ethnic majority populations when considering questions of employment. The overall ethnic minority population is younger than the ethnic majority population. Thus there are fewer retired ethnic minority people yet the proportion who are economically inactive is higher than for the white population, whose inactive members include a large number of retired people. Since this is not the case with the ethnic minorities, because of the differential age structure, there must be another reason for their economic inactivity. The obvious candidate is unemployment, along with the fact that ethnic minority teenagers are much more likely to remain in full-time education after the age of 16, and also, particularly with regard to Pakistani and Bangladeshi girls, notions of domestic responsibility that prevent them from seeking paid employment (Jones, 1993).

Ouseley (1995) argues that it is still the case that career opportunities are unequal. He cites Labour Force Survey figures showing that 62 per cent of young black males in London are unemployed, and points out that while the gap between the white and the ethnic minority unemployment rates narrowed in the boom years of the late 1980s, the gap widened again during the recession of the 1990s.

Exercise 8.2

[i][a] 1. Using publications in your school/college library or the local reference library, look up the official unemployment figures by ethnic group and construct a graph showing the unemployment pattern over the last 10 years.

[i][a][e] 2. Use this graph to test whether the official figures support Ouseley's statement about the changing patterns of unemployment by ethnic group.

Ouseley goes on to argue that there is a 'business case' for equality since customers and business associates are increasingly likely to favour companies with fair employment practices. However he also points out that while a Commission for Racial Equality (CRE) survey found that 88 per cent of the companies surveyed had issued statements committing themselves to racial equality, only 45 per cent had made serious attempts to bring this about. The gap between theory and practice is therefore still large.

There is clear evidence, then, that the ethnic minorities' job market situation is different from that of the ethnic majority. We can investigate this in terms of unemployment levels, job type and level, and pay levels. When considering this issue, however, it is important to be aware that the category 'ethnic minority' covers a variety of groups with important differences.

Job type

Statistics on the distribution of people according to the type of industry they work in reveal that in most instances there are large similarities between the ethnic minorities and the ethnic majority, reflecting the fact that Britain as an industrial society has a particular overall distribution. However there are some notable differences, which can be seen more clearly when broken down by gender. The percentage of ethnic minority females working in manufacturing is 4 percentage points higher than among the ethnic majority (12 per cent rather than 8 per cent), and this is particularly so in the clothing, footwear and textiles sector. Fifty per cent fewer ethnic minority females are employed in education compared with ethnic majority females (6 per cent rather than 12 per cent), but in hospitals and other health institutions the reverse is the case (15 per cent compared with 8 per cent) (Jones, 1993).

The job levels of employees are shown in Items B and C.

Item B

Job levels of female employees by ethnic group, 1988–90 (per cent)

	All origins	White	Total ethnic minority	Afro-Caribbean	African Asian	Indian	Pakis-tani	Bangla-deshi	Chinese	African	Other/mixed
Prof. manager/employer	11	11	9	8	7	10	4	*	16	11	12
Employees and managers, large establishments	6	6	4	5	3	4	1	*	4	5	4
Employees and managers, small establishments	4	4	3	2	2	2	3	*	5	3	4
Professional workers—employees	2	2	2	1	2	4	0	*	7	2	3
Other non-manual	55	56	53	54	58	47	42	*	53	47	63
Skilled manual and foreman	5	5	5	4	9	5	7	*	2	6	3
Semi-skilled manual	22	22	27	25	25	34	45	*	20	32	17
Unskilled manual	7	7	5	9	1	4	2	*	9	4	5
Armed services/inadequately described/not stated	0	0	0	0	0	0	0	*	0	1	0

* Sample size too small.

(Source: Jones, 1993, p. 99, table 4.10.)

Job levels of male employees by ethnic group, 1988–90 (per cent)

	All origins	White	Total ethnic minority	Afro-Caribbean	African Asian	Indian	Pakis-tani	Bangla-deshi	Chinese	African	Other/mixed
Prof. manager/employer	27	27	21	12	27	25	12	12	30	21	30
Employees and managers, large establishments	13	13	7	5	6	9	4	1	7	9	11
Employees and managers, small establishments	7	7	5	3	10	5	4	5	10	3	7
Professional workers– employees	7	7	8	4	11	10	4	6	14	9	12
Other non-manual	20	20	22	19	30	18	16	14	19	34	31
Skilled manual and foreman	32	33	28	39	26	29	34	5	10	20	18
Semi-skilled manual	15	15	23	23	13	24	31	65	36	18	16
Unskilled manual	4	4	5	6	3	4	6	5	4	4	2
Armed services/inadequately described/not stated	1	1	1	1	0	0	1	0	1	3	3

(Source: Jones, 1993, p. 100, table 4.11.)

Exercise 8.3

Study Items B and C and answer the following questions:

[i] 1. Identify the three job levels where there was the greatest disparity between whites and total ethnic minorities for (a) males (b) females.

[i] 2. Identify the two ethnic minority groups with the highest proportion of manual workers.

[i] 3. Identify the ethnic minority group that has a higher proportion of its members in the category 'professional/managerial/employer' than for Britain overall.

[i][a] 4. 'The apparent progress of some specific ethnic minority groups contrasts with the continued disadvantage of others' (Jones, 1993, p. 154). Suggest two ethnic minority groups that might fit into each of the two categories outlined in the preceding quote. Justify your choice.

[i][a][e] 5. To what extent does the information in Items B and C suggest that the differences between ethnic minority groups are as important as the differences between the ethnic majority and the ethnic minorities?

Item D

Percentage of employees working in the secondary sector* by ethnic group, 1988–90

All origins	White	Total ethnic minority	Afro-Caribbean	African Asian	Indian	Pakistani	Bangla-deshi	Chinese	African	Other/mixed
53	53	52	44	53	53	63	80	66	43	53

* The secondary sector is defined here as other manufacturing and distribution; repairs; hotels and catering; small firms with fewer than 25 employees; temporary, seasonal or casual jobs; fixed period jobs.

(Source: Jones, 1993, table 4.22.)

Exercise 8.4

Study Item D and answer the following questions:

1. Explain in your own words the meaning of the term 'secondary sector'.

2. The secondary sector is contrasted with the primary sector. Suggest two types of job that might be categorised as being within the primary sector.

3. To what extent does ethnicity appear to be a factor in relation to location in the secondary employment sector?

Unemployment

We can also look at differences in the economic activity rate by ethnic group. 'Economically active' means being in paid employment or looking for paid employment. This includes those who are registered as unemployed as long as they are looking for work.

Item E

Economic status of all people of working age by ethnic group, 1988–90 (per cent)

	All origins	White	Total minority	ethnic Caribbean	Afro-Asian	African Indian	Pakis-tani	Bangla-deshi	Chinese	African	Other/mixed
All persons of working age											
Economically active	80	81	70	81	79	71	51	52	65	67	70
of which in employment	74	75	60	69	72	63	40	40	60	57	63
Employee (excl. govt scheme)	63	64	49	61	58	48	28	30	42	52	54
Full-time	50	50	41	52	49	41	24	26	33	41	44
Part-time	13	14	8	9	8	7	4	5	9	11	10
Self-employed	9	9	10	6	14	13	9	7	18	4	8
Employed on govt scheme	1	1	2	2	1	1	2	3	0	1	2
YTS – employer based	1	1	0	0	0	0	1	0	0	0	0
YTS – college based	0	0	0	0	0	0	0	1	0	0	0
Other govt scheme	1	1	1	2	1	1	1	2	0	1	1
Unemployed	6	6	9	12	7	8	11	12	5	9	7
Economically inactive	20	19	30	19	21	29	49	48	35	33	30
of which full-time students	3	3	10	6	7	9	11	10	17	17	13
Looking after family/home	9	8	13	6	10	12	29	28	12	9	11

(Source: Jones, 1993, p. 91.)

Exercise 8.5

Study Item E and answer the following questions:

1. Identify the group(s) with the highest percentage(s) in the following categories: (a) economically active, (b) economically inactive, (c) employees, (d) self-employed, (e) unemployed.

2. Suggest reasons for the differences you have identified in question 1.

3. Consider the arguments for and against racial discrimination being the key factor behind the pattern identified above.

Pay

The lower income of ethnic minorities compared with the ethnic majority is due to the greater likelihood of their being unemployed and their general location at a lower level in the job structure. It is important to stress that this generalised statement obscures the inequalities that exist between the ethnic minority communities. The groups with the greatest likelihood of having the lowest income are the Bangladeshi and Pakistani communities, who tend to occupy the lowest-paid jobs. In spring 1994, unemployment among Pakistani/Bangladeshi men stood at 29 per cent and among Pakistani/Bangladeshi women it was 24 per cent (Oppenheim and Harker, 1996). However it is also the case that the richest ethnic minority individuals come from South Asia (Jones, 1993).

According to Oppenheim and Harker (ibid.) the group with the highest level of unemployment in spring 1994 was black men (33 per cent). Among black men aged under 24 the figure was 51 per cent. This shows that the Afro-Caribbean community tends to suffer greater unemployment than the Asian community, and of course this has an effect on household income.

Ethnicity also has an effect on the pay level of those in employment

---

ITEM F

Average earnings of full-time employees by ethnic group and sex, Britain, winter 1993/94 to autumn 1994 (not seasonally adjusted)

Ethnic origin	Average hourly pay (£)			As % of population		
	All	Men	Women	All	Men	Women
All origins	7.42	7.97	6.39			
White	7.44	8.00	6.40			
Ethnic minority groups	6.82	7.15	6.31	92	89	99
Black	6.92	7.03	6.77	93	88	106
Indian	6.70	7.29	5.77	90	91	90
Pakistani/Bangladeshi	5.39	5.47	5.15	72	68	81
Mixed/other origins	7.70	8.45	6.77	103	106	106

(Source: Adapted from Oppenheim and Harker, 1996, p. 118, table 6.2.)

Exercise 8.6

[i] 1. Study Item F and identify the highest- and lowest-paid ethnic groups in terms of (a) men and (b) women.

[i] 2. For which sex does ethnic origin appear to have the greatest effect on the level of pay?

[a] 3. Suggest reasons for the patterns revealed by questions 1 and 2.

The most recent survey on ethnic minorities in Britain was conducted by the Policy Studies Institute (Modood, 1997). One of the key findings was an increase in the degree of interracial integration, with half of the black men and a third of the black women born in Britain having white partners. However the report also shows the continued existence of disadvantages among ethnic minorities.

A particular emphasis of the report is the increasing diversity of identities and experiences within the category 'ethnic minority'. According to the report, Caribbeans identify with their colour, while religion is more likely to be the most important basis for identity among Asian groups. However cultural identity seems to be diminishing among young Asians, with fewer bearing the traditional Hindu bindi (red spot on the forehead), and the arranged marriage system is in decline.

In terms of standard of living there is evidence of continuing inequality, with four out of five Pakistani and Bangladeshi households having incomes of less than half the national average, while unemployment is above the national average among Indian and Caribbean women. However the report also points to some anomalies: African Asians and Chinese are more likely than whites to be earning over £500 per week and they have a lower unemployment rate than whites.

The diversity masked by the term ethnic minority has been the subject of continuing debate, with which Tariq Modood is particularly associated. He argues that the term black should not be used to describe Asians. This contrasts with the argument that the term black should cover all ethnic minorities since it provides them with the basis for political unity in the fight against racial discrimination.

Racial prejudice and discrimination continue to be faced by ethnic minorities, though the PSI report (Modood, 1997) says that young whites are more likely to state that they do not like Asians than they are to say they do not like blacks. Further evidence is the finding that a Pakistani with a university degree is as likely to be living below the poverty line as a white person with no educational qualifications. The survey also points to the number of people who suffer racial harassment: 250 000 people a year.

Racism and racial and ethnic inequality

It is clear that racism exists, and that it has affected the ethnic minorities in this country by damaging their lives in one way or another. Racism is the belief that there are systematic differences between groups based on physical characteristics (phenotype) or genetic characteristics (genotype). For example in the past blacks were considered by some as inferior because of their supposedly smaller brain size, based on pseudo-scientific measurement of skull sizes. The second argument is that our genetic make-up distinguishes us as distinct races and that behavioural differences emerge from this genetic difference. This is the position of sociobiology, which argues that we unconsciously behave on the basis of trying to further our own gene pool.

There are a number of problems with this, the most notable of which are as follows. First, most modern geneticists refute the idea that distinct races can be identified by their genetic make-up. Steven Rose (Rose *et al.*, 1984) argues that 85 per cent of genetic variation occurs *within* racial groupings, and Michael Banton (1988) points out that there are as many as a million different human genes, and therefore on a genetic basis there must be as many as a million races. Second, it is difficult to prove that we somehow act on the basis of genetic programming. Sociobiological theories resort to saying that we unconsciously do so, but this is rather unsatisfactory. Although such arguments are largely discredited, this does not mean that racism is disappearing, although it does mean that any scientific basis for racism is untenable, which is a key achievement of social scientific thinking.

Despite this, classification on the basis of supposed race does take place and is the cornerstone of the oppression of various groups. However the important point is that classifications based on perceived biologically driven differences are translated into hierarchies of superiority and inferiority, which makes racism different from other forms of persecution. Callinicos (1993) points to the difference between this type of oppression and the examples of religious persecution that have been evident throughout history. In this sense Jewish people could escape anti-Semitic persecution by converting to Christianity, but the growth of racial anti-Semitism, which defined the Jews as an inferior race rather than religious group, allowed no such escape. It was this move from anti-Semitism defined in religious terms to anti-Semitism defined in biological terms that led to the Nazis' 'final solution of the Jewish problem': genocide in the concentration camps.

This is one of the most barbaric examples of racism (and of course the main reason for the revulsion at biological theories of race) but the intellectual destruction of the idea of biological race has not prevented it from being used in everyday classification, or indeed in some forms of official classification. Items G to I contain extracts that illustrate two themes: the continued use of such forms of classification, and the illogicalities that result from it.

Racial classification has been used to defend privilege. In Nazi Germany it was used to despoil and isolate a scapegoat group. A law was issued that 'A Jew is anyone who is descended from at least three grandparents who are racially full Jews. A Jew is also one who is descended from two full Jewish parents if (a) he belonged to the Jewish community at the time this law was issued . . .; or (b) was married to a Jewish person; or (c) was the offspring of a union between Jews.' The law stated: 'A Jew cannot be a citizen of the Reich. He has no right to vote in political affairs and he cannot occupy public office.' After the Nazis took power in Austria these laws were applied there. Someone who wished to demonstrate that he was an Aryan had to produce the baptismal certificates of all four grandparents. A friend of the author has described how he shared a school desk in Austria with a boy whose grandparents had all converted to Christianity. Therefore he counted as an Aryan but his parents, who were Christians, were legally 'full Jews'. His parents both perished in the extermination camp at Auschwitz while the son was conscripted at 16 years and died on the Russian front in a uniform several sizes too large for him, defending the values of the Vaterland.

(Source: Banton, 1988, p. 68.)

There is a medical condition known as Nelson's disease in which the skin of 'white' people turns brown, and they become the victims of racial discrimination; they are not of different race if this is defined in terms of their genetic inheritance, but they are if race is defined by reference to differential treatment.

(Source: Banton, 1988, p. 12.)

In 1982–3, Susie Guilory Phipps unsuccessfully sued the Louisiana Bureau of vital Records to change her racial classification from black to white. The descendant of an 18th-century white planter and a black slave, Phipps was designated 'black' in her birth certificate in accordance with a 1970 state law which declared anyone with at least 1/32nd 'Negro blood' to be black.

(Source: Omi and Winant, 1994, p. 53.)

Exercise 8.7

Read Items G to I and then answer the following questions:

[i][a] 1. With reference to Item G, explain in your own words how the Christian converts were defined as 'legally full Jews'. How did conversion to Christianity affect their ability to escape persecution?

[i] 2. With reference to Item H, on what basis are people suffering from Nelson's disease subjected to racial discrimination?

[i][a] 3. With reference to Item I, explain in your own words why Susie Guilory Phipps was legally defined as 'black'. How many past generations did this ruling cover?

[i][a][e] 4. To what extent do these examples undermine the idea that there is such a thing as the scientific definition of race?

It is important to consider the evidence on the level of racism, but also on the resistance to racism. It should not be supposed that ethnic minorities passively accept racism. However the extent to which they are able to organise against racism differs among the groups. Jones (1993) argues that the fact that Pakistanis and Bangladeshis are more recent arrivals in this country may partly explain their relative disadvantage in overcoming the constraints of racism, but the level of human capital in terms of qualifications that ethnic minority groups bring to this country may also play a part, since such qualifications are differentially distributed among immigrant groups and will have an impact on the type of job obtained.

The experience of racism is therefore affected by the level of racism in British society and the extent to which there is resistance against it. The two are of course linked. For example the mobilisations in the 1970s against the National Front largely destroyed any threat of it achieving a mass following, but this can be contrasted with the rise of the Front National in France.

In relation to the level of racial discrimination, Jones (1993) argues that in the mid 1980s this was the same as in the mid 1970s. Since 1983 the British Social Attitude surveys have included a question on racial prejudice (people are asked to assign themselves to one of three categories), and the results of three surveys are presented in Item J.

ITEM J

**People holding various levels of prejudice
(% of whole population)**

	1983	1987	1991
Very prejudiced	4	4	2
A little prejudiced	31	34	29
Not prejudiced at all	64	60	68

(Source: Social and Community Planning Research, British Social Attitude Survey 1983, 1987, 1991.)

ITEM J   *Exercise 8.8*

i 1. Study Item J and then, summarise the changes in attitude between 1983 and 1991.

e 2. To what extent should sociologists accept that the statistics in Item J present a valid picture of the degree of discrimination in Britain?

One specific instance of apparent racial prejudice concerned an advertisement by the motor manufacturer Ford aimed at Eastern Europe in which the faces of the black and Asian workers in the photo were changed to white by computer technology. Ford claimed that this was an administrative error with absolutely no racial motive, but one of the workers, Keith Thomas, told the *London Evening Standard* that 'It affects everyone who works at Dagenham and is black or Asian. It's a sign of just what Ford thinks of us all, and people are angry' (quoted in the *Guardian*, 21 February 1996).

Exercise 8.9

i Explain in your own words why the workers at Ford were so angry about this poster.

Another indication of the extent of racism in Britain can be obtained from police statistics on the number of racially motivated attacks. The report in Item K covers the period 1993–5.

More race attacks reported to police

Reports to the police of racial attacks and intimidation are rising at a rate of 8 per cent a year, according to figures published by the Home Office.

The figures suggest the real level of racial attacks is rising for the first time since 1986 when the police started keeping separate figures on racially-motivated incidents.

Until now ministers have insisted the rapid year-on-year increase of racial attacks has been a reflection of the fact that the police were taking such incidents more seriously, and so victims were more prepared to come forward.

The Home Office figures show 11,878 racial incidents were reported to the police in the year to March 1995, compared with 10,997 in the previous 12 months. The British Crime Survey, which is based on interviews with victims, suggests there are in fact as many as 130 000 racially-motivated incidents, including graffiti and verbal abuse, every year.

Publication of the figures coincides with the opening of the private prosecution at the Old Bailey next Tuesday by the family of 18-year-old black schoolboy, Stephen Lawrence, who was stabbed to death at a south London bus stop in April 1993. His family have so far raised £66 000 from wellwishers to finance the prosecution.

The sharpest rises in official figures were seen in the Northumbria police area, which includes Newcastle, in South Wales, and in Derbyshire, all of which recorded increases of more than 20 per cent. The largest fall, of more than 30 per cent, was recorded in the West Midlands where the number of recorded attacks dropped from 487 to 375.

The shadow home secretary, Jack Straw, has said the figures showed that race was a significant motive in an increasing number of crimes.

'The change in police practice is only part of the explanation,' he said. 'The fact that the numbers are rising underlines our commitment to strengthen the law on racial harassment and racial attacks.'

The figures for 1994/95 do not reflect the introduction of a new offence of intentional harassment in February last year, which was intended to strengthen the law to deal with serious cases of persistent harassment. Mr Straw said it was important that the law specifically recognised racial harassment as a crime.

Police stop and search figures show 37 per cent of those stopped on the streets of London were members of ethnic minority groups despite the fact that they make up only 20 per cent of the capital's population.

Mr Straw said the aggravation of community relations caused by the disproportionate number of black and Asian people stopped by police would not be resolved until there were more officers from ethnic minorities.

Violence round the country

Reported racial incidents (selected forces)	1993/94	1994/95
Derbyshire	221	291
Hampshire	212	210
Lancashire	262	222
Leicestershire	315	366
Greater Manchester	658	637
Metropolitan Police	5124	5480
Northumbria (Newcastle)	405	508
Nottinghamshire	264	259
South Wales	400	517
Sussex	214	247
West Midlands	487	375
West Yorkshire	244	254
England and Wales	10 997	11 878

(Source: Alan Travis, Guardian, 12 April 1996.)

Exercise 8.10

Read Item K and answer the following questions:

[i] 1. According to the British Crime Survey, roughly what proportion of racially motivated attacks are reported to the police?

[i][a] 2. Explain the significance of the figures on police stop-and-search action.

[i][a][e] 3. Summarise the reasons given in Item K for the rise in racial attacks, as shown by the figures, and evaluate the relative importance of each of them.

In the light of the evidence presented above, unfortunately we must conclude that racism and ethnic inequality is still a clear feature of contemporary British society, leading to the lives of ethnic minorities being damaged in one way or another. The next chapter will consider the various theories that have been developed to try to explain this form of inequality.

Exam question

Part (e) of the AEB's June 1994 examination focused on ethnic minorities and social mobility. The question and the source material included in the question are reproduced below, along with the markscheme and an actual answer produced by a student in that exam.

(1) Write detailed comments on the answer provided by the student and use this to:

(2) Plan and write out your own answer to this question.

Item L

In a recent article, Vaughan Robinson of Swansea University reviews the social mobility of British blacks. He uses data derived from the Longitudinal Study of the Office of Population and Censuses to track the mobility of individuals between the 1971 and 1981 censuses.

Robinson commences by reviewing the picture revealed in previous studies, especially the two well-known Policy Studies Institute works by Smith (1977) and Brown (1984). Smith's data showed widespread downward mobility for newly arrived members of ethnic minorities, qualified individuals often being forced to take manual, including unskilled manual work. Brown's later study showed some improvement with all ethnic minorities increasing their representation in white-collar occupations. However, much of this was in routine white-collar work and accountable through occupational change rather than increased opportunities for individual mobility. Moreover, most had not managed to reproduce the class position of themselves or their parents prior to arrival in Britain. This point was confirmed by Heath and Ridge's 1983 analysis of the Nuffield Social Mobility data which showed that 50% of the sample were from petit-bourgeois or farm-owning backgrounds originally but were now concentrated in the working class.

(Source: From 'Gleanings' in Social Science Teacher, 20:2, Spring 1991, Dave Wells.)

Question

(a) With reference to Item L and other sources, evaluate sociological explanations of the class position of ethnic minorities. *(9 marks)*

Mark scheme

0: No relevant points

1–3: Answers will tend to have a limited view of the explanations of the class position of ethnic minorities, perhaps concentrating on racism as the single cause of their class position. The use of material from the ITEM is likely to be unfocused.

4–6: There will be a number of explanations put forward, and where supporting evidence is used, either from the ITEM or elsewhere, it will be well applied and contextualised. Evaluation of the explanations will be present, but it may exist as juxtaposition rather than being explicitly drawn.

7–9: In this band, there will be a good range of explanations included, well contextualised and accurately described. Supporting evidence will be well applied and evaluation will be explicitly drawn about the explanations put forward. At the top, there should also be an awareness of the differential position of various ethnic minorities.

Student answer

(a) There is no doubt that certain ethnic minorities in Britain have remained at the bottom of the social class. Brown Smith as indicated in Item L, states that newly arrived member of ethnic minority groups are being forced into manual and unskilled work.

The consensus view has put forward a host–immigrant model. This suggests that when minorities first enter the country they are seen as strange because they share different cultural values. It is this strangeness rather than prejudice that is the major social barrier which determines acceptability and economic success. It view also emphasises that with time the immigrants become assimilated into British culture and become accepted.

This argument does not put forward a very convincing argument. It doesn't explain how there have been generations of ethnic minorities in Britain (most have made the British culture their own) yet there is still racism and this view does not explain why after all this time minorities still remain at the bottom.

Marxists claim that before examining position of ethnic minorities in the class structure we must first examine the history of minorities with emphasis on imperialism, i.e. exploitation. Today capitalism preserves racism in order to maintain the status quo. They do this by i) legitimising racism, i.e. making the white working class think blacks are inferior ii) divide and rule whereby the working class are divided and iii) scapegoating by making the white working class blame minorities for taking their jobs. Westergaard and Resler consider the working class to be a whole. They claim that too much attention is paid to the 'special problems' e.g. housing and employment. Castles and Kosack are also Marxists and they argue that the working class exists but is divided with the white working class having an economic advantage. Rex and Tomlinson argue that black people as a whole have become the underclass because they do not share the same economic advantages as the white working class. In their Handsworth study they found that black people were not considered in education, housing, employment etc as a result they have become stigmatised as not being wanted and as a threat.

Evidence suggests that the market power of blacks is very poor and that they are more likely to stay in the bottom classes. However there has been evidence to show that other groups like Asians have a better market situation and they remain a separate that is improving economic wise.

Mark: 6

Comment: For you to complete

9 Theories of racial and ethnic inequality

By the end of this chapter you should:

- be aware of a wide range of sociological theories on ethnic inequality;
- be able to distinguish between three broad approaches to explaining ethnic inequality, namely race and ethnicity/race relations models, structural theories of the impact of racism and imperialism, and racial formation approaches;
- have a critical understanding of the strengths and weaknesses of each approach;
- be aware of the variety of theories contained within each broad approach;
- have practised structured exam questions.

Introduction

Early sociological theories of ethnic inequality in this country were largely based on those developed to consider racial and ethnic inequality in the United States, notably by the Chicago School (see Lal, 1986). These thinkers demonstrated that inequality was based not on biological differences but on social and cultural factors, and they used the term ethnicity to denote this, thus differentiating it from the term 'race', which implied biological differences. Inequality was said to arise from the prejudice and discriminatory attitudes associated with cultural differences and spatial competition (competition for space, primarily residential space). The studies focused on the extent to which migrant groups were assimilated into (became an integrated part of) the culture of the host country. This led to a whole tradition of ethnic and race relations research in Britain.

In the 1970s and 1980s this approach came under critical scrutiny from largely Weberian and Marxist oriented sociologists (Rex and Tomlinson, 1979; Miles, 1982), who argued that it ignored the extent to which racial and ethnic inequalities were the result of structural factors in society, notably the existence of racism, which created structural barriers and reinforced existing inequalities. Racism rather than race relations became the focus of concern.

By the late 1980s and 1990s this approach too came under criticism. One criticism was that it tended to portray black people and ethnic minorities as simply the victims of racial discrimination (Gilroy,

1987). Instead it was argued that black people were actively trying both to fight discrimination and to define their identity.

The growth of postmodernist ideas led to an emphasis on differences within ethnic minority groupings and criticism of the use of the term 'black' to describe all racial and ethnic minorities, for example those of Asiatic origin did not feel that 'black' was an identity they could accept (Modood, 1988, 1994).

It was argued that the way in which racially discriminating structures were created by human action and the diverse ways in which they were transformed (sometimes called racial formation – Omi and Winant, 1994) should be considered. For various reasons, sociologists stressed that the division between race and ethnicity established in earlier studies was no longer useful and some writers shifted back to the use of the term race, understood purely as a cultural and ideological construction, but having real effects nonetheless (Gilroy, 1987, 1992; Donald and Rattansi, 1992). The cultural construction of identity and its relation to the creation of and resistance to structures of racial and ethnic inequality became important. Some have argued for the need to move terms such as ethnicity away from their earlier meanings (Hall, 1992). This approach, deriving from postmodernist post-Marxism, is also not without its critics (Callinicos, 1989, 1993).

This chapter will examine the ways in which theories of racial and ethnic inequality have changed over time, and will consider the various approaches to the study of racial and ethnic inequality under four broad headings:

- Biologically based explanations.
- Ethnic and race relations explanations.
- Structures of racism explanations.
- Racial formation explanations.

Biologically based explanations

The idea that there are biologically distinct races is a false one that has gone through a number of modifications. Biological attempts to explain racial and ethnic inequality consist of two broad approaches. The first argues that races can be distinguished on the basis of certain physical or physiological characteristics (phenotype) and attributes psychological and behavioural differences to these. The second argues that the source of racial inequality is to be found in the different genetic structure (genotype) of the races. Again these are assumed to shape cultural and behavioural differences. This approach arose in the late nineteenth century.

So what these two views have in common is the idea that there are different races based on biological differences (either physical characteristics – phenotype – or genes – genotype) and that these result in differential skills, attitudes and behaviours among the races.

1. Phenotype explanations

In relation to the biological explanation of racial differences, O'Donnell (1991) points out that no one has successfully shown that such differences exist. He refers to the studies conducted by biologists working for the United Nations after the Second World War, who concluded that the human race had a single origin, and although it was possible to distinguish groups on the basis of their greater statistical likelihood of possessing certain physical characteristics, for example a certain skin colour, even here there were great overlaps between groups. Gordon (1992) highlights the absence of any study to prove the existence of biological differences between groups and races, other than physical characteristics such as skin pigmentation, which by themselves can not be seen as a basis for racial categorisation. He argues that they become so only when certain personality characteristics are attributed to people with certain physical characteristics. This underlies the social construction of race and therefore racism.

The attempt to distinguish different biological races was undermined by the publication of Charles Darwin's *On the Origin of Species* (1859), which set out to prove that all humans have a common origin. This destroyed the notion that black and white people had separate origins, which had been used to justify the inequalities between them. Darwin pointed out that all humanity is part of one species and that this species changes and adapts over time. This contradicted the attempts to explain racial and ethnic difference on the basis of biology.

2. Genotype explanations

Darwin's ideas led to an attempt to discover how evolution (defined as progress) occurs. This in turn led to the rise of the second, more popular, type of biological explanation, based on the idea of distinct genes. Central to this has been the growth of sociobiology (see Van den Berghe, 1986; Sharp, 1991), which argues that there is a biological basis to social behaviour. Although sociobiology admits to the existence of a complex evolutionary interplay of genetic, environmental and cultural factors, ultimately the approach tends to reduce all behaviour to genetic factors. For example Dawkins (1976) argues that genes are 'selfish' and programme us to act selfishly in order to ensure their survival, while Van den Berghe (1981) sees ethnicity as an extension of kinship – both theories are based on the idea of a genetic predisposition to ensure that our own genes survive and therefore to seek people similar to ourselves and shun others. This offers a biological basis to race and racism. Reproductive success or failure is seen as the principal mechanism of natural selection.

The explanation for racism rests not in the value system or structures of society, but in our genes. The important difference is that while we can change our values and the structures of society, we cannot change our genes. Van den Berghe (1981, 1986) also argues that since culture is carried by humans, biological reproduction is the means by which culture is perpetuated. However he does say that biology does not transmit culture itself, but that culture is somehow genetically evolved. Critics have pointed out that Van den Berghe is equivocal about the extent of biological effects and sociobiology is an attempt to blur the debate about the relative importance of environmental and genetic factors in influencing culture.

The idea that biological differences are at the heart of the social inequalities experienced by ethnic groups returned to the centre of debate after the publication of *The Bell Curve* by two leading new right thinkers in America (Herrnstein and Murray, 1994). According to Herrnstein and Murray, the lower position of some individuals and groups in the United States is due to their lower intelligence. Murray and Herrnstein propose that the key cause of poverty and unemployment is lower cognition (brain processes related to thinking and the capacity for thinking) among an underclass with lower intelligence. They argue that intelligence is at least 60 per cent determined by hereditary factors, leaning heavily (though not entirely) on the idea that biological differences are the causes of inequality. Though they put this in terms of individuals not social groups – because the law of averages means that a bright individual can exist in a group with lower average scores – there is no getting round the fact that they do talk about differences in intelligence between individuals and groups, and that the two groups they mention in the book are classes and races. Gould (1995a) therefore considers that their attempt to argue they are not talking about groups (races) is implausible.

The Bell Curve has been subject to a number of criticisms, not the least from biologists. According to Stephen Jay Gould (1995b), a biologist himself, the book rests on four key arguments, all of which are false. The four arguments are (1) intelligence can be depicted as a single number – an IQ score, (2) such a score can be used to put people into rank order, (3) such intelligence is genetically based and (4) as such it is unamenable to change.

Gould asserts that the first and second arguments can be seen as false since there are at least three different schools of thought on the usefulness of psychometric testing and only one of these supports the notion that a single measure of IQ is possible. He shows that the idea that intelligence is multidimensional and therefore not amenable to a single expression (an IQ score) has majority support amongst biologists.

In relation to the third and fourth arguments, Gould says that their claim that 60 per cent of intelligence is genetic is demonstrably wrong. The link between IQ and various factors such as job and educational qualifications is weak. Gardner (1995) argues that at most 20 per cent of the variance in socioeconomic factors can be put down to intelligence, which means that only 60 per cent of this 20 per cent can be explained by hereditary factors. The rest must be due to environmental, social structural or cultural factors. Since all of these are subject to change, the hereditary case disappears: 'well over 90 per cent of one's fate does not lie in one's genes' (Gardner, 1995).

Nisbett (1995) states that, of the seven key studies looking at the issue of race and IQ, possible backing for the genetic argument can be found in only one of them, and this is the only one quoted by the authors of *The Bell Curve*. Much of the data in *The Bell Curve* originates from articles in *Mankind Quarterly* (see Rosen and Lane, 1995), a controversial publication whose editor believes that racial differences are all-important and whose work draws on the Nazi 'race scientist' Hans Gunther. Billig (1979) shows that there are clear links between the *Mankind Quarterly* and various neo-Nazi and fascist groups operating in Europe.

The vast majority of social scientists do not accept such ideas and seek to locate ethnic inequalities in social factors such as racial discrimination. The biological argument about race has also been subject to much criticism among biologists. For example Steven Rose (Rose *et al.*, 1984) has shown that 85 per cent of genetic variation is due to differences between individuals in the same race, and only 15 per cent is due to variations between peoples or races: 'the genetic variation between one Spaniard and another, or between one Masai and another, is 85 per cent of all human genetic variation, while only 15% is accounted for by breaking people up into groups '... Any use of racial categories must take its justification from some other source than biology'.

Exercise 9.1

[i][a] Compile a list of the criticisms that sociologists have made of the biological concept of race and the use of this concept to explain ethnic inequalities.

Sociological approaches

The recent reemergence of theories based on a notion of biological difference shows the importance of reemphasising the point that race is not a biological entity but a social construction. This is the common starting point of all sociological approaches and sociologists have had to fight hard for it to be recognised. It is for this reason that the word race commonly appears in inverted commas, and there is doubt whether sociologists should use the term at all. Miles (1982) argues that because it is a falsehood and therefore analytically useless, its usage bestows credibility on it and we should not use the term. On the other hand many writers (see Pilkington, 1984; Richardson and Lambert, 1985) have pointed to Thomas's interactionist dictum that 'if people define a situation as real, it is real in its social consequences' (Thomas, 1909) and since race is still a commonsense belief, this false belief will affect people's actions. This section will consider the different ways in which sociologists have conceptualised race and ethnic relations within a shared framework that rejects the biological notion of race.

Exercise 9.2

For each of the three major sociological approaches, write a summary and identify the main authors associated with that approach. Put this information into a table under the following headings:

- Sociological approach.
- Summary of views on ethnic inequality.
- Varieties within this approach.
- Writers associated with this approach.

The following approaches should be covered:

- Ethnic and race relations approaches.
- Structures of racism approaches.
- Racial formation approaches.

1. Ethnicity and race relations explanations

The Chicago School and assimilationism

The study of relations between different ethnic groups started earlier in the United States than elsewhere due to the greater volume of immigration into that country, which presented itself as a 'melting pot'. One of the earliest centres to take an interest in such relations was the University of Chicago, where the idea of symbolic interactionism originated (see Lal, 1986). The spur to the interest was the fact that 80 per cent of the population of Chicago in 1900 were immigrants or the children of immigrants. One of the most famous early studies was conducted by W. I. Thomas and F. Znaniecki on Polish immigrants (Thomas and Znaniecki, 1919).

Exercise 9.3

Suggest any problems that might arise if the findings of this study were to be applied to the situation of black Americans.

Such studies rested on a broadly interactionist framework that stressed the need for ethnographic studies (a detailed description of the way of life of a particular group) of group interaction. They rejected the predominant approach in sociology, structural functionalism, because in their view its emphasis on structures ignored the fluidity and complexity of human relationships. However they broadly shared the functionalist belief that a value consensus was an important basis of society. Misunderstandings emerged over the differences in culture that immigrant groups brought to the United States and this presented a potential problem. There was concern about the effect that retention of separate ethnic identities would have on democracy and national stability.

At the turn of the century there were few African Americans in Chicago (only 1.8 per cent of the population) and sociological studies concentrated mainly on the assimilation of white immigrants from Europe, but by 1930 African Americans made up 7 per cent of the city's population. The ideas developed to explain the assimilation of largely white immigrant groups were then applied to the position of African Americans.

Park (1950) sought to explain the racial conflicts that emerged in terms of a cycle of race relations consisting of four stages: (1) contact, (2) conflict, (3) accommodation and (4) assimilation. What was meant by this was that newcomers would be gradually integrated into the American culture, thereby losing their distinctiveness. This is what is meant by the term assimilation. Rather than social structures, the Chicago School talked in terms of how humans adapt to their environment. This led to the ecological model, which suggested that there is competition for location within the city. Over time the populations of the least desirable areas change as newcomers move in, and as a result these become perpetual zones of transition. These zones of transition are said to be characterised by social disorganisation. Again, since these areas are inhabited by newcomers to the city, the suggestion is that their arrival causes disruption but that over time the groups adapt to each other and consensus is restored. This analysis leads to the conclusion that new groups need to assimilate. The position adopted is that new groups entering the city might destabilise an existing consensus, but this problem can be avoided if they give up their separate identities and assimilate into the majority culture.

Gans (1994) argues that the straight-line version of assimilation presented by Park and others should be modified into what he calls a 'bumpy-line' version to indicate its potentially problematic path, but he still feels that overall this is something positive. Here he talks both of assimilation and acculturation, meaning the giving up of a distinct culture:

> I still think that assimilation and acculturation ... are continuing processes that erode the cultures and groups which immigrants brought, and still bring, to America. This erosion continues, and on

the whole voluntarily, because the old cultures and groups no longer seem relevant to people trying to make their way in America and American culture. For young people especially, immersion in their so-called host culture is easier and socially more rewarding than paying obeisance to an old culture that has little meaning to them, mainly to please their parents and grandparents (Gans, 1994).

Gans is mainly talking about immigrants to the United States rather than black Americans, but the Chicago tradition has been to treat the two groups as undergoing similar processes. Gans' work shows that the notion of assimilation is still present in American sociology. He argues that the elements of ethnicity that remain are mainly symbolic in nature.

The strength of this approach is firstly its break with biologically driven notions of race and secondly its acknowledgement of racial identities and race relations as something in need of consideration. The main weakness of this viewpoint in relation to ethnic relations is the presumption that the culture of newcomers is in some way alien and a potentially destabilising influence on the value consensus that is presumed to exist. It is also assumed that the host community will be willing to accommodate the newcomers, but the well-documented examples of racism tend to negate this assumption. Finally the model assumes that immigrant groups will wish to give up their distinctive culture, which they might not (Richardson and Lambert, 1985). There is also a clear notion of ethnocentrism in this idea, since it presumes that the indigenous culture (which is presumed to be homogeneous) is superior in some way to that of the newcomers and it is therefore their duty to adapt and fit in.

Exercise 9.4

Although the idea of assimilation is often considered to belong to the distant past, Billingham (1995) shows that it is still alive today, particularly in elements of the press. For example in 1989 the *Daily Mail* said that 'We must do nothing through legislation or the use of public money to preserve alien cultures and religions. Likewise, they must seek to be assimilated . . . They have chosen to dwell amongst us. In Rome do as the Romans do' (quoted in Trowler, 1995, p. 108).

 Suggest three reasons why this statement in the *Daily Mail* can be seen as supporting the assimilationist point of view.

In relation to Britain, Patterson (1965) used the notions of accommodation and assimilation in a study of Afro-Caribbean immigrants to Brixton, South London. She argues that the process can be understood in terms of an immigrant–host model where both are required to make accommodations. An important conclusion of the study is that immigrants are required to make more concessions than the host community. Her work is similar to that of the earlier Chicago School and functionalist research in that it argues that the host community is characterised by homogeneity, but one difference is her emphasis on the need for some adjustment by the host community. Although she found that the process of assimilation had not gone very far at the time of her research, she was optimistic about the future.

Exercise 9.5

1. Listed below are a number of evaluative statements on the assimilationist approach. Some gaps appear in the statements and you should fill these with words chosen from the list at the end. Then decide which of the statements are outlining the strengths and which the weaknesses of this approach.

2. Use this material and any other you are familiar with to write your own assessment of the approach (no more than 200 words).

(a) The notion of . . . . is potentially suggestive of the idea that newcomers suffer from . . . . This might be transformed into a theory that suggests the reason for racial inequality is the culture of racial minorities. This view has become more prevalent as the cultural version of the underclass thesis.

(b) The ideas were based on a number of actual . . . . surveys in Chicago and attempted to identify the central . . . . and self-concepts people held that led to racial conflict and prejudice.

(c) The whole approach is marred by the underlying assumption that society is characterised by a value . . . . This inevitably leads to the conclusion that this needs to be upheld, and that therefore . . . . need to adapt and . . . . with the majority.

(d) It has been suggested that the approach failed to distinguish between the different problems faced by white European immigrants to the United States and black Americans moving from the south. The construction of the United States as white meant that while . . . . might find assimilation possible, black Americans probably would not.

(e) The . . . . approach was based on an identification of racial and ethnic groups in clear social terms as opposed to the then prevailing notion of race as a . . . . category.

(f) The whole theorisation of racism is essentially in terms of individual attitudes and breakdowns in . . . . , reflecting the interactionist origin of the idea. The approach is therefore open to the criticism that it ignores the . . . . features of society, notably the inequalities of power, which are seen as a better explanation for racism.

(g) It might be argued that the suggestion that . . . . need to assimilate is racist, in that it is placing much more onus on one group to adapt than on the other. In this sense black people are viewed as the 'problem', rather than white people. Not surprisingly therefore, this approach has not been popular with later, more radical theories.

(h) The approach recognises that society is . . . . by the interactions of humans and is therefore centred on a notion of humans as . . . . constructors of their world. It reinforces the central message of sociology that society is a social construct.

Missing words:

- assimilation
- cultural deficit
- active
- communication
- biological
- constructed
- white immigrants
- ethnographic
- social action
- minorities
- black Americans
- meanings
- assimilate
- structural
- consensus

2. Cultural pluralism

The concept of 'cultural pluralism' was introduced by Horace Kallen (1924). He argued that American culture consists of the cultures of the various immigrant groups. While this perspective shares the assumption of a cultural value consensus, it suggests that separate ethnic identities might be maintained and therefore denies the need for assimilation. This approach avoids the implications of cultural inferiority and superiority that flows out of the assimilationist model. The approach describes the United States as moving towards cultural pluralism, and it is argued that such cultural pluralism needs to complement the pluralism in the US political system.

In relation to Britain, this trend emphasises the idea of the multicultural society. It is argued that Britain has always been a society with a multitude of cultures, reflecting the plurality of social groupings within it. Such a model allows for the possibility that conflict may occur between different social groupings and it can provide the basis for an explanation of racism. It also offers a potential solution to racism through the process of multicultural education, where everyone learns about the diverse cultures in modern Britain. Such an approach may foster understanding and tolerance, and thereby the integration of many cultures into a harmonious society, without the need for any of them to be subsumed under a presumed 'national culture', as in the assimilationist model. Although critical of the assimilationist approach, it centres on changing attitudes as the solution to racism.

Critics point out that this approach still requires immigrant groups to transform their culture and it is sometimes imbued with the notion that the culture of minority groups is in some way deficient (the cultural deprivation model).

3. Primordial and situational ethnicity

A second development in the sociology of ethnicity was debate about the meaning of the term ethnicity. As it was originally applied to immigrant groups moving to the United States, ethnicity was about the possession of a common culture (involving things such as religion and language) and common descent (common ancestral roots with those you identity yourself with). This view of ethnicity has been called the primordialist view since it appears to suggest that ethnic identity arises from a long-shared heritage and is in some way natural. The genuineness of ethnicity has been counterposed to the artificiality of the notion of race.

Such an approach has also arisen in what Martin Barker (1981) has called the 'new racism'. The basis of this is a definition of Britishness in cultural terms that acts to prevent ethnic and racial minorities from ever being seen as really British. Racism can therefore be disguised as patriotism and can exist without recourse to discredited notions of biological difference. Instead the nation is construed in cultural terms, but in such a way that Britishness effectively become whiteness, without ever actually having to use such a word. Different cultures are not overtly viewed as inferior, merely different, but since such differences are long-standing and almost permanent, people with different cultures can never really become British.

In contrast situational views of ethnicity tend to suggest that 'common descent' is not necessarily real, but is socially constructed. This development has allowed an important rethinking of the the notion of ethnicity and new theories based on the concept. These are very different from the old ethnicity/assimilation approach. Here ethnic groups arise from a sense of shared identity. However this might not be genuine or reflect a common descent. In this analysis, the important thing to discover is the ways in which ethnicity is constructed in particular situations. It is therefore seen as dynamic. It is also seen as something that may be relevant to all aspects of someone's identity, or only some parts of it. Ethnicity and ethnic identity are therefore flexible. This approach builds on the work of the anthropologist Frederick Barth (1959, 1969), who argues that the most important element to consider is the formation of boundaries between groups and the way these are constructed. This approach can be seen most recently in the work of Banton (1983, 1988) and Sandra Wallman (1979).

Wallman sees race as simply one of the ways in which boundaries might be constructed and therefore views it as a subset of ethnicity. The setting of boundaries reflects the resources and options available to groups at any one time. The problem with this is that while the situational notion of ethnicity demands that it be seen as flexible, it tends to be presented as almost universal, and therefore merges into the primordial notion of ethnicity (Solomos and Back, 1994). A second criticism of this approach is that it tends to view ethnic identity as a positive resource that can be used for boundary creation and maintenance. This ignores the fact that ethnic identification can be a negative thing, since it can also occur through the imposition of identities and therefore becomes a way of justifying oppression on ethnic or racial grounds (Rex, 1986a). Rex (1986b) further argues that the subject of ethnic conflict is missing from Barth's account, leading to a consensus view of society and ethnic relations, which Rex sees as accepting the *status quo* in ways similar to classical functionalism.

A further use of ethnicity has been proposed by Hall (1992). He argues that it is time to reappropriate the term from its meaning and usage in the early sociology of ethnicity. That is, the problems faced by black people were assumed to be the same as that of white immigrant workers. This was criticised by those who argued that racism would limit the possibility of assimilation by black groups and as such the ethnicity approach could not explain the position of black people. Implicit was the assumption that race was a subcategory of ethnicity. The concept of ethnicity is being resurrected in the light of criticism of the idea of black unity (which grew up in the 1970s and 1980s) for lumping together very diverse groups under the banner of 'black'. Hall suggests that the notion of ethnicity within the category of black might be a useful way around this. Ethnicity in this sense becomes a subcategory of race understood purely as a social and ideological construction.

Exercise 9.6

[i][a] Explain in your own words the difference between primordial and situational ethnicity and provide one example of each.

4. Foucault and the return to Weberian social action theory

Jenkins (1994) argues that in recent years there has been an important shift in the work of thinkers such as Barth (1984, 1989), who has moved away from the interactionist approach and back towards a standard Weberian social action approach. The reason for this is the adoption of a notion of history as something that constrains actions. Jenkins uses this, along with others such as discourses derived from Foucault (1980), to argue that there needs to be a shift of emphasis in ethnicity models from the past concern with self-ascription and self-identification (looking at how people identify themselves) to a greater emphasis on external categorisation (how people are categorised by others) in ethnic relations. He therefore argues that the concept of power to devise and impose classifications needs to be incorporated into the study of ethnic groups. This can be done by incorporating Weber's concept of power and authority into the classification of ethnicity.

The importance of this is that Jenkins is able to deal with the main drawback of the interactionist-based approaches – the complete absence of any notion of power. His model includes both macro sociological notions of power (from Weber) and micro conceptions of power (from Foucault). This brings his model close to the racial formation approaches by viewing identity as changeable and dynamic, but it scores over the interactionist approach by incorporating a notion of power.

The Weberian notion of social action also lies at the heart of John Rex's (1986a) approach to the study of race relations. However his theory is an attempt to relate social action to the structural features of society, and therefore his work will be considered under the heading 'structures of racism explanations'.

Evaluation of the ethnicity approach

The underlying theme of this approach is social interaction and the way this constructs meanings. Consequently it draws on anthropological studies and applies the concept of ethnicity to relations between groups in advanced industrial societies.

The key benefit of the approach is that it breaks with the notion that race is a biological reality. The criticisms of the approach are however increasing in number. Firstly it is argued that analysing 'race' as a particular type of ethnicity tends to risk confusing two different processes. Since the approach was first developed to explain relations between white Americans and white European immigrants, it failed to grasp the racial aspects of discrimination faced by black Americans and Afro-Caribbean migrants to Britain. Crucially, the approach failed to take into account the historical experiences of black people, notably the experience of slavery and colonialisation.

Secondly it is argued that while the whole concept of ethnicity is invoked to place social and cultural processes at the centre of the stage, some of the terminology used can lead to confusion. For example, although the early theorists tended not to distinguish between white immigrants and black migrants within the United States, they still tended to use the terms race and ethnicity. If one explanation suits both, why use both terms. This problem can be seen with the term 'race relations'. If race is conceived purely as a social and cultural construction, then it is clearly by definition a relational matter, and the term race relations becomes a mere tautology.

The third criticism of this approach is that it sees black people as a problem. This is particularly clear with the assimilationist approach, which assumes the existence of value consensus in society. It also assumes that slavery led to the destruction of black culture (Sowell, 1983). Although Sowell uses this notion to point to the great advances black people have made, bearing in mind their experience of slavery, the assumption of some kind of cultural deficit is still there. This process of acculturation has been questioned and some have argued that black Americans retain a cultural heritage.

The main problems with the assimilationist approach can be addressed by adopting the cultural pluralist approach, but this still focuses on culture.

More recent studies in the field of ethnicity have tried to deal with these criticisms but they remain rooted in an analysis that has culture at the centre of the explanations, and are thus open to the criticism that they ignore the structural aspects of inequality.

Structures of racism explanations

Proponents of the structural approach to the study of ethnic and racial inequality reacted against the interactionist-driven ethnicity and race relations approaches because they incorporated no notion of power, and as a result no explicit notion of the way that racism has been a structural feature of society and may affect interactions between social groups. There are two broad structural approaches, deriving from Weberian and Marxist frameworks.

1. Weberian analysis

The Weberian-inspired approach can be seen in the work of John Rex (Rex, 1970, 1986a, 1986b; Rex and Moore, 1967; Rex and Tomlinson, 1979). Rex and Moore (1967), in a study conducted in Birmingham, located race relations within the social structural issue of housing allocation and argued that different ethnic groups constituted different housing classes. The reason for this was racism, leading to immigrants being allocated inferior housing. Specifically, the local council adopted a policy of allocating houses on the basis of length of residence, and due to their recent arrival immigrants received inferior housing.

Rex and Tomlinson (1979), in their study of Birmingham, also argued that ethnic minorities were incorporated into employment in different ways from the ethnic majority. They said that there was a dual labour market and ethnic minority groups were largely represented in the secondary labour market, which offered insecure, poorly paid work. Therefore ethnic minorities constituted an underclass that was distinct from the ethnic majority, and their lack of participation in traditional working-class political organisations further enforced their separation.

Both these studies went beyond consideration of culture and interaction to incorporate an understanding of the way racial discrimination had become a structural feature of British society. What Rex meant by structure were the actions of the state both nationally and locally and the intervention of the state in society, through things such as the planned economy and the welfare state. Race relations therefore emerged as a result of the intersection of economic and political factors in society.

His conclusion was that welfare rights were often denied to immigrant groups, leaving them with the worst housing, jobs and schools: 'To some extent, therefore I saw them as constituting an underclass in the specifically British sense of those who did not benefit from incorporation in the welfare state' (Rex, 1986a). Since they did not share in the rewards of the white working class and did not generally identify with its culture and organisation, they were separate in the sense of developing their own organisations, committed either to achieving social mobility or to the construction of a black identity.

The notion of class utilised here is clearly Weberian, in that it is about the distribution of economic rewards (either through the marketplace or the welfare state) rather than the Marxist notion of class as an objective position in relation to the means of production.

Rex has pointed out that since the time of his studies in Birmingham, some important changes have occurred, notably the cut-back of the welfare state. As a result many white people have found themselves in the underclass, along with the ethnic minorities who remain there. This, he argues, might encourage the formation of class unity between black and white, or it might encourage whites forced down into the underclass to compete against the ethnic minorities, which could lead to racial conflict (Rex, 1986a). He also argues that this change means that the term underclass as a description of the position of ethnic minorities is now overstating the break between them and white people, and that there is an overlap between the structural situation of whites and that of ethnic minorities. He calls this the pyramid model (Rex, 1986b; see also Taylor et al., 1995).

2. Marxist analysis

A similar focus on structural factors to account for the inferior social position of ethnic minorities is advanced by Marxist sociologists, though here the crucial structure is the capitalist economy.

Racism is seen as promoted by the state (both of which are viewed as instruments of the bourgeoisie) to divide the working class, force though cuts in wages and resist demands for improved working conditions. Racism as a specific ideology based on the notion of the inferiority of some biologically identified groups is seen as developing only with the rise of capitalism. Racist ideas have the effect of masking the basic conflict in society between the bourgeoisie and the proletariat by posing the idea that there are differences, based on race, between groups of workers.

A prominent Marxist explanation of racism is provided by Robert Miles (1982, 1984, 1989). Miles argues that racism needs to be central to the analysis of ethnic relations in capitalism and this means we should dispense with the notion of race. Use of this term opens up the danger of legitimating the idea that there are real biological entities called races and justifying some form of racism.

Racism is seen as an ideology (both in the sense of a set of ideas, and in the sense that these are false) that is actively constructed by some people. The question is why? According to Miles, this ideology can be explained by capitalism's need for a global labour force. This leads to the process of migration in the first place, but also to the need to define citizenship and its associated rights, and racial notions provide a means to do this. At the same time it divides the working class and lessens the chance of a united working-class challenge to capitalism. Miles also claims that black nationalism with its attempt to invert the negative characteristics associated with black into positive ones, poses the potential danger that divisions of race will be seen as real.

In relation to this, Banton (1987) has argued that since the notion of race has been shown to be false, we should no longer talk of racism since this rests on the belief that races are real. Miles strongly disagrees with this position: 'One therefore has the choice of concluding either that racism has disappeared, as Banton and others have done, or that the definition of racism should be revised in order to express the claim that racism is an ideology that takes a number of forms' (Miles, 1989).

Miles believes that the standard definition of racism as prejudice plus power, which suggests that only white people can be racist since only they have power, is wrong. He argues that this, plus the development of the notion of institutional racism, are examples of the way the concept of racism has been inflated, and this is not helpful. The notion of racism has become so wide as to almost encompass the whole of stratification and it risks obscuring other divisions in society. He suggests that many working-class people falsely rationalise their situation by recourse to racism, and this is an example of the way it serves as a common-sense ideology. More importantly, it diverts attention away from the real source of the problem, capitalism.

In order to explain the social processes from which racism emerges (which Miles claims the race relations approach fails to do) he utilises the concept of racialisation developed by Franz Fanon (1967, 1986). This involves the study of processes where significance is attached to certain biological differences to define and construct social collectivities. The important thing is that this process has varied over time and therefore racism needs to be studied in relation to concrete circumstances.

Racism hides the reality of economic relations and allows certain fractions of the working class to be racialised. It therefore splits the working class. Miles argues that the same effect can be caused by expanding the politics of race beyond a concern with fighting racism. In other words, black nationalist and separatist black political movements also have the effect of splitting the working class. The view remains Marxist since it sees economic relations as fundamental, but recognises the effect racism can have and utilises the concept of racialisation to stress the dynamic nature of racism.

In a critique of this position, Anthias (1990, 1992) states that Miles' argument is essentially a variant of the 'false consciousness' argument about ideology and she rejects his attempt to relate racism to class categories. She stresses the centrality of the concepts of nation and ethnicity in understanding racial formation. She also disagrees with Miles' argument that we can dispense with the concept of race. While she agrees that race and racism need to be separated, she argues that Miles' identification of racism as an ideology (not actions) based on biological difference excludes the concept of inferiority based on supposed cultural differences. Here again she argues for the need for a concept of ethnicity to encompass these divisions.

Miles explains the position of black workers in Britain by Marxist class analysis, whereby class is an objective structure that exists whether people recognise it or not. Miles argues that all the evidence on the positioning of black migrant workers shows that they are disproportionately represented in the lower end of the class structure. Therefore it is not enough to argue that they are working class and to ignore the differences between white and black workers as some other Marxists have tended to do (for example Westergaard and Resler, 1975). Instead black workers have to be seen as a fraction of the working class. Marxist analysis shows that all classes are fractionalised, and black workers provide one example of this (women are cited as another example).

This approach has implications for the combatting of racism. Firstly, since Marxists assert that racism is a set of ideas that arises from the economic structures of capitalism, and more importantly only arose with capitalism, the way to eliminate racism is to destroy the system that created it, namely capitalism.

Miles' idea of class fractions can be contrasted with the notion that there are permanent structural divisions within the working class, as suggested by Castles and Kosack (1973). They see the working class as permanently divided by racism, and in this case the idea that black workers form an underclass is more likely.

ITEM A

According to *The Economist* (1 October 1994) it costs $35 per hour to employ a production worker in Germany, compared with $5 in South Korea and $0.50 in China, Indonesia and India.

ITEM B

The World Development Movement (1996) broke down the cost of a £50 pair of Nike trainers as follows:

Retailer's costs and profits	£23.00
Nike's costs and profits	£16.39
Materials	£6.56
Administration and overheads	£2.01
Subcontractor's profits	£0.85
Labour	£1.19

ITEMS A AND B *Exercise 9.7*

[i] 1. With reference to Item A, calculate the number of production workers it is possible to employ in China for an hour for the same cost as one production worker in Germany for an hour.

[i] 2. With reference to Item B, calculate the percentage of the price of a pair of trainers that is paid to the labourer who makes them.

[i][a][e] 3. To what extent do you agree that these examples provide evidence of the exploitation of Third World workers.

In contrast Miles implies that, while racism creates real divisions within the working class, these divisions can be overcome and therefore a united working class, cleansed of racism, is still possible. In a study conducted in Willesden by Phizacklea and Miles (1980), about 75 per cent of the white working-class respondents made negative comments, albeit often vague, about black people, usually in relation to housing and employment. The authors argue that while this illustrates a substantial degree of racism, it can also be seen as one of the ways in which the white working class has understood (however mistakenly) the effect of economic recession caused by capitalism. The reality of financial shortages and material inequalities formed the basis of their beliefs. Such views cannot be countered simply by a campaign to change attitudes, since this would do nothing to remove the material inequality at the heart of the problem. Racism can therefore only be overcome by a radical class consciousness that deals with both the causes (material inequalities) and the racism they create.

Miles is also critical of the Weberian approach of John Rex (1970, 1986a, 1986b). He argues that by using the category of immigrant, Rex's work contains a trace of the host–immigrant model, even though Rex rejected that model. More importantly, the term immigrant is not accompanied by analysis of the reason why black people moved here: they were concerned to find jobs, and were encouraged to come to

Britain to help remedy the labour shortage. It is this process that Miles sees as central to explaining the position of black workers in Britain. He argues that the Weberian emphasis on distribution (via the welfare state) tends to depict black workers simply as the objects of racial discrimination. This obscures their position as workers, which affects their attitudes and behaviour.

3. Neo-Marxism and autonomy from class

The usefulness of the Marxist class framework for explaining ethnic and racial inequalities led to a debate among Marxist-oriented sociologists. Neo-Marxist writers tend to argue that racial inequality and racism have a greater degree of autonomy from the processes of class formation and class exploitation than Miles allows for. The best exposition of this view came from the Centre for Contemporary Cultural Studies (CCCS, 1982). They relate the racialisation of political debate in Britain in the 1970s to the crisis, both economic and ideological, of capitalism at that time. In the 1970s economic crisis hit much of the advanced industrial world, accompanied by mass unemployment and high inflation. Although their analysis is Marxist in orientation, it draws largely on Gramsci (1971) and Althusser (1971) and therefore places more emphasis on how ideas such as racism can operate with some degree of autonomy from strictly economic factors. The authors argue that racism has to be interpreted within a framework of political, cultural and ideological factors as well as economic ones.

However they differ from other approaches in their treatment of the sociology of race relations, which they attack for portraying ethnic minorities as suffering from cultural deprivation. The whole race relations approach, they argue, sees ethnic minorities as passive victims rathern than active creators of their own destiny, and the problem with this approach is that it leads to notions of cultural deprivation that are popular among the new right, especially the cultural version of the underclass thesis, as expounded by Charles Murray (1984). According to the CCCS, black people in the Britain should instead be seen as active citizens for whom the official structures of the race relations industry are an irrelevance.

In the CCCS approach, then, race is seen as relatively autonomous of class relations but remains subject to the laws of capitalist development. The authors argue that there is a need to consider the ideological and cultural processes that arise out of this and led to race being created as a social problem in 1970s Britain. Racism is seen as a central element of the attempt to deal with the economic crisis of that era, but the resulting racism, racial inequality and the responses to it cannot be seen purely as part of a class struggle. According to Gilroy (1982), approaches based on class struggle tend to ignore those cultural factors that cannot be seen as simply epiphenomena (that is, things that are direct reflections of something else and have no autonomy or causal power of their own) of the economic class struggle. Secondly, such an approach, with its emphasis on the workplace, cannot capture the struggles taking place in the local community or among the unemployed.

The CCCS analysis builds on the earlier work of Hall (1978, 1980), who argued that the important thing to consider is how racism is relatively autonomous from other social relations. Nonetheless it still has an impact upon those relations, which has led it to take specific historical forms. This implies the need to consider several racisms rather than just one form of racism. The notion that racism is multifaceted and actively constructed in the midst of changing circumstances was a key influence in the later development of racial formation approaches.

Since the publication of its 1982 work the centrality of Marxism in CCCS analyses has been largely replaced by postmodernist notions. This has been evident in the increasing stress on the autonomy of racism and a greater focus on cultural factors to explain it, leading to attempts to reappropriate the concept of culture from the view presented in cultural versions of the underclass thesis. The fixed nature of culture in the underclass version is challenged by the postmodern view of culture as a fluid and dynamic entity. These ideas have been utilised to provide an alternative analysis that is not rooted in primordialist (long ago in history) notions of ethnicity. Nor does it reduce ethnic and racial relations to passive reflections of the wider class structure. This will be examined in the section entitled 'Racial formation approaches'.

4. Autonomy and post-Marxism

The trend away from structural analyses in the wake of post-structuralist ideas can be seen in the rise of post-Marxist ideas. These are not really structural but they do show the end point of some debates that started within the Marxist approach.

This presents notions of racism as more autonomous of class relations than the relative autonomy to be seen in the neo-Marxist approaches. Gabriel and Ben-Tovim (1978, 1986) argue that the notion of relative autonomy still locates the struggle against racism in an economic framework and is therefore 'economistic'. Instead it is necessary to consider racism as the product of struggles that go beyond the economic struggle.

For Solomos (1986) this drift towards pluralism is dangerous. Although he supports the general proposition that it is necessary to locate racism and antiracism in concrete local struggles, he considers that a more developed notion is needed of how the structures of capi-

ITEM C

Racial designations preferred by blacks in detroit

	1968	1971
Coloured	12	6
Negro	59	38
Black, Afro-American or Black-American	23	53
Other	6	3

(Source: Banton, 1985.)

ITEM C   *Exercise 9.9*

[i] 1. In Item C, which racial designation had the greatest support in 1968 and in 1971?

[i][a] 2. Suggest reasons for the changing level of support for each designation.

[i][a] 3. Suggest some labels that might be included in the 'Other' category.

While often drawing on Marxism, black nationalists criticised Marxism as Eurocentric, that is, it was developed on the basis of the European experiences and assumed that this was an adequate reflection of all experiences. Robinson (1983) argues that Marxism as a product of Europe has failed to provide an adequate analysis of racism and that black intellectuals such as W. E. B. Du Bois, Richard Wright and C. L. R. James have had to draw on Africa for an alternative tradition of ideas and resistance.

Ultimately black nationalism rested on the idea that all white people were inherently and irredeemably racist. It posited an unbridgeable division between black and white. This cut across the Marxist analysis, which sees class as the key division, and as a result the approach has been criticised by Marxists.

Firstly, Marxists have argued that as a political strategy it was a non-starter. Alexander (1987) writes that black people account for about 11 per cent of the US population, but despite this large representation organisations such as the Black Panthers were suppressed and destroyed, so if black nationalists could not achieve their aims in the United States, it is unlikely they could do so in Britain, where the ethnic minority population is only about 5 per cent.

What these accounts share is the construction of 'nation' on a cultural basis. They serve to illustrate the reemergence of the centrality of culture in analysis. This idea can best be seen in the work Paul Gilroy (1987, 1992, 1993). Gilroy argues that we need to consider the process of race formation, in which the meanings of race and racism are open to contestation and therefore racial messages can change. He rejects any unitary notion of racism and instead talks about racisms.

In relation to political struggle, Gilroy suggests that the language of class analysis cannot provide a basis for mobilisation since it is too closely linked to production and represents only a minority of the possible bases for identity that people have. He also argues that antiracism is problematic, not only because it operates on the basis that black people's existence is determined solely by racism, but also because it is based on absolute and unchanging notions of race. The way that antiracism is often bureaucratically implemented may lead to a backlash. Central to the struggle against racism are the new social movements, since they are based on the local community and retain autonomy from the local state.

Gilroy emphasises that culture needs to be understood not in absolute terms, as is the case with new racism and some variants of antiracism, but as fluid and heterogeneous (composed of many different elements). Culture is syncretic, that is, the result of complex interactions between different groups (Gilroy, 1993).

This approach undermines the attempt of new racism to construct Britishness as a culturally homogeneous and fixed commodity. The fluid and syncretic nature of culture is stressed, as is the way in which contemporary culture both transforms and builds upon earlier notions of resistance to racism and thus allows the construction of culture and cultural resistance to be seen as central to political resistance, both to racism and to other oppressive structures.

Culture is also a central element in postmodernist analysis and this can be seen in a number of works. Rattansi and Westwood (1994) consider the way in which postmodern ideas concentrate on breaking up the notion of structure and how social structures are actually 'constructs' of various discourses. This can help us to understand the active construction and formation of racial and ethnic identities, and the way these have been transformed by the process of globalisation. The construction and reinvention of the notion of 'the West' and the implications of this for changing patterns of racial formation and identity are seen as important elements that need to be considered.

The artificial and constructed nature of categories such as black and white are also considered by Donald and Rattansi (1992). They examine how class, gender, ethnicity and race intersect and how static conceptions of ethnicity are problematic. There is a need to study the historical specificity of the many types of racism, all reflecting socially constructed identity and social categorisations. However Brah (1992) points to the potential problems with the notion of difference, which is a central concept of postmodernism. It arose in the attempt to avoid all struggles being reduced to one theory, notably versions of Marxism. However the problem is that if difference is taken to its full conclusion, oppressed groups will be fragmented. Some have therefore argued for a joining together, rather than emphasising difference, in order to create a political alliance. The problem here is, on what basis? The use of the word black as a unifying political symbol led to arguments about whether it should include those of Asiatic origin and to debates between white and black feminists. Once the concept of difference is used, it is difficult to avoid a headlong rush into fragmentation. If the aim is self-identity this is fine, but if the aim is to fashion a political movement to challenge racism and change society, then collective mobilisation is required.

The concept of difference can be employed not only to differentiate struggles against racism from struggles against capitalism but also to identify differences between ethnic and racial minorities. Here the question of identity is central. Do people describe themselves as black, Afro-Caribbean, Afro-American, African-American, African-Caribbean, Asian or something else, and are there important differences between the groups so identified? This point can be linked to developments in the feminist movement.

This has led to the growth of what has been called identity politics, where groups are formed around specific identities to defend their cultural autonomy. The problem with this is that it promotes fragmentation, and therefore strategies based on a culture of resistance may divide rather than unite black people (Callinicos, 1993). Furthermore, as Goldberg (1994) argues, although the use of concepts such as identity and difference have some use, they are also problematic. Identity can be exclusionary as well as inclusionary.

Solomos (1993) has argued that while we should consider the postmodernist approaches to race and ethnicity, they are highly abstract and theoretical are hence cannot explain the development of racial and ethnic identities in specific locations. He says there is a need for more local empirical research, which is what he has done in Birmingham and his work arguably fits into the second approach – focusing on political struggle as the key factor in racial formation. Omi and Winant's work in the United States (1994) is perhaps the best known example of this approach.

Exercise 9.10

As we have seen, the idea that culture is at the heart of contemporary racial theories can be found in a number of works.

 1. Draw up a list of the differences between the accounts given by the new right, black nationalists and Gilroy (1987, 1992, 1993). (For instance those in the new right tend to view culture as arising from past traditions and tend to adopt a more static view of culture than Paul Gilroy's notion of syncretic culture, which implies almost constant modification and interchange as the basis of culture.)

2. Consider how Robert Miles (1989) would respond to the arguments of the new right, black nationalism and Paul Gilroy and write a short critique of them based on his work.

 3. Consider how Michael Banton (1987) would respond to the three arguments and write a short critique of them based on his work.

2. Racial formation: stress on politics

The most influential example of this approach is that by Omi and Winant (1994), who have popularised the term 'racial formation'. Their work contains a particular interpretation of that process, and they focus on the way the state, through political and legal relations, has caused the existence of racial categories.

They refer to a court case in Louisiana in the United States, where a woman unsuccessfully petitioned the state authorities to have the racial classification on her birth certificate changed. She was classified black because of a 1970 law which declared that anyone with at least '1/32nd Negro blood' was black. This reflects the legacy of slavery and sexual liaisons between white slaveowners and slaves. The fact that such classifications were made more than 100 years after slavery was abolished shows 'how the racial legacies of the past – slavery and bigotry – continue to shape the present . . . It demonstrates how deeply Americans both as individuals and as a civilisation are shaped, and indeed haunted, by "race"' (Omi and Winant, 1994).

This example highlights the involvement of state authorities in defining race and their central involvement in the process of racial formation. It is for this reason that Omi and Winant disagree with those (notably Miles) who argue that we should dispense with the concept of race. They say that while it does not hold up as a scientific category, it still exists in the real world and plays an important part in structuring the world. The court case cited above is a prime example of this. Race exists because of the process of racial formation which Omi and Winant define as 'the sociohistorical process by which racial categories are created, inhabited, transformed and destroyed'.

This means that racial formation is part of both the social structure and the culture of society. Omi and Winant suggest that the difficulties arise when we see racial formation as either structural or cultural. Structural approaches are unable to explain the origins or transformation of racial difference, while cultural accounts seem unable to comprehend structural phenomena such as racial stratification in the jobs market.

Racial formation theory sets out to provide a link between micro analysis and macro analysis. Omi and Winant argue that state policy on such issues as affirmative action (positive discrimination) is not fixed but arises from the legacy of previous political contests, and is therefore itself a political struggle. This is affected by the way people think about race in common-sense terms, which is in turn affected by notions of race embedded in the social structure, for example in the law 'ideological beliefs have structural consequences, and that social structures give rise to beliefs' (Omi and Winant, 1994).

It is therefore important to consider the way in which race and racism are developed and used in social interactions and the social structures that underlie these beliefs. This leads to the idea that race and racism have changed over time, and as fluid entities they can be fought over. Using Gramsci's (1971) notion of hegemony, Omi and Winant (1994) suggest that racial rule in the United States has shifted over time from being based on coercion to being based more on consent. This is not to say that coercion no longer exists, or that its legacy has disappeared, since the common-sense ideas of today are buttressed by structural legacies from the past, for instance the legacy of slavery in the United States.

By arguing that racism has changed in form, Omi and Winant (1994) are also arguing against the black nationalist notion of an unchanging white racism. They reject both the argument that racism is only engaged in by white people in relation to black people and the definition of racism as prejudice plus power, since (1) it is not true to say that racial minorities have no power and (2) white people are sometimes the victims of racism, for example Jewish people.

They go on to argue that there are many types of racism. The arguments of the black leader Louis Farrakhan meet their criteria for a racist discourse. However his arguments do not fit as easily into the hegemonic racial formation of the United States as those of white supremacists.

Politics is central to Back and Solomos' analysis of race and racism in Britain (Back and Solomos, 1992; Solomos and Back, 1994, 1995). Solomos (1993) argues that we should consider the impact of the growth of racist ideologies and of various discourses such as antiracism and British nationalism, the latter often being seen as the basis of the new racism. We should examine how these discourses have affected political action, for example the way that racial discourse often relies on the perceived threat that the black community poses to national homogeneity, rather than overt references to biological notions of superiority. He also argues that we should extend our consideration of politics beyond the conventional terrain of the nation-state and refer to the actions of local communities and new social movements.

He considers that the CCCS (1982) analysis should be supplemented by more concrete questions about how the British political structure serves to reproduce or overcome racism, influences how racism is formed and transformed, and determines how racism shapes or affects other social relations, for example those concerned with class and gender.

In all these respects Solomos argues that we should conduct studies at the local level, which can then provide the basis for more generalised accounts. Such research is necessary to counteract the abstract nature of some theories of race and racism.

In relation to political mobilisation by black and Asian groups, Solomos thinks it is likely that both struggles based on community organisations (as emphasised by Gilroy) and attempts to gain recognition through the Labour Party (for example through the Labour Party's Black sections) will continue to be important. In their study of the politics of race in Birmingham, Solomos and Back observed the actions of black and Asian groups who were trying to gain representation inside the Labour Party, as well as the actions of councillors. They focused in particular on Small Heath, where black people and Asians (mainly of Pakistani origin) make up nearly half the population and much of the membership of the local Labour Party. There was a debate about whether an Asian candidate should be selected to replace the retiring Labour MP, and Solomos and Back describe the way the Labour Party dealt with the affair, leading to a white trade unionist being selected as parliamentary candidate (Back and Solomos 1992; Solomos and Back 1995).

The racial formation approaches: an evaluation

Strengths

This approach clearly allows us to consider the way that racial and ethnic identities are fluid and are constructed through social interaction, either through cultural exchanges or political and legal judgments.

Exercise 9.11

 Write your own summary of other strengths of this approach to complete this section.

Weaknesses

First in many instances the ideas are developed at a very abstract level, despite the authors' often avowed belief that the different types of racism need to be studied in their specific historical contexts. As a result, very little empirical work has so far developed from this approach.

Second, the centrality of postmodernist notions leads to a downplaying of the importance of structural factors. While the emphasis on the way structures are created and transformed is important and acts as a corrective to structuralist accounts, which tend to view humans as mere dupes and therefore eliminate all notions of human agency, the postmodernist emphasis on fluidity and contingency arguably does not sufficiently capture the way some structures survive and continue to have an impact.

Third, in some works the concern with identity sometimes occurs at the expense of more mundane material facts of inequality.

Fourth, strategies for dealing with racism are not always provided. This is not true of some, for example Solomos, Back and Gilroy are clear about the need for local political action, though they seem to differ on what that might be, from community-based new social movements (Gilroy) to the local state and political parties (Solomos and Back). However the more postmodernist-influenced accounts talk in rarefied terms of differences, discourse and identity, but seem to offer no clear strategy. Perhaps this is a result of the postmodernist view that it is impossible and/or dangerous to provide or attempt to arrive at generalised pictures of the whole of society, but presumably it would be possible to develop some local narratives, that is, to provide some concrete strategy based on these ideas.

Exercise 9.12

1. Add to, amend or disagree with this list of weaknesses.

2. Write your own evaluative conclusion of the strengths and weaknesses of the racial formation approach.

Exam question

The following question is taken from the Interboard Syllabus Summer 1995 examination. Use material from this chapter and other material you are familiar with to answer this question.

ITEM D

Male and female earnings

In 1983, women's average full-time earnings were only two-thirds of men's. One reason for this is that men tend to work longer basic hours than women, even when women are engaged in full-time work. A second reason lies in the effects of overtime, since men work substantially more overtime than women. A third reason why women's weekly earnings are on average lower than men's is that women tend to be concentrated in low-paying industries and in sexually segregated occupations.

(Source: Adapted from Veronica Beechey, 1986, 'Women's Employment in Contemporary Britain', in Beechey and Whitelegg, Women In Britain Today.)

White and Black workers earnings

White men on average earn a good deal more than black men, although the differences between the groups of women is much less. A study conducted in the early 1970s found that non-manual ethnic minority workers earned 77 per cent of the earnings of their white colleagues; skilled manual earned 89 per cent; while for semi-skilled and unskilled manual workers the earnings were the same. However, in this last case, in order to achieve this equality of earnings, ethnic minority workers have to do more shift work because their jobs are intrinsically worse paid. These differences derive from a number of factors. For example, black workers are concentrated in certain industries which traditionally pay low wages. Again, it is the case that in certain occupations, older people are paid more than younger ones. The black population is younger than the white, and this will in itself depress wages. Further, within any broad socio–economic category, white workers tend to occupy more promoted positions. But lastly, having eliminated all these factors, black workers seem to be paid less than white ones simply because they are black.

(Source: Adapted from Abercrombie and Warde et al., Contemporary British Society, 1994.)

Questions

(a) Using Item D, describe in your own words two reasons why full-time women workers earn less on average than full-time male workers. *(4 marks)*

(b) Using the information in Item E, outline the reasons for differences in earnings between white and black workers. *(4 marks)*

(c) Identify and explain two other areas of social life where black people suffer disadvantage. *(6 marks)*

(d) Critically assess sociological explanations of racism which seek to show why 'black workers seem to be paid less than white ones simply because they are black' (Item E). *(16 marks)*

10 Age, disability, locality and inequality

By the end of this chapter you should:

- be aware that there are important causes of inequality other than class, gender and ethnicity;
- be familiar with the various aspects of age inequality in contemporary British society and understand the way in which theories of age inequality have developed;
- be familiar with the various aspects of inequality caused by disability in contemporary British society and understand the way in which concern about inequality caused by disability has developed;
- be familiar with the various aspects of regional or locational inequality in contemporary British society and understand the way in which theories of locational inequality have developed.

Introduction

There are other aspects of structured social inequality that need to be considered in an overall account of social stratification, not all of which can be covered in this book. This chapter seeks to consider age, disability and locality as causes of inequality and how these interact with and modify patterns of inequality based on the more familiar class, gender and ethnicity.

Age and inequality

Harriet Bradley (1996) refers to age as the neglected dimension of inequality and there is no doubt that there is some truth in this, albeit something she and other sociologists are seeking to rectify.

The easiest way to investigate how age affects inequality is to compare the status and material resources allocated to the oldest members of society. Vincent (1995) quotes the example of the Tiwi Aborigines of northern Australia, where the greatest status and power is accorded to male elders. As such this tribal society can be described as a gerontocracy (rule by the eldest). A similar example is provided by Bradley (1996) in relation to the Beaver tribe in North-West Canada, where because of their experience the elders are treated as a valuable social resource.

In contrast, in relation to Britain, Oppenheim and Harker (1996) show that while those over pension age accounted for 18 per cent of the population in 1993, they made up 21 per cent of the poor (those living on less than 50 per cent of average earnings) and the value of the state pension that many of them had to survive on fell from 23.2 per cent of average earnings in 1979 to 17.5 per cent in 1994. This indicates that in Britain the elderly are overrepresented among the poor and government action in the 1980s and 1990s has meant that their financial resources have fallen compared with younger groups in work. Insofar as this reflects the status and value society places on the elderly in this country, it contrasts sharply with the examples from other societies quoted above.

This points to the basic but important sociological observation that since the status of the elderly varies across societies, the treatment of different age groups cannot be seen as natural or to flow inevitably from biological wear and tear – they must be socially constructed. The same biological phenomena – the process of aging and being chronologically old – elicit two different social responses that need to be explained. Inequality in old age, just like other bases of inequality such as race and sex, is assumed to be biological but is in fact social, so we need to consider age as a cause of inequality and an important part of the study of social stratification. Or as Harris (1987) puts it, age only assumes significance through a social process of imputing characteristics to various age groups and of itself has no intrinsic significance.

1. The effect of age on social inequality

The examples given in the literature suggest a broadly evolutionary process, whereby in preindustrial societies the elderly were valued but since industrialisation and the rise of the work ethic, those who do not work (including the elderly) are no longer accorded high status. Such an evolutionary view oversimplifies the reality of the way age brings social inequality. Fennell *et al.* (1988) show that there was in fact a fair degree of variation in the treatment of the elderly in preindustrial societies, undermining simple linear evolutionary theories. They also suggest that age combines with other bases of social inequality such as class, gender and ethnicity, so that only some old people will experience the problems of poverty associated with old age. For instance according to Oppenheim and Harker (1996), while 73 per cent of male full-time workers have occupational pensions, only 68 per cent of female full-time workers and 31 per cent of female part-time workers have one. This inequality during the working life will affect their standard of living after retirement.

We will therefore explore sociological work on age stratification while bearing in mind that it does not act totally independently of other causes of social inequality.

Age and paid employment

For most of us, in order to survive above the very basic level we need to work, and here age plays an important part. Kohli (1991) suggests that our society is characterised by a powerful three-fold age division, defined in relation to work, namely pre-work, work, post-work. The length of the pre-work stage is largely determined by compulsory schooling and may be extended by post-compulsory education. What characterises this period is economic dependence on parents and perhaps the state through student grants (if they haven't disappeared by the time you read this book). Work offers a period of economic independence, though the extent of this differs greatly. Arrival at the post-work stage is determined by the age of retirement, and for many it is a time of economic dependence on the state through the pension system. It is important to note that the growth of occupational pensions and the fact that these are very unequally distributed means that the extent of dependence on the state is unequal.

ITEM A

Percentage of jobs where employer provides benefits, by gender

	Male full-timers	Female full-timers	Female part-timers
Pensions*	73	68	31
Sick pay*	66	58	27
Paid time off	64	48	30
Unpaid time off	54	54	57
Company car or van	30	10	5
Free/subsidised transport	31	24	17
Goods at a discount	47	40	31
Free or subsidised meals	39	47	25
Finance/loans	21	20	12
Accommodation	14	17	5
Life assurance	39	19	5
Private health insurance	31	22	9
Recreation facilities	40	36	24
Maternity pay	n/a	31	16
Childcare	1	13	10

* In addition to the basic government scheme.

(Source: Oppenheim and Harker, 1996, p. 105.)

ITEM A **Exercise 10.1**

[i] 1. According to Item A, which groups are most likely to receive an occupational pension and which are least likely?

[i][a] 2. How do the inequalities shown in Item A modify the effect of age as a factor in structuring social inequality?

Vincent (1995) argues that although it is clear that age interacts with other causes of inequality, it can be seen as an independent factor in inequality since in the late 1980s, which was a period of prosperity for many in Britain, the rise in income among the elderly was on average not as great as that among the middle aged.

ITEM B

Average (median) disposable household income by age, per week

	Age of head of household				
	17–30	31–50	51–65	66–75	Over 75
Household expenditure (£s)					
1985	168.33	237.97	206.77	130.82	88.20
1992	229.07	321.81	243.57	142.18	98.38
Expenditure per capita (£s)					
1985	69.18	71.37	87.85	75.08	62.78
1992	103.91	105.26	116.52	87.67	71.89

(Source: Vincent, 1995, table 1.1, p. 23.)

ITEM B   *Exercise 10.2*

[i][a] 1. Explain in your own words the effect of age on household expenditure according to the figures shown in Item B.

[a] 2. How might the growth of occupational pensions change the figures in Item B over time?

[i][a] 3. Why do the figures for expenditure per capita (that is, per person) in Item B show a slightly different pattern from those for household expenditure?

[a] 4. Suggest reasons why those over 75 have considerably lower expenditure than those aged 66–75.

The majority of people's standard of living will be highest during the period of employment, and therefore in relation to age, during the middle part of their lives. Young people and old people are on average relatively disadvantaged, though it could be argued that young people suffer less from this as they can look forward to an improvement in the future, something that is largely denied to the elderly.

If Kohli (1991) is right about the three-fold age division, then there is an important debate to be had about the changing proportion of the population in each of the three stages. This reflects longer periods in education and longer life expectancy, but also the growing phenomenon of early retirement. Laczko and Phillipson (1991) report that in 1965, 90 per cent of men between 60 and 65 were working, but by the late 1980s this had fallen to 60 per cent and it would appear that this trend is continuing. In relation to this Vincent (1995, p. 61) comments: 'If the age of retirement keeps coming down and the average age of leaving education keeps going up, somewhere around the age of 38 they should eventually meet. This proposition, which is of course impossible, serves to caution against simple extrapolation of current trends into the future' (extrapolation is the process whereby current trends are extended into the future without further changes).

Exercise 10.3

Reread the quote from Vincent and answer the following questions:

i 1. At what age does Vincent suggest the age of retirement and the age of leaving education might eventually meet?

i *a* 2. Suggest reasons why Vincent says that this proposition is 'of course impossible'.

While Vincent points to the impossibility of the two points ever meeting, the duration of the pre-work and post-work stages is increasing, the latter made worse in the 1980s and 1990s by companies 'downsizing', that is, making people redundant. Some of the growth in early retirement is a result of this, since it is more expensive older employees and middle managers who have suffered most from 'downsizing'. This means that the proportion of the population dependent on pensions (either occupational or state) is increasing.

Old age therefore affects people's command over material resources, though it does so in a way that reproduces the inequalities affecting people earlier in their lives. Thus Victor and Evandrou (1987) argue that there is no evidence that class inequalities diminish with age, and the experience of old age is therefore structured by class. It is also affected by gender and ethnicity, as the following table from the United States shows (Item C).

ITEM C

Median income of persons aged 65 and older by age, race and sex in the United States, 1984 ($)

	All races	White	Black	Hispanic
Both sexes				
65–69	8 250	8 655	5 431	5 033
70+	6 556	6 889	4 217	4 754
Male				
65–69	11 837	12 180	7 079	6 551
70+	8 663	9 109	5 114	5 289
Female				
65–69	5 782	5 966	4 477	4 289
70+	5 540	5 765	3 850	4 346

(Source: Vincent, 1995, table 1.4, p. 29.)

i a e

Study Item C and assess the relative importance of age, gender and ethnicity as factors in social inequality.

The elderly and the future of the welfare state

The growth in the number of people of pensionable age has partly contributed to talk of the crisis of the welfare state. It is argued that the number of pensioners is increasing so rapidly that the working population will not be able to support them if the level of benefit and taxation remain constant. In many ways, talk of the increasing burden posed by the elderly has reached the level of a 'moral panic' (a situation where a perceived problem is blown up out of all proportion but serves to create pressure for action and change). One example of this was an article in the *Guardian* (27 March 1990), which talked of the possibility of the Third World War being a war between generations due to the resentment of young people at having to pay the increasing cost of caring for an increasing number of elderly people.

Johnson *et al.* (1989), writing from a new right perspective, argue that there will be an increasingly bitter battle between workers and pensioners, though Vincent (1995) sees this as an attempt to provide a justification for cutting back the welfare state, which has been government policy since 1979.

In contrast Hutton (1996) argues that the financial burden imposed by the elderly will not increase substantially. He quotes figures showing that, in order to maintain the current value of pensions in relation to average earnings, taxation needs to rise by 2.3 per cent of GDP by the year 2030, when the elderly will be at their largest as a proportion of the population.

Exercise 10.5

a

Why will the proportion of the population who are elderly fall after 2030?

Manning (1990) quotes research by the Organisation for Economic Cooperation and Development (OECD), which shows that the overall ratio of welfare dependents to contributors will remain fairly stable, since although the elderly are increasing in number, the number of children is declining. Taylor-Gooby (1996) makes a very similar point in relation to the fall in the number of young people dependent on state expenditure. The notion of a 'demographic timebomb', which suggests that the change in the structure of the population with the rise in the number of the elderly will in time create an intolerable pressure on society, is misplaced since between 1951 and 1991 the number of pensioners increased from 6.5 million to 10 million but this growth was absorbed without any major problems. This is made more significant by the real value of benefits more than doubling over this period. A rise in the number of the elderly is therefore something that has happened before and it did not cause the end of the welfare state.

Vincent (1995) argues that the question of welfare expenditure needs to be seen in terms of political decisions, and there remains the possibility of funding the increased expenditure on the elderly through cuts in other expenditure, for example defence. He provides evidence to show that expenditure on pensions is relatively low in Britain, amounting to only 7.7 per cent of the national income compared with 14.3 per cent in France and 16.9 per cent in Italy. His second point is that calculations of the increasing burden of expenditure on the elderly assume that only those born in this country will work here. This creates an artificial figure due the declining birth rate here. Migrants to this country will contribute to the national coffers, and he argues that ignoring this results in distorted figures. Finally he points out that if the productivity of workers in this country could be raised to the level that prevails in Germany, there would be no problem with paying larger pensions to the elderly.

Exercise 10.6

i *a* *e* 1. Explain in your own words the arguments for and against the proposition that the increasing proportion of the elderly in the population means we will no longer be able to afford to keep pensions at the present level.

e 2. Provide your own evaluative conclusion on this debate.

Youth and inequality

The previous section focused on the elderly and the inequalities they face from the way old age is socially constructed in our society. It must be remembered that as economic dependency is at the heart of these inequalities, this is also a problem faced by the young in our society. This section will therefore consider some evidence relating to the command over material resources by the young and the inequalities they face.

Youth and paid employment

Coles (1995) points out that the transition from pre-work to work, which is seen as the basis of the transition from youth to adulthood, was relatively unproblematic until recently. This is confirmed by Kiernan (1992), whose analysis of the longitudinal National Child Development Survey showed that in 1976, when those in the study reached 18, more than two thirds had a job. Coles (1995) also points out that

90 per cent of those who left school at 16 obtained a job within six months.

This picture changed with the subsequent rise in youth unemployment. Finn (1987) shows that in the late 1970s, while overall unemployment grew by 40 per cent, for those under 20 it grew by 120 per cent, and Ashton (1986) reports that in 1981 the unemployment rate among those under 25 reached 21.4 per cent.

It is probable that the lack of jobs is one of the factors that has encouraged young people to stay on in education, and the rise in unemployment among the young has led to the development of a plethora of training schemes and vocational educational initiatives, which add greater complexity to the route from youth to adulthood.

Exercise 10.7

|a| 1. Devise a questionnaire to give to students at your school or college about their experience of part-time jobs. Your survey should include questions about pay levels (bearing in mind that this may be a sensitive topic) and other benefits. You should also ask them what type of job they do and about the social characteristics of the other people who do these jobs.

|i||a||e| 2. Analyse the data by considering what it tells you about pay levels for young people, and whether female students take jobs that are predominantly undertaken by adult females or whether gender divisions break down. You can also look at ethnic and class divisions and see how these impact on part-time jobs for young people.

|a||e| 3. If you can, interview some people who have had experience of the government's Welfare to Work initiative and consider whether this scheme is qualitatively different from previous schemes, as the government claims.

Theories of age inequality

The earliest theories of age inequality derive from anthropological considerations of the difference between the treatment of the elderly in preindustrial societies and industrial societies. Such views were taken up by functionalist sociologists, who argued that there are a number of distinct life-stages with functions associated with each. This led to consideration of the number of these stages and the transition from one to another, the most famous accounts being those by Erickson (1965, 1982). The most fully developed version of this approach came to be known as disengagement theory.

In the 1970s and 1980s the approach came under criticism from Marxist-influenced thinkers who argued that the differing experiences and inequalities associated with age groups needed to be understood in the context of the structures of capitalism. However the Marxist approach has been criticised as seeing the elderly as merely victims.

Postmodernist analysis has focused on the great diversity of individual experiences, and the ways in which people can act to shape their bodies in the face of biological processes that were seen as inevitable in the past. Postmodernists have also emphasised that there has been a decrease in the importance of the transition stages that form the basis of age stratification. However those who argue that age is still important consider that age stratification needs to be approached from a life-course perspective.

This section investigates the theories relating to age stratification. The first focuses on socialisation and disengagement, centring on the process of socialisation as a key explanation of age inequalities. The second approach involves theories about capitalism and ageism and the third can be described as the life-course approach.

Age inequality – socialisation and disengagement

The functionalist Eisenstadt (1956) argues that age groups assume significance when society is organised around universalistic principles or general rules, in contrast to societies where particularistic principles determine integration. Thus age becomes important when kinship and place of origin is not the determining element of a person's place in society. In societies where all activities are organised in kinship groups, separation according to age group is rare since kin relationships determine everything. However in societies where life is not lived in kinship groups, there is room for age groups to assume some significance.

Take contemporary British society. When we are children our lives are centred on the family, but at some point we move out from this environment to work, go to university or form another family, at which point our place in society is no longer determined by family relationships. This is essentially arguing that age is more important in societies based on achievement (universalistic rules) than on ascription. The standard functionalist argument that such a move has largely occurred as a result of the growth of industrial society and the process of modernisation leads to the conclusion that age is more important now than it was in the past.

The second point Eisenstadt makes is that age groups contribute to integration and stability in society, another classic functionalist idea. They effectively operate as a link between the narrow kinship group and the much wider society. Youth is seen as an important transitional stage that allows people to try out certain roles outside the family and this prepares them for independent adult life.

This theory therefore suggests that age is important as a mechanism of societal integration, allowing people to evolve unproblematically from one age group to the next.

Exercise 10.8

1. Identify the elements of classical functionalist theory contained in the above account of age groups in society.

2. Those in youth age groups are seen as being in a transitional stage. Explain in your own words what they are in transition from and in transition to.

Exercise 10.9

Listed below are a number of activities for which there are specific legal age limits. Guess the relevant age for each one and check whether you are right by referring to material in your school/college or local reference library.

- Age you can vote.
- Age you can ride a motorbike.
- Age you can purchase alcohol.
- Age you can get married.
- Age you can obtain paid employment.

While the notion of youth as a transitional stage is easy to reconcile with the main functionalist themes of socialisation and everything playing a role, it is less easily applied to the other group affected by age stratification: the elderly.

Bradley (1996, p. 158) summarises the problem as follows: 'The situation of the old poses something of a problem for the functionalist theory of age-groups, since it is hard to see how the segregation and relative poverty of the elderly could serve as a mechanism of social integration.' She states that this can be seen in the functionalists' concentration on youth when talking about age groups and points out that Eisenstadt (1956) has largely ignored the elderly.

This issue was tackled by 'disengagement theory', developed by Cumming and Henry (1961), who argue that the elderly make room for the young and in this way retirement helps the integration of society as a whole. Bradley (1996) describes this as not very convincing. Another explanation, centred on subcultures, suggests that the elderly prefer their own company.

Vincent (1995) points to modifications to the original theory that add a more positive dimension to retirement through the notion of substitute roles (that is, roles that replace the roles played when working and allow retirement to be viewed in a more positive way than simply the time after work has ended). Vincent argues that this reflects the notion of selective engagement and disengagement, though he says the theory is still full of ageist stereotypes that portray the elderly as 'incompetent role players subject to inevitable decline' (ibid., p. 154). This arises because the theory assumes a homogeneity of experience among elderly people that is not consistent with the facts. Since this ability to provide a universal theory of age transition is seen as one of the strengths of the theory, this still leaves the debate unresolved. The theory is strongest in suggesting that all societies have and need some mechanism to facilitate the disengagement of people from certain roles at certain points, but it is less strong in its description of how those mechanisms operate. Vincent puts this down to its ethnocentric (judging something from the point of view of our own culture) and chronocentric (viewing something from our own point in time) nature, making it less useful since it is unable to deal with historical changes in the status of old people.

Exercise 10.11

1. The following extract is taken from Bradley (1996). Some of the words have been removed and spaces left. Using the knowledge you have gained from the previous section, select words from the list below to complete the extract.

2. Summarise the three points made in the extract (no more than 25 words).

Disengagement theory has been substantially criticised. It ignores the
. . . . effects of such a process for . . . . people themselves and
implies that . . . . and segregation are . . . . Moreover it can easily
be established as . . . . inaccurate. Even if older people are forced to give up
. . . . employment, many of them remain active . . . . in other spheres of
social life such as voluntary and . . . . work, ... and leisure
activities. Persistent carping at the . . . . of the . . . . bill casts doubt
on the proposition that retirement is unproblematically . . . . for society.

Missing words

- participants
- cost
- politics
- functional
- pensions
- community
- disengagement
- voluntary
- negative
- empirically
- older
- paid

Strengths of the socialisation and disengagement approach

- It recognises the importance of age as a possible basis for inequality and stratification.
- It recognises the need to see age as a social construction, with cultural and social patterns affecting the way the biological process is experienced and reacted to.
- It views the transition from one age-group to another as particularly important.

Weaknesses of the socialisation and disengagement approach

- It assumes that the social constructions around age groups and the process of transition from one to another are always functional, generally smooth and help societal integration.
- It tends to focus more on youth than any other age group.

Exercise 10.12

1. Add to the above list of weaknesses of the socialisation and disengagement approach on the basis of your reading of this section.

2. Write your own overall conclusion on this approach to age inequality.

2. Age inequality – capitalism and ageism

The relative neglect of the elderly in functionalist theories and the assumption of social homogeneity among the elderly led others to integrate the experiences of the elderly into a framework that recognises that such inequalities build on other inequalities, such as those related to class, gender and ethnicity.

Such an approach allows us to consider the variety of experiences of the elderly and the way divisions among the workforce created by capitalism continue to have an effect after retirement. It recognises the existence of key structures in society that lead to inequalities being generated on the basis of age as well as other factors.

Vincent (1995) points to two broad tendencies within this overall approach, which roughly correspond to the division between the Weberian and Marxist approaches.

Weberian age stratification

The major work adopting a broadly Weberian approach is that of Matilda Riley (1979, 1988) who developed the term cohort (all those born in a particular time period). She shows that the way individuals live their lives is affected by the structures built up and changed by each particular cohort. Vincent (1995, p. 159) summarises this notion as follows: 'Society changes, and therefore people in different age cohorts age in different ways. The ageing process is altered by social change.'

Riley (1988) points to the division of society into different age strata, which in a sense are the same as Weber's status groups. While each cohort experiences each age stratum, the effect of this will vary for each cohort because of the effect of social change on the age strata. For example being old today is different from being old in times past due to the existence of state pensions and other benefits, but the threat to the future of these benefits means the experience might change again in the future.

Vincent (1995) argues that the cohort model is an example of the long-range notion of social figurations (connections between people who do not necessarily know each other) developed in the work of Norbert Elias (1982, 1985). Both models have complex sets of human relationships at the heart of their theories of social change. According to Vincent, a weakness of this approach is that while it explains how age stratification works, it provides no explanation of why age stratification develops in a certain way. It is this that is at the heart of more Marxist-oriented theories of age stratification, which adopt a political economy approach.

Marxism and the political economy of ageing

Vincent provides the following summary of the political economy approach:

> Political economy can be understood to be the study of the inter-relationships between polity, economy and society or, more specifically in modern society, the reciprocal influences between government, economic institutions and interests, and social classes and status groups. The central problem addressed by writers using political economy perspectives is the manner in which the economy and polity interact in a relationship of reciprocal causation affecting the distribution of social goods (Vincent, 1995, p. 162).

The key writers in this traditon are Walker and Phillipson (Phillipson, 1982; Phillipson and Walker, 1986), who developed the concept of 'structured dependency'. This draws upon a broadly Marxist understanding of the way society works.

They argue that the logic of capitalism is the key process. This is centred on the need to make profits, and the labour market is structured and restructured in line with this aim. This has a clear influence on inequality in old age, since age is one of the key ways in which the labour market is structured, for instance through the notion of a retirement age. A distinction is made between those who are in the labour market and able to make profits for capitalism, and those who are unemployed. The latter are the reserve army of labour – a cheap, easily controlled group of potential workers who can be called upon if the pursuit of profit requires it, but can be just as quickly dispensed with. Retirement has many similarities with unemployment. This shows how age is a factor in structuring the labour market, and how the political economy of capitalism structures the distribution of reward and therefore creates inequality. The fact that the elderly consistently represent a large proportion of those in poverty illustrates how this works.

The Marxist approach also investigates the ideologies of age in capitalist society, and in particular the way that the transition from worker to retired person is not viewed positively. Retirement is seen as a series of losses of identity. This is an effect of the centrality of work and labour in the ideology of capitalism. From the viewpoint of capitalism, the retired are people who no longer produce surplus value, but instead impose a cost on society in the form of pension and other social security payments. The whole debate on the potential crisis of the welfare state as a result of the ageing population can be seen as an ideologically motivated attempt to reduce the cost of the elderly on the rest of society and therefore reduce the cost on capitalism. Because of the emphasis on fulfilling the needs of capitalism, capitalism is seen as unlikely to meet the needs of the elderly.

Vincent (1995) argues that a weakness of this approach is that it is centred on paid employment and hence those without employment, including those who are retired, are not seen as central to society. He goes on to ask whether we can really accept the notion that 20 per cent of society are historically irrelevant in the sense that the retired in Marxist theory don't have a role and are not seen as part of the vanguard of social change.

Attempts to view them as a reserve army of labour and the attempt to analyse the changes in the welfare state using a political economy approach, do seek to integrate the elderly into a broad framework that explains inequality and the unequal social distribution of societal rewards.

The criticicms made of this approach have partly spurred the development of the life-course approach to the study of age inequality, the approach favoured by Vincent (1995).

Strength of the capitalism and ageing approach

- The key strength of this approach is its recognition of the importance of social structural factors in determining age and other forms of inequality. Therefore we cannot simply focus on the reaction of individuals since it is their location within a preexisting social structural context that is important.
- The life-course approach explicitly seeks to include the notion of the elderly as active creators and not simply passive products of a structure beyond their control. As such it seeks to overcome the action–structure division in a similar way to Giddens's structuration theory.

Weaknesses of the capitalism and ageing approach

Exercise 10.14

Summarise in your own words, using the material in the above subsections and other sources, the weaknesses of the life-course and capitalism and ageism approaches. (Hint: the age inequality approach is closely related to Marxism and this is a source of criticism, and the life-course approach is similar to the structuration theory of Giddens. The criticisms of that theory also apply to this approach.)

3. Age inequality – the life-course approach

Vincent (1995) argues that the problem with the political economy approach is that it stresses the economy and the productive sphere as the essential aspect of society, and this creates problems because children and the retired are not part of this sphere of society.

He therefore suggests that a cultural and moral dimension to the study of inequality in old age needs to be added to the insights of the political economy approach. This builds upon the notion that the process of retirement, pensions policies and policies relating to residential care serve to place the elderly in a position of 'structured dependency', that is, their living standards depend on decisions made by others. On this basis he argues that it is possible to identify three broad strands of thinking about the elderly:

> It has been suggested that there has been a dialectical progression advancing the understanding of the social position of the elderly. The original thesis was provided by the first generation of social gerontological theories such as disengagement and activity theories. These approaches . . . are individualistic and psychological in orientation. The antithesis came with second-generation theories such as age stratification and structured dependency, which saw elderly people within a social structural framework and within a modernizing context. The third-generation or synthesis theories are theories that can bridge both structure and action (Vincent, 1995, p. 171).

Vincent has retained the Marxist-based notion of structured dependency but seeks to build into his analysis the notion of the elderly as active beings with subjectivities, identities, cultural traditions and patterns of behaviour. He also considers the creation of dominant ideas about the elderly through the use of Gramcsi's notion of hegemony.

He argues that the key form of domination contributing to the social reproduction of inequality in old age is that of ageism, which can be seen both in the economic exploitation of the elderly and in the creation of cultural and ideological stereotypes of the elderly that contribute to the process of hegemonic domination.

The other aspect of social reproduction is differentiation, that is, ways of understanding and classifications that lead us to differentiate the elderly from the young, just as we differentiate male from female, working class from upper class and so on. The important point here is that the meaning and significance of these processes of differentation can change. On this basis there are similarities between the creation of inequalities based on age and those based on class, gender and ethnicity. Vincent summarises these in a table, which is reproduced in Exercise 10.13.

Exercise 10.13

The following table is taken from Vincent (1995). Some of the words have been omitted and appear as a list after the table.

 1. Correctly identify which missing words fit which spaces.

 2. Summarise the meaning of the table (no more than 150 words).

Patterns of Inequality

Differentiation	Historical process	Institution	Hegemonic relations	Exploitative relations
. . . .	Patriarchy	Family	. . . .	Domestic labour Labour market segmentation Consumer weakness
Ethnicity/race	. . . .	Nation	Racism/ nationalism	Imperialism Unequal exchange Labour market segmentation Consumer weakness
Property	. . . .	. . . .	Class ideology	Capitalism Wage labour Labour market segmentation Labour market exclusion Consumer weakness
. . . .	Chronologisation	Age strata	. . . .	Labour market exclusion Domestic labour Consumer weakness

Missing words

- Gender • Imperialism • Class • Ageism • Sexism • Capitalism • Age

Central to Vincent's explanation of how these processes are created and renewed is the concept of the life-course. This considers the way in which individual lives are impinged upon by the structures of inequality identified in the table above, but also the way in which individuals and groups respond to these pressures, and as a result do not necessarily accept the inequalities inflicted on them. In other words, the concept of the life-course adds the component of the active subjective individual or social group, and through this a process of historical and social change.

The concept of the lifecourse can therefore add to and strengthen other theories that seek to combine structural and action perspectives, for example Giddens's structuration theory:

The original perspective elaborated through this book is that people should be understood in terms of their life-course – as producer and as product of a life course. That which people have become in the present, and that potential they have for the future, is the creation of their life course. Thus from a sociological perspective, issues of inequality should be seen as a life-course phenomenon. People should not be divided up and thought about by individual characteristics of age or gender or class or race or disability or other single strands of identity. They should be looked at as the current expression of a life course that obviously includes a wide range of attributes each and all of which impact on the course of that life (Vincent, 1995, p. 193).

Disability, inequality and society

As Davies (1994) points out, the issue of disability was largely ignored by sociologists until the 1990s, and considering the number of lives affected this cannot be justified. The ethnic minority make up 5.5 per cent of the British population, while the disabled number over six million, or more than 14 per cent of the population (Davies, 1994). Hence there is a sharp contrast between the amount of space that has been devoted to ethnicity and inequality and that to disability and inequality.

Perhaps this is because the disabled population did not actively campaign or protest about the their situation until recently, and because of the perception that theirs was a medical and not a sociological problem. Developments in the sociology of health and illness, and the view that well-being and illness are socially constructed undermine this (see Senior and Viveash, 1998). This means that the whole issue of exactly what we mean by disability and therefore exactly who is disabled is one that can be debated sociologically.

Barton (1996) argues that if we look at the disabled through the concept of citizenship, then it is important to consider how disability is defined, who it is defined by and for what purposes such a definition is arrived at. Such a view is centred not on fixed medical notions of disability but on social constructions of disability and who has the power to make such distinctions, leading to inequality:

Disability is a significant means of social differentiation. To be disabled means to be discriminated against and involves experiencing varying degrees of stereotyping, social isolation and restriction . . . This perspective is a key aspect of a social model of disability, one which seeks to identify the ways in which society disables people. The task then is to remove those disabling material, economic, ideological, attitudinal barriers that cumulatively prevent disabled people from experiencing the entitlements of citizenship. This includes challenging the mythology of the rhetoric of democracy in the light of the position and experiences of marginalised and oppressed groups (Barton, 1996, p. 180).

Barton argues that historically the medical model, with its notion of deficit, has meant that the voice of the disabled themselves has been excluded from decisions that affect their lives and a primarily custodial approach involving incarceration in institutions has been the norm, alternating with a similar outcome motivated by a notion of the disabled as vulnerable and in need of protection.

In either case, the disabled were viewed as powerless objects of policy rather than as citizens. This has been described as the deficit view of disability. As a result, one of the most important aspects of the struggle by disabled people has been to develop and promote a positive self-identity. As Barton (1996, p. 184) says: 'The focus of criticism and concern . . . needs to move from an individualized, deficit model to one in which the institutional barriers can be challenged and the rights and value of disabled people as equal citizens can be achieved.'

Barton points to the emergence of the disability movement as one result of this change, but it is a movement that builds upon the importance of the concept of difference within the universalist notion of citizenship. Using the example of 'inclusive education' he highlights the difficulties involved. The notion of inclusive education relates to social justice, equality and choice and means a concern for the well-being of all children. It rejects the notion of segregated special schools. However Barton argues that:

> Inclusive education is not about 'dumping' pupils into existing conditions and relations with the intention that schools will have to cope with these additional responsibilities. Schools will need to change. This process may comprise changes to the physical structure of the building in terms of access and appropriate facilities. But it is much more than this. It will also affect the curriculum, ethos and teaching practices. Importantly, it will also require carefully planned, adequately resourced and monitored staff development policies and practices. Teachers are key to this change and must therefore be adequately supported and encouraged (ibid., p. 189).

As well as the problems identified by Barton, the evidence that those who are disabled suffer from unequal treatment and an inferior place in societal structures compared with the able-bodied can be discussed in relation to a number of aspects of society.

Barnes (1991) points out that while 21 per cent of the non-disabled workforce hold professional or managerial positions, only 12 per cent of the disabled workforce do so. Since for most of us, our job is the main or only source of income and affects our standard of living, this is bound to create inequality.

In relation to women and inequality, Lonsdale (1988) states that women who are disabled are often encouraged not to have children and see their sexuality as being denied. Therefore disability might result in loss of the sense of self, leading to difficulties in forming and maintaining relationships and a greater dependence on others.

One of the insights of sociologists is that normality and abnormality are in fact socially constructed notions and therefore the study of disability has to take into account that it is not a purely medical definition of disablement that is needed, but one that takes into account the effects of social reaction to a particular medical condition.

Ryan and Thomas (1980) show that, through the process of socialisation and the creation of stereotypes, disabled people are seen primarily in terms of what is wrong with them, rather than in terms of their potential as human beings. The fact that the disabled are largely segregated from able-bodied society means there is little chance that these stereotypes will be undermined.

However in the 1990s such stereotypes have been combatted by the growth of disabled campaigning groups that use direct action tactics to protest against the lack of rights for disabled people, and the fact that many buildings and transport systems are constructed in such a way as to effectively exclude disabled people. Through these activities they have also challenged the view of disabled people as passive victims.

The British Council of Organisations of Disabled People and the Disabled Peoples International have argued that rather than charitable handouts, disabled people need specific rights, an argument that echoes that of the black civil rights movement and the women's liberation movement.

In an attempt to secure their rights in the early 1990s, groups of disabled people began to engage in a number of direct action protests, such as blocking roads and chaining themselves to buses. Their anger was fuelled by the lack of legislation to outlaw discrimination against disabled people and the Conservative government's attempts to stop such legislation being passed because of the cost of the proposed alterations to buildings, transport systems and so on. Despite this governmental opposition the protests continued and led to the introduction of a modest set of proposals, which at least provided a legal basis for outlawing discrimination on the basis of disability.

The Disability Discrimination Act 1995 made it illegal for employers to discriminate against disabled people and they are now required to take reasonable measures to ensure they do not do so. (Of course, as with all anti-discrimination legislation the key word here is 'reasonable' – exactly who is to define what is and what is not reasonable?) The Act does not however apply to employers with fewer than 20 employees, and this is important given the growth of small firms in the economy. It is also the case that the Disabled Quota Scheme, which required employers to employ a certain proportion of disabled staff, was ended by this Act. Although this scheme was largely unenforced, its demise did nothing to enhance the employment rights of disabled people.

In relation to the provision of goods and services, the Act made it illegal to refuse to provide someone with a good or service, or to provide a service on terms that are different for disabled people. The Act also made it illegal for people selling or letting property to discriminate against disabled people, and it contains clauses allowing the government to set minimum standards for new public transport vehicles so that disabled people can use them. It also requires schools and colleges to produce statements about their provision for disabled students.

While there are limits to the effect of such legislation (the Sex Discrimination Act 1975 and the Race Relations Act 1976 have been on the statute book for over twenty years, but we still have gender and ethnic inequality), the Act does provide some rights to disabled people and with some basis for legal redress.

Whether the Act is extensive enough radically to change the lives of disabled people remains to be seen, but its existence illustrates the fact that disabled people are no longer, as a result of their campaigning activities, invisible or content to let society make them invisible.

Locality and inequality

We can demonstrate the existence of inequality as a result of locality with the help of official government publications, and there are also a few tables and figures available that compare Britain with other nation-states. However, these are average figures for the whole of Britain and obscure the inequalities that exist within Britain in terms of locality or region. The New Earnings Survey shows that in 1995 a male manual worker in the East Midlands earned only 90.9 per cent of the earnings of a male manual worker in the South East. Thus two people in the same social class and of the same gender have different income levels and therefore locality is a factor in creating inequality. The figures on regional pay are reproduced in Item D.

Average gross weekly pay for full-time workers

Region	Male manual	Male non-manual	Female manual	Female non-manual
South East	310.7	506.3	208.5	326.1
East Anglia	283.3	402.7	175.3	264.0
South West	276.5	410.0	178.0	267.3
West Midlands	285.2	410.2	186.4	264.2
East Midlands	282.4	395.8	177.2	262.8
Yorkshire and Humberside	285.5	390.6	176.2	259.3
North West	290.4	414.4	182.0	270.6
North	286.4	385.4	180.3	258.7
Wales	284.4	386.8	185.4	264.9
Scotland	284.5	413.2	186.0	272.7

(Source: New Earnings Survey, 1995.)

ITEM D · *Exercise 10.15*

1. Study Item D, then for each of the four columns write down the order of pay by region, with the highest first and the lowest last.

2. Summarise any patterns you have found and make a note of any differences that emerge.

3. For each column, work out the percentage of the pay in the highest paid region that is obtained by those in the same class and of the same gender in the region with the lowest pay. Upon which group does locality seem to have the greatest impact?

4. Using information in this section and in other books, try to explain the patterns revealed in this exercise.

There are important questions about the effect of these differences, for example does the pay differential mean that working-class males in the South East do not feel they have a common identity with working-class males in the North or the North West? The answer to this question is important in terms of whether or not a unified working class and a unified middle class exist, and whether locality or regional differences have an impact on the process of class formation.

Secondly, it is important to consider the explanations given for the rise of inequalities on the basis of locality. Why is it that incomes in the South East are higher than elsewhere in Britain? If we look at wealth then the regional disparity is even greater. *The Sunday Times* survey of the richest 500 people in 1996 (see Beresford and Boyd, 1996) shows that the rich in Britain are unequally distributed geographically: 49 per cent of the richest 500 live in London and the South East. According to Beresford and Boyd there are also pockets of rich people in the North West, Yorkshire and Scotland, and outside London the greatest concentration of millionaires is in the Cheshire town of Alderly Edge.

Despite the fact that the South East and London accommodate a large proportion of the very richest people in Britain, they house some of the poorest as well. The London Boroughs of Hackney, Tower Hamlets, Newham and Southwark regularly come near to the top of the list of areas of urban deprivation and poverty. It is therefore likely that London is the locality with the greatest degree of all forms of inequality.

ITEM E

Low pay

Labour says more than 1m paid less than £2.50 an hour

Keith Harper

More than a million people in Britain are earning less than £2.50 an hour, according to research released yesterday by the Labour Party.

Using information compiled from income data in the Government's Labour Force Survey, the shadow employment secretary Harriet Harman claimed that 328,000 people across the country are paid less than £1.50 a hour.

In all, 1,143,000 receive an hourly rate of less than £2.50, of whom 670,000 are women, she said. "We are all paying the price – in the cost of topping up low pay rates through the benefits system, and through social and economic problems – of a policy which is pushing more people into low pay."

She also published a "low pay map of Britain" which reveals that the regions with the highest proportion of low paid are Yorkshire and Humberside, where nearly 150,000 people – 51,000 men and 93,000 women – earned less than £2.50. The

Wage slaves
People earning less than £1.50 an hour and £2.50 an hour

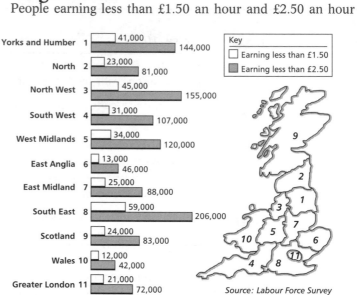

Key
☐ Earning less than £1.50
▣ Earning less than £2.50

Source: Labour Force Survey

South-east – the traditional Tory heartland – was also badly affected, with 206,000 people earning less than £2.50.

In Scotland, 83,000 people earned less than £2.50 and 24,000 people less than £1.50. In Wales 42,000 people earned less than £2.50, with 12,000 on less than £1.50. It costs £2.44 billion a year to provide benefits to top up such incomes, Ms Harman said.

The figures suggest that the highest payout was family credit at £1.091 billion. Then came £627 million for income

support, £600 million for housing benefit and £126 million for council tax relief.

She said Labour would end "this vicious circle" by introducing a national minimum wage to set a floor under wages and make a start on ending poverty pay.

Labour, though, is facing problems with the unions on this. Although both are committed to a legally enforceable low pay policy, the Labour leader Tony Blair wants to leave a decision about what target he would set until after the election.

(Source: Guardian, 20 March 1995.)

Exercise 10.16

i 1. Which region has the highest number of people earning (a) less than £1.50 per hour, (b) less than £2.50 per hour?

i 2. Which region has the lowest number of people earning (a) less than £1.50 per hour, (b) less than £2.50 per hour?

i a e 3. To what extent does this study support the argument that the South East is the region with the greatest degree of inequality in Britain?

This still leaves us with the question of why this regional inequality occurs.

Explaining locational inequality

One way of starting is to study the movement of capital around the regions of Britain and the way in which the availability or otherwise of jobs in certain areas has an impact on the creation of regional inequality. This is essentially the approach taken by the Marxist geographers Doreen Massey (1984) and David Harvey (1973, 1982, 1989). Their work concentrates on the way that capitalism, in its search for profit, is a key factor in the reconstruction of certain areas and the way that this leads to the development of regional and locational inequalities.

Harvey argues that, for capitalists, land is a commodity and that the cyclical (boom–slump) nature of capitalism has a specific impact on different localities. In boom times when there is a crisis of over-production, idle capital that cannot be invested in production is invested in land and buildings, usually in the construction of large office blocks. This might attract other investment, but not if the surrounding buildings are old and rundown. Hence the economic processes of capitalism and the condition of the urban environment are linked, and this will have an impact on the number and type of jobs available and therefore the standard of living in a particular region or city.

Massey (1984) considered the strategies individual companies adopt in order to maximise their profits, and in particular the way that companies restructure, which often leads to geographical relocation. This led her to propose a geography of class resulting from the spatial division of labour, that is, the concentration of certain jobs and occupations in particular regions. According to Massey the South East is the dominant region for the location of 'control functions', leading to a concentration of managers, professionals and specialist technicians in that area since these are the types of people who carry out the control function. The magnetic nature of the South East has much to do with the seat of government being located in that region, as well as the historical importance of the City of London.

Hence because London and the South East contain the highest concentration of 'control functions', and since such people tend to be highly paid, there is a concentration of the upper middle class in that region, with a consequent underconcentration of highly paid people elsewhere in Britain.

There are also historical factors in locational inequality. During the Industrial Revolution industry grew up along an East–West belt running broadly from South and West Yorkshire across to Lancashire and resulted in the growth of large cities such as Leeds, Bradford, Manchester and Liverpool. (The location of raw materials such as coal in these areas had something to do with this.) Ever since that time these areas have been associated with heavy industry, and the impact on them of the economic crises from the 1970s onwards was severe. In the early 1980s roughly one third of British manufacturing industry was shut down and the northern regions were particularly affected. Shortly thereafter the government started to close coalmines, and after the 1984–5 miners' strike the rate of closure increased. In July 1997 it was announced that the Ashfordby superpit in Leicestershire was to be closed, leaving no more than 30 pits in operation nationwide.

Newspaper reports have shown that of the miners working at the start of the 1984–5 miners' strike over 90 per cent are no longer miners, a figure that underlines the scale of the devastation wreaked on the mining industry. Dramatic events such as this naturally affect the standard of living in the areas concerned, and the concentration of closures in heavy industry in certain regions has led to a decline in the average standard of living and a growth in mass unemployment in those areas.

Harvey and Massey's approach has been criticised by Savage et al. (1992), who argue that the problem with the Marxist geography approach is that it depicts capital as the key geographically mobile factor and tends to present workers as relatively immobile and largely passive in the face of capital movements. Instead, they argue, there is a need to study the effect of migration as people do in fact move around the country. Their study focuses on the extent of geograpical mobility and the effect of this on class formation. In their opinion the emphasis on the dominance of the South East, based on the number of middle-class people in that area, is problematic since it tends to underplay the fact that middle-class people also live in other regions and furthermore they tend to move around.

The authors identified more regional mobility among the service class than among other sections of the middle class, such as the petty bourgeoisie. Regional mobility of service-class workers was also higher than that of manual workers, and they also found a fairly strong link between geographical movement and upward social mobility into the service class.

It is important to consider changes in job structure and how these jobs are filled. In relation to this Savage *et al.* argue that it is necessary to see the South East as an 'escalator region', with young middle-class workers starting out there, but then moving to other regions. Focusing on a static picture of the occupational structure of each region overlooks the fact that geographical mobility means that there is not a distinctive middle class in each region. Rather the movement of middle-class people around the country creates a more homogeneous national middle class.

This debate shows the importance of considering locality and regional issues in relation to the question of class formation.

Until the 1990s, most considerations of geography in sociology were developed around the concept of 'community', as exemplified in the notion of the loss of community, a belief originally associated with such thinkers as Tönnies (1890) and Durkheim (1893). However criticisms of this led to a growing attack upon the use of the term community. An alternative approach is presented by Cooke (1989), who argues that the term community needs to be replaced with the term locality. The main reason for this is the romantic notions attached to community (particularly in the loss of community thesis), while the term locality allows us to consider the diverse ways in which regions or individual towns and cities have historically developed. This in turn allows us to consider the part locality plays in the creation of inequalities. This allows a dynamic historical account of the role played by localities in the creation of other forms of inequalities, thereby integrating this often ignored aspect of stratification.

Bibliography

Abbott, P. and C. Wallace (1990) *An Introduction to Sociology: Feminist Perspectives* (London: Routledge).

Abbott, P. and C. Wallace (1997) *An Introduction to Sociology: Feminist Perspectives*, 2nd edition (London: Routledge).

Abercrombie, N. and J. Urry (1983) *Capital, Labour and the Middle Classes* (London: George Allen & Unwin).

Abercrombie, N., A. Warde, K. Soothill, J. Urry and S. Walby (1994) *Contemporary British Society*, 2nd edn (Cambridge: Polity).

Abercrombie, N., A. Warde, K. Soothill, J. Urry and S. Walby (1988) *Contemporary British Society* (Cambridge: Polity).

Acker, J. (1989) 'The problem with patriarchy', *Sociology*, vol. 23, no. 2.

Alcock, P. (1993) *Understanding Poverty* (London: Macmillan).

Alexander, J. (ed.) (1985) *Neofunctionalism* (Beverley Hills, CA: Sage).

Alexander, J. (1990) 'Between progress and apocalypse', in J. Alexander and P. Sztompka (eds), *Rethinking Progress* (London: Unwin Hyman).

Alexander, P. (1987) *Racism, Resistance and Revolution* (London: Bookmarks).

Alexander, S. and B. Taylor (1980) 'In defence of patriarchy', *New Statesman*, 1 February.

Althusser, L. (1966) *For Marx* (London: Verso).

Althusser, L. (1968) *Reading Capital* (London: Verso).

Althusser, L. (1971) *Lenin and Philosophy and Other Essays* (London: Verso).

Amin, K. and C. Oppenheim (1992) *Poverty in Black and White* (London: CPAG/Runneymede Trust).

Anthias, F. (1990) 'Race and class revisited – conceptualising race and racisms', *Sociological Review*, vol. 38, no. 1.

Anthias, F. (1992) 'Connecting "race" and ethnic phenomena', *Sociology*, vol. 26, no. 3.

Anthias, F. and N. Yuval-Davis (1993) *Racialized Boundaries* (London: Routledge).

Arber, S., A. Dale and N. Gilbert (1986) 'The Limitations of Existing Social Class Classifications of Women' in A. Jacoby (ed.), *The Measurement of Social Class* (Guildford: Social Research Association).

Archer, M. (1988) *Culture and Agency* (Cambridge: Cambridge University Press).

Archer, M. (1995) *Realist Social Theory: the morphogenetic approach* (Cambridge: Cambridge University Press).

Ashton, D. (1986) *Unemployment under capitalism* (Brighton: Wheatsheaf).

Back, L. and J. Solomos (1992) 'Black politics and social change in Birmingham, UK: an analysis of recent trends', *Ethnic and Racial Studies*, vol. 15, no. 3.

Ball, G. (1996) 'Blacks less intelligent, says racist lecturer', *Independent on Sunday*, 14 April.

Balls, A. (1997) 'Study shows "unprecedented" rise in inequality', *Financial Times*, 28 July.

Banton, M. (1967) *Race relations* (London: Tavistock).

Banton, M. (1983) *Racial and Ethnic Competition* (Cambridge: Cambridge University Press).

Banton, M. (1985) 'Racial Classification in the Census', *Social Studies Review*, vol. 1, no. 1.

Banton, M. (1986) 'Racial Classification in History', *Social Studies Review*, vol. 1, no. 5.

Banton, M. (1987) *Racial theories* (Cambridge: Cambridge University Press).

Banton, M. (1988) *Racial Consciousness* (London: Longman).

Banton, M. (1994) *Discrimination* (Buckingham: Open University Press).

Barash, D. (1979) *The Whisperings Within* (New York: Harper & Row).

Barker, M. (1981) *The New Racism* (London: Junction Books).

Barnes, C. (1991) *Disabled People in Britain and Discrimination: A case for Anti-Discrimination Legislation* (London: Hurst & Co.).

Barrett, M. (1980) *Women's Oppression Today: Problems in Marxist Feminist Analysis* (London: Verso).

Barrett, M. and A. Phillips (eds) (1992) *Destabilising Theory: Contemporary Feminist Debates* (Cambridge: Polity).

Barron, R. D. and G. M. Norris (1976) 'Sexual Divisions and the Dual Labour Market', in S. Allen and D. L. Barker (eds), *Dependence and Exploitation in Work and Marriage* (London: Longman).

Barth, F. (1969) *Ethnic Groups and Boundaries: The Social Organisation of Cultural Difference* (London: George Allen & Unwin).

Barth, F. (1984) 'Problems in conceptualising cultural pluralism', in D. Maybury-Lewis (ed.) *The Prospects for Plural Societies*, Proceedings, American Ethnographical Society.

Barth, F. (1989) 'The analysis of culture in complex societies', *Ethnos*, vol. 54.

Barton, L. (1996) 'Citizenship and Disabled People: A Cause for Concern', in J. Demaine and H. Entwistle (eds), *Beyond Communitarianism: Citizenship, Politics and Education* (London: Macmillan).

Bates, S. (1992) 'Trouble brews on exoneration of psychologist', *Guardian*, February 26.

Bauman, Z. (1990) *Thinking Sociologically* (Cambridge: Polity).

Beechey, V. (1977) 'Some Notes on Female Wage Labour in Capitalist Production', *Capital and Class*, vol. 3.

Beechey, V. (1986) 'Women's employment in Contemporary Britain', in V. Beechey and E. Whitelegg (eds), *Women in Britain Today* (Buckingham: Open University Press).

Beechey, V. (1987) *Unequal Work* (London: Verso).

Bell, D. (1973) *The Coming of Post-Industrial Society* (New York: Basic Books).

Beresford, R. and S. Boyd (1996) *The Sunday Times – Britain's Richest 500* (London: Times Newspapers).

Bernstein, E. (1899) *Evolutionary Socialism* (New York: Stochen Books, 1961 edn).

Best, S. (1997) 'Agency and Structure in the Writings of Anthony Giddens', *Social Science Teacher*, vol. 26, no. 3 (Summer).*

Billig, M. (1979) *Psychology, Racism and Fascism* (London: AF and R Publications).

Billingham, S. (1995) 'Racism, ethnicity and education', in P. Trowler, *Investigating Education and Training* (London: Collins Educational).

Blumer, H. (1973) 'Reflections on a Theory of Race Relations', in A. Lind (ed.), *Race Relations in World Perspective* (Westport, Conn.: Greenwood Press).

Bottomore, T. (1993) *Political Sociology*, 2nd edn (London: Pluto).

Bourdieu, P. (1984) *Distinction* (London: Routledge).

Bourdieu, P. (1990) *In Other Words* (Cambridge: Polity Press).

Bourdieu, P. and J. C. Passeron (1977) *Reproduction in Education, Society and Culture* (London: Sage).

Bowles, S. and H. Gintis (1976) *Schooling in Capitalist America* (London: Routledge).

Bradley, H. (1989) *Men's Work, Women's Work* (Cambridge: Polity).

Bradley, H. (1996) *Fractured Identities* (Cambridge: Polity).

Brah, A. (1992) 'Difference, Diversity and Differentiation', in J. Donald and A. Rattansi (eds), *Race, Culture and Difference* (London: Sage).

Braverman, H. (1974) *Labour and Monopoly Capital* (New York: Monthly Review Press).

Brown, C. (1984) *Black and White in Britain: The Third PSI Survey* (London: Heinemann).

Brownmiller, S. (1976) *Against Our Will* (Harmondsworth: Penguin).

Burris, V. (1995) 'The Discovery of the New Middle Classes', in A. J. Vidich (ed.), *The New Middle Classes* (London: Macmillan).

Butler, T. and M. Savage (1995) *Social Change and the Middle Classes* (London: UCL Press).

Callinicos, A. (1989) *Against Postmodernism* (Cambridge: Polity).

Callinicos, A. (1993) *Race and Class* (London: SWP).

Carby, H. (1982) 'White women listen: black feminism and the boundaries of sisterhood' in CCCS (eds), *The Empire Strikes Back* (London: Hutchinson/CCCS).

Cardechi, G.(1977) *On the Economic Identification of Social Classes* (London: RKP).

Carter, B. (1997) 'The Restructuring of Teaching and the Restructuring of Class', *British Journal of Sociology of Education*, vol. 18, no. 2.

Castles, S. and G. Kosack (1973) *Immigrant Workers and Class Structure in Western Europe* (Oxford: Oxford University Press).

CCCS (1982) *The Empire Strikes Back* (London: Hutchinson).

Chauvet, J.-M., E. B. Deschamps and C. Hillaire (1996) *Chauvet Cave: The discovery of the World's Oldest Pictures* (London: Thames & Hudson).

Church, J. and C. Summerfield (1996) *Social Focus on Ethnic Minorities* (London: HMSO).

Cliff, T. (1984) *Class Struggle and Women's Liberation* (London: Bookmarks).

COI (1996) *Women in Britain*, 2nd edn (London: HMSO).

Coles, B. (1995) *Youth and Social Policy* (London: UCL Press).

Cooke, P. (ed.) (1989) *Localities: The Changing Face of Urban Britain* (London: Unwin & Hyman).

Craib, I. (1992) *Modern Social Theory*, 2nd edn (Hemel Hempstead: Harvester Wheatsheaf).

Crewe, I. (1985) 'Can Labour rise again?', *Social Studies Review*, September.

Crewe, I. (1987) 'Why Mrs. Thatcher was returned with a landslide', *Social Studies Review*, September.

Crewe, I. (1992) 'Why did Labour lose (yet again)?', *Politics Review*, September.

Crewe, I. (1993) 'The changing basis of party choice 1979–92', *Politics Review*, February.

Crewe, I., B. Sarlvik and J. Alt (1977) 'Partisan dealignment in Britain, 1964–1974', *British Journal of Political Science*, vol. 7.

Crompton, R. (1989) 'Class, theory and gender', *British Journal of Sociology*, vol. 40, no. 4.

Crompton, R. (1993) *Class and Stratification* (Cambridge: Polity).

Cumming, E. and W. Henry (1961) *Growing Old: The Process of Disengagement* (New York: Basic Books).

Dahrendorf, R. (1959) *Class and Class Conflict in an Industrial Society* (London: RKP).

Darwin, C. (1859) *On the Origin of Species* (London: Murray).

Davies, T. (1994) 'Disabled by society', *Sociology Review*, vol. 3, no. 4.

Davis, K. and W. Moore (1945) 'Some principles of stratification', *American Sociological Review*, vol. 10.

Davis, K. and W. E. Moore (1967) 'Some principles of stratification', in R. Bendix and S. M. Lipset (eds), *Class Status and Power*, 2nd edn (London: Routledge).

Dawkins, R. (1976) *The Selfish Gene* (Oxford: Oxford University Press).

Deem, R. (1980) *Schooling for Women's Work* (London: Routledge).

Deem, R. (1988) *Work, Unemployment and Leisure* (London: Routledge).

Delamothe, T. (1989) 'Class Dismissed', *British Medical Journal*, vol. 299.

Delphy, C. (1984) *Close to Home* (London: Hutchinson).

Delphy, C. and D. Leonard (1992) *Familiar Exploitation* (Cambridge: Polity).

Dennis, N. and G. Erdos (1992) *Families without Fatherhood* (London: IEA).

Devine, F. (1992) *Affluent Workers Revisited* (Edinburgh: Edinburgh University Press).

Devine, F. (1997) *Social Class in America and Britain* (Edinburgh: Edinburgh University Press).

Donald, J. and A. Rattansi, (eds) (1992) *'Race', Culture and Difference* (London: Sage).

Draper, H. (1978) *Karl Marx's Theory of Revolution, Volume 2: The Politics of Social Classes* (New York: Monthly Review Press).

Dunleavy, P. and C. Husbands (1985) *British Democracy at the Crossroads* (London: George Allen & Unwin).

Durkheim, E. (1893) *The Division of Labour in Society* (1960 edition) (New York: The Free Press).

Edgell, S. (1993) *Class* (London: Routledge).

Egerton, M. and A. H. Halsey (1993) 'Trends by social class and gender in access to higher education in Britain', *Oxford Review of Education*, vol. 19, no. 2.

Ehrenrich, J. and B. Ehrenrich (1977) 'The Professional–Managerial Class', *Radical America*, vol. 11.

Eisenstadt, S. N. (1956) *From Generation to Generation* (London: Macmillan).

Elias, N. (1982) *The Civilising Process* (Oxford: Blackwell).

Elias, N. (1985) *The Loneliness of Dying* (Oxford: Blackwell).

Elliott, L., P. Wintour and R. Kelly (1994) 'Tory taxes favour rich says study', *The Guardian*, 9 February.

Elster, J. (1985) *Making Sense of Marx* (Cambridge: Cambridge University Press).

Erickson, E. (1965) *Childhood and Society* (Harmondsworth: Penguin).

Erickson, E. (1982) *The life cycle completed* (New York: Newton).

Etzioni, A. (1995) *The Spirit of Community* (London: Fontana).

Fanon, F. (1967) *Towards the African Revolution* (Harmondsworth: Penguin).

Fanon, F. (1986) *Black Skin, White Masks* (London: Pluto Press).

Fauldi, S. (1992) *Backlash: The Undeclared War against Women* (London: Chatto & Windus).

Featherstone, M. and M. Hepworth (1989) 'Ageing and old age: reflections on the postmodern life course', in W. Blytheway (ed.), *Becoming and Being Old: sociological approaches to later life* (London: Sage).

Fennell, G., C. Phillipson and H. Evers (1988) *The Sociology of Old Age* (Buckingham: Open University Press).

Finch, J. and D. Groves (1983) *A Labour of Love* (London: Routledge).

Finn, D. (1987) *Training without Jobs* (London: Macmillan).

Firestone, S. (1972) *The Dialectic of Sex* (Harmondsworth: Penguin).

Flax, J. (1987) 'Postmodernism and gender relations in feminist theory', *Signs*, vol. 12, no. 4.

Foucault, M. (1980) *Power/Knowledge: Selected Interviews and Other Writings 1972–77* (Brighton: Harvester).

Fraser, S. (ed.) (1995) *The Bell Curve Wars* (New York: Basic Books).

Frobel, F., J. Heinrichs and O. Kreye (1980) *The New International Division of Labour* (Cambridge: Cambridge University Press).

Fryer, P. (1984) *Staying Power* (London: Pluto Press).

Gabriel, J. and G. Ben-Tovim (1978) 'Marxism and the concept of racism', *Economy and Society*, vol. 7, no. 2.

Gabriel, J. and G. Ben-Tovim (1986) *The Local Politics of Race* (London: Macmillan).

Gallie, D. (1994) 'Are the unemployed an underclass? Some evidence from the Social Change and Economic Life Initiative', *Sociology*, vol. 28, no. 3.

Gans, H. J. (1994) 'Symbolic ethnicity and symbolic religiosity: towards a comparison of ethnic and religious acculturation', *Ethnic and Racial Studies*, vol. 17, no. 4.

Gardner, H. (1995) 'Cracking Open the IQ Box', in S. Fraser (ed.) (1995) *The Bell Curve Wars* (New York: Basic Books).

George, V. (1996) 'The Demand for Welfare', in V. George and P. Taylor-Gooby (eds), *European Welfare Policy: Squaring the Circle* (London: Macmillan).

German, L. (1988) 'Child Abuse', *Socialist Worker Review*, September.

German, L. (1989) *Sex, Class and Socialism* (London: Bookmarks).

Giddens, A. (1973) *The Class Structure of the Advanced Societies* (London: Hutchinson).

Giddens, A. (1980) *The Class Structure of the Advanced Societies*, 2nd edn (London: Hutchinson).

Giddens, A. (1984) *The Constitution of Society* (Cambridge: Polity).

Giddens, A. (1993) *Sociology*, 2nd edn (Cambridge: Polity).

Giddens, A. and G. MacKenzie (eds) (1982) *Social Class and the Division of Labour* (Cambridge: Cambridge University Press).

Giddens, A. and J. Turner (eds) (1987) *Social Theory Today* (Cambridge: Polity).

Gill, S. and D. Law (1988) *The Global Political Economy* (Hemel Hempstead: Harvester Wheatsheaf).

Gilroy, P. (1982) 'Steppin out of Babylon – race, class and autonomy', in CCCS, *The Empire Strike Back* (London: Hutchinson).

Gilroy, P. (1987) *There ain't no Black in the Union Jack* (London, Routledge).

Gilroy, P. (1992) 'The end of antiracism', in J. Donald and A. Rattansi, *'Race', Culture and Difference* (London: Sage).

Gilroy, P. (1993) *The Black Atlantic* (London: Verso).

Ginn, J., S. Arber, J. Brannen, A. Dale, S. Dex, P. Elias, P. Moss, J. Pahl, C. Roberts and J. Rubery (1996) 'Feminist fallacies: a reply to Hakim on women's employment', *British Journal of Sociology*, vol. 47, no. 1.

Gittins, D. (1985) *The Family in Question* (London: Macmillan).

Glass, D. V. (ed.) (1954) *Social Mobility in Modern Britain* (London: Routledge).

Glyn, A. and D. Miliband (eds) (1994) *Paying for Inequality* (London: Rivers Oram/Institute for Public Policy Research).

Goldberg, D. T. (1992) 'The semantics of race', *Ethnic and Racial Studies*, vol. 15, no. 4.

Goldberg, D. T. (ed.) (1994) *Multiculturalism: A Critical Reader* (Oxford: Blackwell).

Goldberg, S. (1979) *Male Dominance* (London: Abacus).

Goldthorpe, J. (1980) *Social Mobility and Class Structure in Modern Britain* (Oxford: Clarendon Press).

Goldthorpe, J. (1982) 'On the service class, its formation and future', in A. Giddens and G. MacKenzie (eds), *Social Class and the Division of Labour* (Cambridge: Cambridge University Press).

Goldthorpe, J. (1987) *Social Mobility and Class Structure in Modern Britain*, 2nd edn (Oxford: Clarendon Press).

Goldthorpe, J., D. Lockwood, J. Platt and F. Bechhofer (1968) *The Affluent Worker* (Cambridge: Cambridge University Press).

Gordon, P. (1992) 'The Racialization of Statistics', in R. Skellington and P. Morris, *'Race' in Britain Today* (London: Sage).

Gorz, A. (1982) *Farewell to the Working Class* (London: Pluto).

Gould, S. J. (1981) *The Mismeasure of Man* (Harmondsworth: Penguin).

Gould, S. J. (1995a) 'The unfinished revolution', *New Statesman and Society*, 15 September.

Gould, S. J. (1995b) 'Curveball', in S. Fraser (ed.), *The Bell Curve Wars* (London: Basic Books).

Gould, S. J. (1996) 'In the beginning', *Observer*, 14 April.

Goy, R. and C. H. Phoenix (1971) 'The effects of testosteronepropionate administered before birth on the development of behaviour in genetic female rhesus monkeys', in C. H. Sawyer and R. A. Gorski (eds), *Steroid Hormones and Brain Function* (Berkeley: University of California Press).

Gramsci, A. (1971) *Selections from the Prison Notebooks* (edited by Q. Hoare) (London: Lawrence & Wishart).

Gouldner, A. (1979) *The Future of Intellectuals and the Rise of the New Class* (New York: Seabury Press).

Habermas, J. (1989) *The New Conservatism* (Cambridge: Polity).

Hadfield, G. and M. Skipworth (1994) *Class: Where do you stand?* (London: Bloomsbury).

Hakim, C. (1992) 'Explaining Trends in Occupational Segregation: The Measurement, Causes, and Consequences of the Sexual Division of Labour', *European Sociological Review*, vol. 8, no. 2.

Hakim, C. (1995) 'Five feminist myths about women's employment', *British Journal of Sociology*, vol. 46, no. 3.

Hall, S. (1977) 'Marx's theory of Classes', in A. Hunt (ed.), *Class and Class Structure* (London: Lawrence & Wishart).

Hall, S. (1978) 'Racism and reaction', in Commission for Racial Equality, *Five Views of Multi-Racial Britain* (London: Commission for Racial Equality).

Hall, S. (1980) 'Race, articulation and societies structured in dominance', in UNESCO, *Sociological Theories: Race and Colonialism* (Paris: UNESCO).

Hall, S. (1992) 'New Ethnicities', in J. Donald and A. Rattansi, *'Race', Culture and Difference* (London: Sage).

Hall, S. and M. Jacques (eds) (1989) *New Times* (London: Lawrence & Wishart).

Hall, S. and J. Jefferson (eds) (1976) *Resistance Through Rituals* (London: Hutchinson).

Halsey, A. H., A. Heath and J. M. Ridge (1980) *Origins and Destinations* (Oxford: Clarendon Press).

Hamilton, M. and M. Hirszowicz (1993) *Class and Inequality* (London: Harvester Wheatsheaf).

Hanmer, J. and S. Saunders (1984) *Well Founded Fear: A Community Study of Violence to Women* (London: Hutchinson).

Harding, S. (1986) *The Science Question in Feminism* (Ithaca, NY: Cornell University Press).

Harris, C. (1987) 'The Individual and Society: A Process Approach', in A. Bryman, W. Blytheway, P. Allatt and T. Keil (eds), *Rethinking the Life Cycle* (London: Macmillan).

Harris, N. (1983) *Of Bread and Guns* (Harmondsworth: Penguin).

Hartmann, H. (1981) 'The unhappy marriage of marxism and feminism: towards a more progressive union', in L. Sargent (ed.), *The Unhappy Marriage of Marxism and Feminism* (London: Pluto Press).

Hartmann, H. (1982) 'Capitalism, patriarchy and job segregation by sex', in A. Giddens and D. Held (eds), *Classes, Power and Conflict* (Basingstoke: Macmillan).

Hakim, C. (1980) 'Census reports as documentary evidence: the Census commentaries 1801–1951', *Sociological Review*, vol. 28, no. 3.

Harvey, D. (1973) *Social Justice and the City* (London: Edward Arnold).

Harvey, D. (1989) *The Condition of Postmodernity* (Oxford: Blackwell).

Harvey, L. and M. MacDonald (1993) *Doing Sociology* (London: Macmillan).

Hayek, F. von (1944) *The Road to Serfdom* (London: Routledge).

Hayek, F. von (1960) *The Constitution of Liberty* (London: Routledge).

Heath, A., R. Jowell and J. Curtice (1985) *How Britain Votes* (Oxford: Pergamon).

Heath, A., J. Curtice, R. Jowell, G. Evans, J. Field and S. Witherspoon (1991), *Understanding Political Change* (Oxford: Pergamon).

Heaton, T. and T. Lawson (1996) *Education and Training* (London: Macmillan).

Hechter, M. (1986) 'Rational Choice theory and the study of race and ethnic relations', in J. Rex and D. Mason (eds), *Theories of Race and Ethnic Relations* (Cambridge: Cambridge University Press).

Herrnstein, R. (1989) 'IQ and falling birth rates', *The Atlantic*, May.

Herrnstein, R. and C. Murray (1994) *The Bell Curve* (New York: The Free Press).

Hill, S. (1976) *The Dockers* (London: Heinemann).

Hilton, R. H. (1978) *The Transition from Feudalism to Capitalism* (London: Lawrence & Wishart).

Hills, J. (1995) *Inquiry into Income and Wealth* (York: Joseph Rowntree Foundation).

Hirst, P. (1990) *Representative Democracy and its Limits* (Cambridge: Polity).

Hirst, P. and G. Thompson (1995) 'Globalisation and the future of the nation state', *Economy and Society*, vol. 24, no. 3.

HMSO (1966) Census 1961: Occupation Tables (London: HMSO).

Hobsbawm, E. (1962) *The Age of Revolution* (London: Abacus).

Hobsbawm, E. (1977) *The Age of Capital* (London: Abacus).

Hobsbawm, E. (1987) *The Age of Empire* (London: Abacus).

Hobsbawm, E. (1994) *Age of Extremes* (London: Michael Joseph).

Hood-Williams, J. (1996) 'Goodbye to sex and gender', *Sociological Review*, vol. 44, no. 1, February.

Hutton, W. (1996) *The State We're In* (London: Vintage).

Jenkins, R. (1994) 'Rethinking Ethnicity: identity, categorization and power', *Ethnic & Racial Studies*, vol. 17, no. 2.

Jobey, L. (1996) 'Solanas and son', *Guardian*, 24 August.

Johnson, P., C. Conrad and D. Thomson (eds) (1989) *Workers versus pensioners: intergenerational justice in an ageing world* (Manchester: Manchester University Press).

Johnson, P., A. Goodman and S. Webb (1997) *Inequality in the UK* (London: Institute for Fiscal Studies).

Jones, T. (1993) *Britain's Ethnic Minorities* (London: PSI).

Kallen, H. (1924) *Culture and Democracy in America* (New York: Boni & Liveright).

Kellner, P. and P. Wilby (1980) 'The 1:2:4 rule of class in Britain', *The Sunday Times*, 13 January.

Kelly, A. (1985) 'The construction of masculine science', *British Journal of the Sociology of Education*, vol. 6.

Kessler, S. J. and W. McKenna (1978) *Gender: An Ethnomethodological Approach* (New York: John Wiley).

Keys, D. (1996) 'Ancient Voyage of discovery', *Independent*, 8 April.

Kiernan, K. (1992) 'The impact of family disruption in childhood on transitions made in young adult life', *Population Studies*, vol. 46.

Kirby, M. (1995) *Investigating Political Sociology* (London: Collins Educational).

Kohli, M. (1991) 'Retirement and the moral economy: an historical interpretation of the German case', in M. Minker and C. Estes (eds), *Critical Perspectives on Aging: the political and the moral economy of growing old* (New York: Baywood).

Laclau, E. and C. Mouffe (1985) *Hegemony and Socialist Strategy* (London: Verso).

Laczko, F. and C. Phillipson (1991) *Changing Work and Retirement* (Buckingham: Open University Press).

Lal, B. B. (1986) 'The "Chicago School" of American sociology, symbolic interactionism, and race relations theory', in J. Rex and D. Mason (eds), *Theories of Race and Ethnic Relations* (Cambridge: Cambridge University Press).

Landry, B. (1987) *The New Black Middle Class* (Berkeley, CA: University of California Press).

Laqueur, T. (1990) *Making Sex* (London: Harvard University Press).

Lash, S. and J. Urry (1987) *The End of Organised Capitalism* (Cambridge: Polity).

Lash, S. and J. Urry (1994) *Economies of Signs and Space* (London: Sage).

Lawn, M. and G. Grace (eds) (1987) *Teachers: the culture and politics of work* (London: Falmer Press).

Lawrence, E. (1982) 'In the abundance of water the fool is thirsty: sociology and 'black pathology', in CCCS, *The Empire Strike Back* (London: Hutchinson).

Lawson, T. (1986) *Sociology: A Conceptual Appraisal* (London: Checkmate).

Layder, D. (1995) *Understanding Social Theory* (London: Sage).

Lee, D., D. Marsden, P. Rickman and J. Duncombe (1990) *Scheming for Youth* (Buckingham: Open University Press).

Lenin, V. I. (1969) *Selected Works* (London: Lawrence & Wishart).

Lewis, O. (1968) *La Vida* (Harmondsworth: Penguin).

Lister, R. (1991) 'Concepts of Poverty', *Social Studies Review*, vol. 6, no. 5.

Lockwood, D. (1964) 'Social Integration and System Integration', in G. K. Zollschan and W. Hirsch (eds), *Explorations in Social Change* (London: RKP).

Lonsdale, S. (1988) *Women and Disability* (Basingstoke: Macmillan).

MacKinnon, C. (1982) 'Feminism, Marxism, method and the state: an agenda for theory', *Signs*, vol. 7, no. 3.

Madry, N. and M. Kirby (1996) *Investigating Work, Unemployment and Leisure* (London: Collins Educational).

Mann, K. (1995) 'Work, Dependency and the Underclass', in M. Haralambos (ed.), *Developments in Sociology*, vol. 11 (Ormskirk: Causeway Press).

Mann, M. (1986) *The Sources of Social Power*, vol. 1 (Cambridge: Cambridge University Press).

Mann, M. (1993) *The Sources of Social Power*, vol. 2 (Cambridge: Cambridge University Press).

Mann, N. (1995) 'Britain "second among unequals"', *New Statesman and Society*, 16 January.

Manning, N. (1990) 'Social Policy', in M. Haralambos (ed.), *Developments in Sociology*, vol. 6 (Ormskirk: Causeway Press).

Marable, M. (1991) 'Black America in search of itself', *The progressive*, November.

Marshall, G. and A. Swift (1993) 'Social Class and Social Justice', *British Journal of Sociology*, June.

Marshall, G., H. Newby, D. Rose and C. Vogler (1988) *Social Class in Modern Britain* (London: Hutchinson).

Marshall, T. H. (1963) 'Citizenship and Social Class', in T. H. Marshall (ed.), *Sociology at the Crossroads* (London: Heinemann).

Marsland, D. (1996) *Welfare or Welfare State?* (London: Macmillan).

Martin, J. and C. Roberts (1984) *Women and Employment: A Lifetime Perspective* (London: HMSO).

Marx, K. (1975) *Theories of Surplus Value*, Part 2 (Moscow: Progress Publishers).

Mason, D. (1995) *Race and Ethnicity in Modern Britain* (Oxford: Oxford University Press).

Massey, D. (1984) *Spatial Divisions of Labour* (London: Macmillan).

McDonnell, B. (1990) 'The Beginning and End of Social Class', *Social Science Teacher*, Autumn.*

McGarr, P. (1992) 'Why IQ does not equal intelligence', *Socialist Worker*, 21 March.

McGuire, R. (1997) 'Typecast to start on £19,000 a year', *TES*, 19 June.

McKaughan, M. (1987) *The Biological Clock* (New York: Doubleday).

McRobbie, A. (1991) *Feminism and Youth Culture* (London: Macmillan).

Melucci, A. (1989) *Nomads of the Present* (London: Hutchinson).

Melvin, O. and T. Shapiro (1996) *Black Wealth/White Wealth* (London: Routledge).

Mervin, D. (1990) 'Black "Progress" in the USA', *Social Studies Review*, vol. 5, no. 4.

Mihill, C. (1997) 'Heart illness risk for poor', *Guardian*, 24 July.

Miles, R. (1980) 'Class, race and ethnicity: a critique of Cox's theory', *Ethnic and Racial Studies*, vol. 3, no. 2.

Miles, R. (1982) *Racism and Migrant Labour* (London: RKP).

Miles, R. (1984) 'Marxism versus the sociology of race Relations?', *Ethnic and Racial Studies*, vol. 7, no. 2.

Miles, R. (1989) *Racism* (London: Routledge).

Miles, R. (1990) 'Racism, Ideology and Disadvantage', *Social Studies Review*, vol. 5, no. 4.

Miles, R. and A. Phizacklea (1984) *White Man's Country: racism in British politics* (London: Pluto Press).

Miliband, R. (1973) *The State in Capitalist Society* (London: Quartet).

Mirza, H. S. (ed.) (1997) *Black British Feminism* (London: Routledge).

Millett, K. (1970) *Sexual Politics* (New York: Doubleday).

Mitchell, J. (1971) *Woman's Estate* (Harmondsworth: Penguin).

Modood, T. (1988) '"Black" racial equality and Asian identity', *New Community*, vol. 14, no. 3.

Modood, T. (1994) 'Political Blackness and British Asians', *Sociology*, vol. 28, no. 4.

Modood, T. (1997) *Ethnic Minorities in Britain: Diversity and Disadvantage – the Fourth National Survey of Ethnic Minorities* (London: PSI).

Moore, R. (1979) 'Foreword', in M. Billig, *Psychology, Racism and Fascism* (London: AF & R Publications).

Morgan, D. (1986) 'Gender' in R. Burgess (ed.), *Key Variables in Social Investigation* (London: Routledge & Kegan Paul).

Morris, L. (1993) 'Household finance management and the labour market: a case study in Hartlepool', *Sociological Review*, vol. 4, no. 3.

Munch, R. (1987) 'Parsonian Theory Today: in search of a new synthesis', in A. Giddens and J. Turner (eds), *Social Theory Today* (Cambridge: Polity).

Murdock, G. P. (1949) *Social Structure* (New York: Macmillan).

Murray, C. (1984) *Losing Ground* (New York: Basic Books).

Nanda, P. (1988) 'White attitudes: the rhetoric and the reality' in A. Bhat, R. Carr-Hill and S. Ohri (eds) *Britain's Black Population* (Aldershot: Gower).

Newson, J. and E. Newson (1963) *Patterns of Infant Care in an Urban Community* (London: George Allen & Unwin).

Nicolaus, M. (1970) 'Proletariat and Middle Class in Marx', in J. Weinstein and D. Eakins (eds), *For a New America* (New York: Random House).

Nietzsche, F. (1969) *Thus Spake Zarathustra* (Harmondsworth: Penguin).

Nisbett, R. (1995) 'Race, IQ and Scientism', in S. Fraser (ed.), *The Bell Curve Wars* (New York: Basic Books).

Norwood, C. (1985) 'The Baby Blues: How Late Should You Wait to Have a Child?' Mademoiselle, October.

Nozick, R. (1974) *Anarchy, State and Utopia* (Oxford: Blackwell).

Oakley, A. (1972) *Sex, Gender and Society* (London: Maurice Temple Smith).

Oakley, A. (1974) *The Sociology of Housework* (Oxford: Martin Robertson).

Oakley, A. (1981) 'Interviewing Women: A Contradiction in Terms', in H. Roberts (ed.), *Doing Feminist Research* (London: Routledge).

O'Donnell, M. (1985) *Age and Generation* (London: Tavistock).

O'Donnell, M. (1991) *Race and Ethnicity* (London: Longman).

O'Donnell, M. (1992) *A New Introduction to Sociology*, 3rd edn (Walton-on-Thames: Nelson).

O'Higgins, M., J. Bradshaw and R. Walker (1988) 'Income Matters over the Life Cycle', in R. Walker and G. Parker (eds), *Money Matters: Income, Wealth and Financial Welfare* (London: Sage).

Ohri, S. (1988) 'The politics of racism, statistics and equal opportunity', in A. Bhat, R. Carr-Hill and S. Ohri (eds), *Britain's Black Population* (Aldershot: Gower).

Omi, M. and H. Winant (1994) *Racial Formation in the United States*, 2nd edn (London: Routledge).

Oppenheim, C. and L. Harker (1996) *Poverty: the Facts*, 3rd edn (London: CPAG).

Ouseley, H. (1995) 'Talent Spotting', *Guardian*, 25 February.

Outhwaite, W. and T. Bottomore (eds) (1993) *Twentieth-Century Social Thought* (Oxford: Blackwell).

Owen, D. (ed.) (1997) *Sociology after Postmodernism* (London: Sage).

Ozga, J. and M. Lawn (1981) *Teachers, Professionalism and Class* (London: Falmer Press).

Pahl, R. (1984) *Divisions of Labour* (Oxford: Blackwell).

Pahl, J. (1989) *Money and Marriage* (Basingstoke: Macmillan).

Park, R. (1950) *Race and Culture* (New York: Free Press).

Parkin, F. (1968) *Middle Class Radicalism* (Manchester: Manchester University Press).

Parkin, F. (1971) *Class Inequality and Political Order* (London: Paladin).

Parkin, F. (1979) *Marxism and Class Theory: A Bourgeois Critique* (London: Tavistock).

Parsons, T. (1937) *The Structure of Social Action* (Glencoe: The Free Press).

Parsons, T. (1951) *The Social System* (New York: The Free Press).

Parsons, T. (1954) *Essays in Sociological Theory* (Glencoe, Ill.: The Free Press).

Parsons, T. (1977) *The Evolution of Societies* (Englewood Cliffs, NJ: Prentice-Hall).

Pateman, C. (1988) *The Sexual Contract* (Cambridge: Polity).

Patterson, S. (1965) *Dark Strangers* (Harmondsworth: Penguin).

Payne, G. (1991) 'The Classless Society?', *General Studies Review*, November.

Pearce, F. (1989) *The Radical Durkheim* (London: Unwin Hyman).

Perkin, J. (1993) *Victorian Women* (London: John Murray).

Phillips, A. (1992) 'Must Feminists Give upon Liberal Democracy?', in D. Held (ed.), *Prospects for Democracy* (Cambridge: Polity).

Phillips, A. (1991) *Engendering Democracy* (Cambridge: Polity).

Phillips, A. (1993) *Democracy and Difference* (Cambridge: Polity).

Phillipson, C. (1982) *Capitalism and the Construction of Old Age* (London: Macmillan).

Phillipson, C. and A. Walker (1986) *Ageing and Social Policy: a critical assessment* (Aldershot: Gower).

Phizacklea, A. and R. Miles (1980) *Labour and Racism* (London: RKP).

Pilkington, A. (1984) *Race Relations in Britain* (Slough: UTP).

Pilkington, A. (1992) 'Is there a British Underclass?', *Sociology Review*, vol. 1, no. 3.

Pollert, A. (1996) 'Gender and class revisited; or, the poverty of "patriarchy", *Sociology*, vol. 30, no. 4.

Poulantzas, N. (1973) 'The problem of the capitalist state', in J. Urry and J. Wakeford (eds), *Power in Britain* (London: Heinemann).

Poulantzas, N. (1975) *Classes in Contemporary Capitalism* (London: Verso).

Poulantzas, N. (1978) *State, Power, Socialism* (London: Verso).

Rattansi, A. (1992) 'Changing the subject? Racism, culture and education', in J. Donald and A. Rattansi, *'Race', Culture and Difference* (London: Sage).

Rattansi, A. and S. Westwood (eds) (1994) *Racism, Modernity and Identity: On the Western Front* (Cambridge: Polity).

Reid, I. (1989) *Social Class Differences in Britain* (London: Fontana).

Renvoize, J. (1978) *Web of Violence* (London: RKP).

Rex, J. (1970) *Race Relations in Sociological Theory* (London: Weidenfeld & Nicolson).

Rex, J. (1986a) 'The role of class analysis in the study of race relations – a Weberian perspective', in J. Rex and D. Mason (eds), *Theories of Race and Ethnic Relations* (Cambridge: Cambridge University Press).

Rex, J. (1986b) *Race and Ethnicity* (Buckingham: Open University Press).

Rex, J. and R. Moore (1967) *Race, Community and Conflict* (Oxford: Oxford University Press).

Rex, J. and S. Tomlinson (1979) *Colonial Immigrants in a British City: A Class Analysis* (London: RKP).

Richardson, J. and J. Lambert (1985) *The Sociology of Race* (Ormskirk: Causeway Press).

Riley, M. W. (ed.) (1979) *Ageing from Birth to Death* (Boulder, CO: Westview Press).

Riley, M. W. (1988) 'On the significance of age in sociology', in M. W. Riley, B. J. Huber and B. B. Hess (eds), *Social Structures and Human Lives* (London: Sage).

Roberts, K., F. Cook, S. Clark and E. Semenoff (1977) *The Fragmentary Class Structure* (London: Heinemann).

Robertson, R. and B. S. Turner (1991) *Talcott Parsons: Theorist of Modernity* (London: Sage).

Robinson, C. J. (1983) *Black Marxism* (London: Zed Press).

Roemer, J. (1982) *A General Theory of Exploitation and Class* (Cambridge, Mass.: Harvard University Press).

Rose, S., L. J. Kamin and R. C. Lewontin (1984) *Not in Our Genes: Biology, Ideology and Human Nature* (Harmondsworth: Penguin).

Rosen, J. and C. Lane (1995) 'The Sources of the Bell Curve', in S. Fraser (ed.), *The Bell Curve Wars* (New York: Basic Books).

Rowbotham, S. (1981) 'The trouble with "patriarchy"', in Feminist Anthology Collective (ed.), *No Turning Back: Writings from the Women's Liberation Movement 1975–1980* (London: Women's Press).

Rowntree, S. (1901) *Poverty: A Study of Town Life* (London: Macmillan).

Rubery, J. (1980) 'Structured Labour Markets, Worker Organisation and Low Pay', in A. Amsden (ed.), *The Economics of Women and Work* (Harmondsworth: Penguin).

Russell, D. (1984) *Sexual Exploitation: rape, child sexual abuse and workplace harassment* (Beverly Hills: Sage).

Ryan, J. and F. Thomas (1980) *The Politics of Mental Health* (Harmondsworth: Penguin).

Ryan, T. (1985) 'The roots of masculinity' in A. Metcalf and M. Humphries (eds), *The Sexuality of Men* (London: Pluto Press).

Sarsby, J. (1983) *Romantic Love and Society* (Harmondsworth, Penguin).

Saunders, P. (1990) *Social Class and Stratification* (London: Routledge).

Saunders, P. (1995a) 'Might Britain be a Meritocracy?', *Sociology*, vol. 29, no. 1.

Saunders, P. (1995b) *Capitalism: A Social Audit* (Buckingham: Open University Press).

Savage, M., J. Barlow, P. Dickens and T. Fielding (1992) *Property, Bureaucracy and Culture* (London: Routledge).

Schwartz, D. and M. J. Mayaux (1982) 'Female Fecundity as a function of Age', *New England Journal of Medicine*, February 18.

Scott, J. (1991) *Who Rules Britain?* (Cambridge: Polity Press).

Scott, J. (1992) 'Deconstructing Equality-versus-Difference: or, the uses of post-structuralist theory for feminists', in L. McDowell and R. Pringle (eds), *Defining Women* (Cambridge: Polity).

Senior, M. and B. Viveash (1998) *Health and Illness* (Basingstoke: Macmillan).

Shaiken, H. (1979) 'Numerical control of work: workers and automation in the computer age', *Radical America*, vol. 1, no. 6.

Sharp, K. (1991) 'Sociobiology', *Sociology Review*, vol. 1, no. 1 (September).

Sharpe, S. (1976) *Just Like a Girl* (Harmondsworth: Penguin).

Sivanandan, A. (1990) *Communities of Resistance* (London: Verso).

Skellington, R. and P. Morris (1992) *'Race' in Britain today* (London: Sage).

Small, S. (1993) 'Key Thinkers – WEB Du Bois', *Sociology Review*, vol. 3, no. 1.

Small, S. (1994) 'Black people in Britain', *Sociology Review*, vol. 3, no. 4.

Smart, C. (1894) *The Ties that Bind: Marriage and the Reproduction of Patriarchal Relations* (London: Routledge).

Smith, A. (1776) *The Wealth of Nations*, 1910 edn (London: Dent).

Smith, D. (1977) *Racial Disadvantage in Britain* (Harmondsworth: Penguin).

Solomos, J. (1986) 'Varieties of Marxist conceptions of "race", class and the state: a critical analysis', in J. Rex and D. Mason (eds), *Theories of Race and Ethnic Relations* (Cambridge: Cambridge University Press).

Solomos, J. (1990) 'Changing forms of Racial Discourse', *Social Studies Review*, vol. 6, no. 2.

Solomos, J. (1993) *Race and Racism in Britain*, 2nd edn (London: Macmillan).

Solomos, J. and L. Back (1994) 'Conceptualising Racisms: Social Theory, Politics and Research', *Sociology*, vol. 28, no. 1.

Solomos, J. and L. Back (1995) *Race, Politics and Social Change* (London: Routledge).

Sowell, T. (1983) *The Economics and Politics of Race: An International Perspective* (New York: William Morrow).

Spencer, H. (1874) *The Study of Society* (London: Appleton).

Spencer, H. (1896) *The Principles of Sociology* (London: Appleton).

Spender, D. and E. Sarah (eds) (1980) *Learning to Lose: Sexism and Education* (London: Women's Press).

Spender, D. (1983) *Invisible Women: Schooling Scandel* (London: Women's Press).

Stanley, L. and S. Wise (1983) *Breaking Out: feminist consciousness and feminist research* (London: Routledge).

Stanworth, M. (1983) *Gender and Schooling* (London: Hutchinson).

Stroller, R. (1968) *Sex and Gender: On the development of Masculinity and Femininity* (New York: Science House).

Szreter, S. (1984) 'The genesis of the Registrar-General's social classifications of occupations', *British Journal of Sociology*, vol. 35, no. 4.

Taylor, F. W. (1947) *Scientific Management* (New York: Harper & Row).

Taylor, P., J. Richardson, A. Yeo, I. Marsh, K. Trobe, A. Pilkington, G. Hughes and K. Sharp (1995) *Sociology in Focus* (Ormskirk: Causeway Press).

Tang Nain, G. (1991) 'Black women, sexism and racism: black or antiracist feminism', *Feminist Review*, no. 37.

Taylor-Gooby, P. (1996) 'The United Kingdom: Radical Departures and Political Consensus', in V. George and P. Taylor-Gooby (eds), *European Welfare Policy: Squaring the Circle* (London: Macmillan).

Thomas, W. I. (1909) *The Child in America* (New York: Alfred Knopt).

Thomas, W. I. and F. Znaniecki (1919) *The Polish Peasant in Europe and America* (Chicago: University of Chicago Press).

Thompson, E. P. (1968) *The Making of the English Working Class* (Harmondsworth: Penguin).

Thompson, E. P. (1978) *The Poverty of Theory and other Essays* (London: Merlin).

Tiger, L. and R. Fox (1972) *The Imperial Animal* (London: Secker & Warburg).

Tompkins, R. (1997) 'Where a bad hair day breaks the rules', *Financial Times*, 16 August.

Tönnies, F. (1890) *Community and Association* (London: Routledge & Kegan Paul) (1955 edition).

Touraine, A. (1982) *The Voice and the Eye* (Cambridge: Cambridge University Press).

Touraine, A., M. Wieviorka and F. Dubet (1987) *The Workers' Movement* (Cambridge: Cambridge University Press).

Townsend, P., N. Davidson and M. Whitehead (1987) *Inequalities in Health and The Health Divide* (Harmondsworth: Penguin).

Trowler, P. (1995) *Investigating Education and Training* (London: Collins Educational).

Tuchman, G., A. K. Daniels and J. Benet (eds) (1978) *Hearth and Home: Images of women in the mass media* (New York: Oxford University Press).

Turner, B. (1983) 'Outline of a theory of human rights', *Sociology*, vol. 27, no. 3.

Tuttle, L. (1986) *Encyclopedia of Feminism* (London: Longman).

Urry, J. (1993) 'The Middle Class', in W. Outhwaite and T. Bottomore (eds), *Twentieth-Century Social Thought* (Oxford: Blackwell).

Van den Berghe, P. (1981) *The Ethnic Phenomenon* (New York: Elsevier Press).

Van den Berghe, P. (1986) 'Ethnicity and the sociobiology debate', in J. Rex and D. Mason (eds), *Theories of Race and Ethnic Relations* (Cambridge: Cambridge University Press).

Victor, C. and M. Evandrou (1987) 'Does class matter in later life?', in S. di Gregorio (ed.) *Social Gerontology: New Directions* (London: Croom Helm).

Vincent, J. (1995) *Inequality and Old Age* (London: UCL Press).

Walby, S. (1986) *Patriarchy at Work* (Cambridge: Polity).

Walby, S. (1990) *Theorizing Patriarchy* (Oxford: Blackwell).

Walker, M. (1996) 'Editor Sullivan quits with HIV', *Observer*, 14 April.

Walker, P. (ed.) (1979) *Between Capital and Labour* (Brighton: Harvester).

Wallman, S. (ed.) (1979) *Ethnicity at work* (London: Macmillan).

Warde, A. (1990) 'Domestic Divisions of Labour', *Social Studies Review*, vol. 6, no. 2.

Waters, M. (1997) 'Inequality after Class', in D. Owen (ed.), *Sociology after Postmodernism* (London: Sage).

Weber, M. (1921) *Economy and Society* (New York: Bedminster Press, 1968 edn).

Westergaard, J. (1995) *Who gets What?* (Cambridge: Polity).

Westergaard, J. and H. Resler (1975) *Class in a Capitalist Society* (Harmondsworth, Penguin).

Wheelock, J. (1990) *Husbands at Home* (London: Routledge).

Willis, P. (1977) *Learning to Labour* (Farnborough: Saxon House).

Wilmott, P. and M. Young (1975) *The Symmetrical Family* (Harmondsworth: Penguin).

Willmott, R. (1996) 'Resisting sex/gender conflation: A Rejoinder to John Hood-Williams', *Sociological Review*, November, vol. 44, no. 4.

Wilson, A. (1978) *Finding a voice* (London: Virago).

Wilson, E. O. (1975) *Sociobiology* (Cambridge, Mass.: Harvard University Press).

Wilson, E. (1983) *What is to be Done about Violence to Women?* (Harmondsworth: Penguin).

Wilson, W. J. (1987) *The Truly Disadvantaged* (Chicago, Ill.: University of Chicago Press).

World Development Movement (1996) *Corporate Giants* (London: WDM).

Wright, E. O. (1976) 'Class boundaries in advanced capitalist societies', New Left Review, 98.

Wright, E. O. (1979) *Class, Crisis and the State* (London: Verso).

Wright, E. O. (1985) *Classes* (London: Verso).

Wright, E. O. (ed.) (1989) *The Debate on Classes* (London: Verso).

Wright, E. O. (1995) *Interrogating Inequality* (London: Verso).

Wright, E. O. (1997) *Class Counts* (Cambridge: Cambridge University Press).

Young, I. (1980) 'Socialist feminism and the limits of dual systems theory', *Socialist Review*, vol. 10, no. 2/3.

Zimbalist, A. (1979) *Case Studies on the Labor Process* (New York: Monthly Review Press).

* *Social Science Teacher* is the Journal of the Association for the Teaching of the Social Sciences (ATSS). For further details write to ATSS, PO BOX 61, Watford, WD2 2NH.

Author index

Subject index

age   3–5, 137, 151, 195–211
ageism   203–10
assimilation   170–4, 177

berdache   122
biological theories   118–22, 134–7, 157, 166–9, 177
black nationalism   5, 37, 127, 180, 185–7
black women   66, 119, 133
bourgeoisie   18, 41, 58–9, 61, 179
British Crime Survey   108
British Nationality Act 1981   147–8
British Social Attitudes Survey   159–60
bureacracy   63–64

Cambridge University   28–9
capitalism   32–3, 37, 45, 51, 54, 57–8, 62, 64, 66, 75–6, 81, 83, 88, 103, 107, 111–12, 119, 126–7, 130–1, 133–4, 179–82, 184–5, 203, 206–8, 217
Census   7, 13–14, 34, 147, 150
child abuse   109
childcare   65, 104–5, 120–2, 197
chronocentric   205
citizenship   45, 48, 52, 54, 57, 148, 180, 183, 211–12
class   3–96, 107, 109, 111, 128, 130, 132, 181, 184–5, 187, 191, 195–6, 199, 206–7, 209–11, 214
class boundaries   9, 41
class formation   4, 22, 47, 67–76, 183, 215
class structure   4, 6, 8, 10, 19–22, 57, 59, 67–76, 181
classless society   84, 88, 90
clerical workers   10, 14–15, 38, 45, 59, 99–101
Commission for Racial Equality   152
communitarianism   56
consumption   15–16, 37, 75, 81
contradictory class locations   40–1, 72

dependency culture   43–5
deskilling   38–9, 59, 103
disability   3–5, 211–14
Disability Discrimination Act 1995   213

disengagement theory   202–5, 209
domestic labour/sphere   65, 97, 103, 106, 109, 111, 126, 127, 140, 151, 210
dual labour markets   102–5, 114, 141, 178
dual-system theories   81, 107, 130–2

Economic and Social Research Council   7, 11–12
embourgeoisement   42, 58
employers   13, 102–103
Employment Gazette   31
equality of opportunity   48, 88–9
Equal Opportunities Commission   99–100
Equal Pay Act 1970   110
ethnic boundaries   175–6
ethnic minorities   146–94
ethnicity/race   3–5, 16, 44, 62, 77, 80, 83, 132–3, 146–96, 199, 206, 209–11
ethnocentrism   172, 205
Eton   28–9
exam questions   2, 45–6, 77–9, 93–6, 113–17, 140–5, 162–4, 193–4
exploitation   23, 57, 81, 83, 106–7, 130, 132, 183, 209

Family Expenditure Survey   26
femininity   122–5, 134
feminism   4–5, 18, 21, 23, 59, 65–6, 80–1, 97, 106–8, 110–11, 127–8, 133–4, 137, 139, 189
flexibility   32, 103
Fordism   32
fragmentation   83, 94
Frankfurt School   37
functionalism   30, 47–9, 56, 77, 80, 105, 171, 173, 176, 202–6

General Household Survey   87
gender/sex   3–5, 16, 19, 22, 62, 65–6, 77, 83, 92–3, 97–145, 189, 191, 195–6, 199, 206, 209–11, 214
gerontocracy   195
globalisation   32–3, 82, 88, 188

Harrow   28–9
hegemony   72, 75

Hope–Goldthorpe scale   17–18
horizontal segregation   99–101, 103
housework/wives   21, 23, 59, 65, 98, 105, 109, 111, 126

ideology   66, 107, 132, 166, 179, 180–1, 183, 185, 191, 207–11
immigration   146–9, 171–2, 177–8, 182
income   10, 18, 20, 24–6, 51, 57, 62, 65, 149, 155, 198, 212, 215–6
Institute of Fiscal Studies   25–6
Institute of Practitioners in Advertising   6, 15, 17
interactionism   170–1, 176
intermediate class   17, 86, 91
International Labour Organisation   98
IQ tests   88–92, 168–9

Labour Force Survey   98, 100–1, 150–1, 216
labour market segregation   99–102, 130, 193, 210
life chances   11, 18, 62–3, 99, 146
life course approach   203, 208–11
lifestyles   16, 19, 82, 93, 105
locality/region   3–5, 28–9, 214–19

managerial workers   7, 9, 13–15, 19, 39, 40, 45, 58, 72, 100–2, 113, 152–3, 212
manual workers   7–10, 13, 18–19, 21, 27, 30, 34, 36, 38–9, 42–43, 59, 64, 86, 88, 92, 99–100, 102, 150, 152–3, 162, 194, 215, 218
manufacturing   30, 31–3, 45, 87, 150, 152, 218
market   50–1, 53–4, 57, 62, 75, 179
masculinity   122–5, 134
Marxism   4, 14, 18, 22, 30, 34, 44, 57, 60, 80, 103, 106–7, 127–8, 130–1, 134, 165, 179, 180–6, 188, 202, 206, 209, 217
mean average   26–7
measuring social class   6–23
median average   26–7
meritocracy   47, 48, 55, 57, 84, 86–7, 89, 91
middle class   6–10, 13–14, 20–1, 30, 33–5, 37, 40–1, 43–4, 58–9, 64, 89, 93–4, 119, 133, 215, 218–19

National Child Development Survey   201
neofunctionalism   48, 55–6
New Earnings Survey   25, 214–15

New Left Realism   48, 52–5
New Right   24, 43, 48, 50–1, 53–7, 75, 84, 92, 109
new social movements   185, 188, 191
non-manual workers   7–10, 13, 18, 21, 27, 34–5, 37, 59, 88, 152–3, 215
norms   4, 55
NSPCC   109

objective measures of class   4, 6–7, 10, 23, 61, 76, 81
Office of Population Censuses and Surveys   11, 162
official statistics   67, 72
oppression   23, 83, 97, 105, 107–9, 111–12, 119, 125, 127–8, 130, 132–4, 175, 212
Oxford University   28–9, 110

part-time work   103, 104, 154, 196–7
patriarchy   65–6, 81, 83, 105, 107, 112, 119, 126, 129–34, 137–8, 210
pensions   197, 200, 209
petty bourgeoisise   14, 34, 38–40, 64, 162, 218
Policy Studies Institute   149, 156, 162
post-class society   83–4
post-Fordist   31–32, 42–3, 103
post-industrial   30–1, 33, 82
postmodernism   15–17, 63, 69, 75, 81–4, 119, 134, 137, 139, 166, 184–6, 188, 192–3, 203
post-structuralism   75, 134, 138–9, 184
poverty   16, 43–5, 88, 114, 150, 168, 196, 207, 216
power   22, 23, 61, 63, 71, 82, 109, 119, 125–6, 128, 176, 178, 180
primary labour market   102, 141
professional workers   7–10, 13, 15–16, 18–19, 36, 37, 39, 40, 45, 58–9, 72, 88, 99–101, 113, 120–1, 129, 152–3, 212, 217
proletarianisation   34, 37–8, 40, 59, 88
proletariat   18, 38, 40, 42, 58, 61, 179
psychoanalysis   125, 134

qualitative   21–3, 71, 73
quantitative   22, 67, 72–3

race formation   5, 166, 185–93
Race Relations Act 1976   214

racism   4, 23, 45, 127, 130–1, 133, 146, 148–151, 156–62, 165–6, 168–9, 174–5, 178–185, 186–8, 191, 210
rape   65, 108–9
Registrar-General   7, 9–13, 17, 57, 59
reserve army of labour   103–5, 111, 207–8

secondary labour market   65, 102, 114, 141, 153, 178
self-employment   14, 18–19, 25, 36, 39, 98, 154
service class   17, 34–6, 58, 64, 86, 89, 91–2, 218
service sector   30, 32–3, 38, 87, 103
sex and gender formation   5, 119
Sex Discrimination Act 1975   110, 214
sexism   127–31, 210
skill   1, 14, 35, 84, 91
skilled workers   9, 13, 18–19, 38, 45, 92, 99, 102, 150, 152–3, 194
slavery   177, 190–1
social closure   64, 70, 85
social mobility   5, 17, 64, 70–1, 84–93, 162, 218
Social Trends   27
socialisation   4, 118, 123–5, 127, 134–5, 203
sociobiology   120, 157, 167
socioeconomic groups   7, 13, 17, 102
stakeholder society   53–4
state   82, 108–9, 126, 128, 130, 178–9, 190, 191–3, 197, 199–200, 207
status   10, 16, 61–3, 82–4, 196, 206–7

structuration   68–76, 208–9
structure–action debate   68–76, 208–9
subjective measures of class   4, 7, 10, 20, 22–3, 47, 61, 83
surplus value   39, 132
Surrey occupational scale   18–19

tax   26, 32, 200
trade unions   42, 88

underclass   11, 43–5, 114, 168–9, 178–9, 183–4
unemployment   26, 98, 149–51, 154–5, 168, 183–4, 202, 207, 218
unskilled workers   8–9, 13, 18–19, 45, 92, 100, 102, 152–3, 162, 194
upper class   14, 35, 59

values   4, 55, 77, 171–7, 177, 196
vertical segregation   100–3
violence against women   97, 108–9, 128–29, 131

wealth   16, 24, 26–8, 57, 90, 215
Weberianism   4, 18, 30, 34–5, 44, 60, 80, 102, 165, 176, 178–9, 183, 185, 206
welfare state   32, 43–5, 50, 54, 88, 178–9, 200–1, 208
white-collar workers   35, 37–9, 64, 94, 98–9, 162
women's movement   5, 37, 127, 129, 133
working class   6, 8–10, 13, 17, 20–1, 34, 34–42, 43, 58–9, 64, 66, 86, 91–3, 111, 119, 162, 178–83, 215

youth   201–2, 205